P9-DMH-514

Finding the Dragon Lady

Finding the Dragon Lady

THE MYSTERY OF VIETNAM'S MADAME NHU

MONIQUE BRINSON DEMERY

PUBLICAFFAIRS
New York

Published in the United States by PublicAffairs™,
a Member of the Perseus Books Group

Printed in the United States of America.

PublicAffairs books are available at special discounts for bulk purchases in the U.S. by corporations, institutions, and other organizations. For more information, please contact the Special Markets Department at the Perseus Books Group, 2300 Chestnut Street, Suite 200, Philadelphia, PA 19103, call (800) 810–4145, ext. 5000, or e-mail special.markets@perseusbooks.com.

Book design by Cynthia Young

Library of Congress Cataloging-in-Publication Data
Demery, Monique Brinson, 1976–
Finding the Dragon Lady : the mystery of Vietnam's Madame Nhu /
Monique Brinson Demery.
pages cm
Includes bibliographical references and index.
ISBN 978-1-61039-281-5 (hardcover)—ISBN 978-1-61039-282-2 (e-book)
1. Tran, Le Xuan, 1924–2011. 2. Politicians' spouses—Vietnam (Republic)—
Biography. 3. Vietnam (Republic)—Politics and government. I. Title.
DS556.93.T676D46 2013
959.7'7043092—dc23

2013021155

First Edition

10 9 8 7 6 5 4 3 2 1

Contents

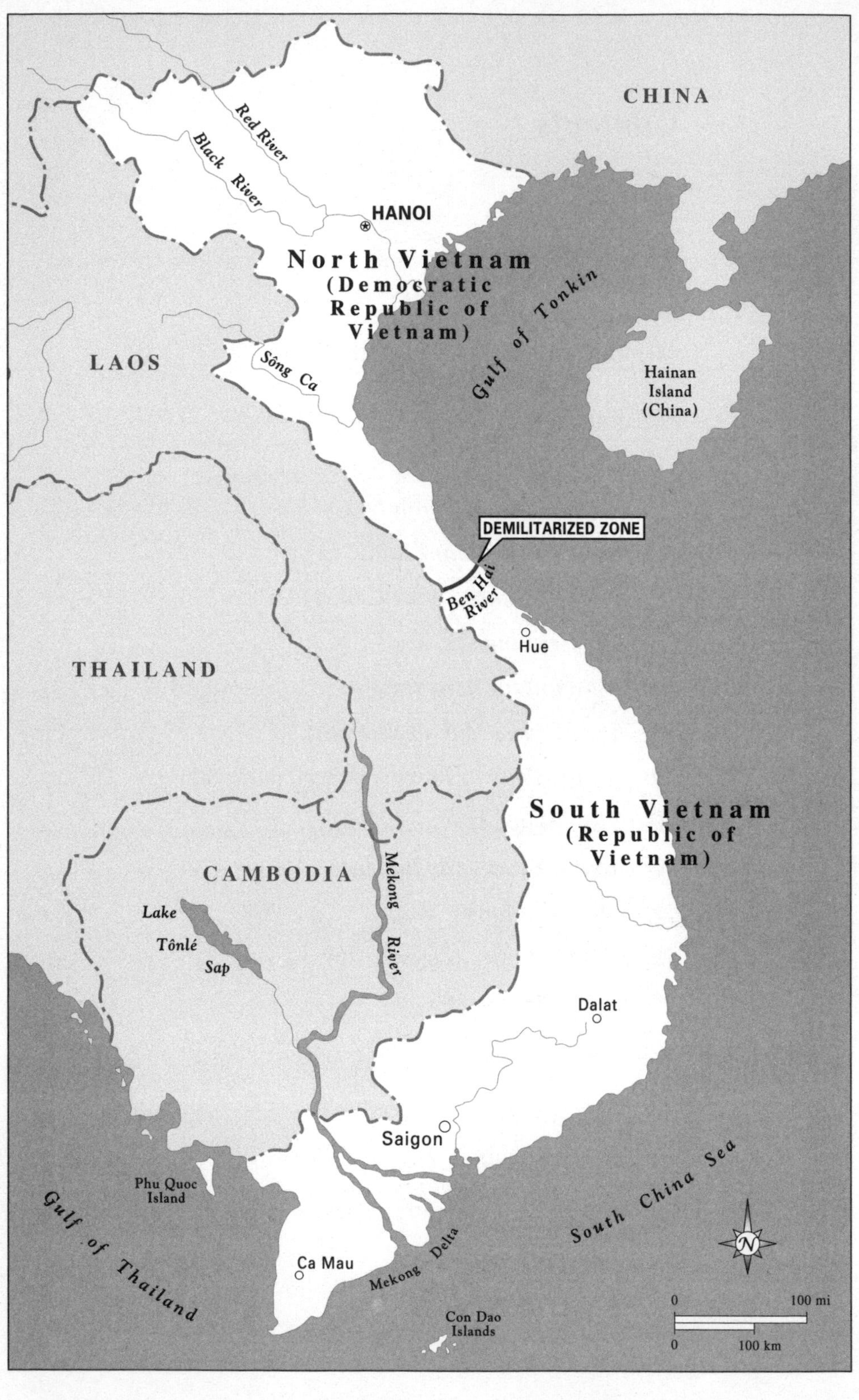
CHINA
Red River
Black River
HANOI
North Vietnam
(Democratic
Republic of
Vietnam)
Gulf of Tonkin
LAOS
Sông Ca
Hainan
Island
(China)
DEMILITARIZED ZONE
Ben Hai
River
Hue
THAILAND
South Vietnam
(Republic of
Vietnam)
CAMBODIA
Mekong River
Lake
Tônlé
Sap
Dalat
Saigon
Phu Quoc
Island
South China Sea
Gulf of Thailand
Ca Mau
Mekong Delta
N
0
100 mi
0
100 km
Con Dao
Islands

List of Illustrations

A Note on Vietnamese Names

TO READERS ENCOUNTERING them for the first time, Vietnamese names can seem confounding. The family name comes first, followed by the middle name—or names—and then the first, or given, name. Additionally, an overwhelming number of people share relatively few last names. Tran and Ngo are more common in Vietnam than Johnson or Smith in the United States. The middle name is no help in distinguishing among brothers and sisters, as parents often give their offspring the same middle names. That was the case in the Ngo family; the six male siblings all had the middle name Dinh, and in the case of the Chuongs's daughters, Madame Nhu and her sister had the same two middle names, Thi and Le. Thi is a common middle name for girls, but in the case of Madame Nhu and her sister, they dropped the Thi in practice and used Le as a prefix to their given names.

The accepted way to refer to a Vietnamese person is by their given name, even in the most official settings—hence, the president of the Republic of South Vietnam was called President Diem and not President Ngo. One notable exception to this rule is Ho Chi Minh. In his case, he has been decreed so esteemed and so well known that his last name is sufficient.

I struggled over what to call various Vietnamese people in this book, but when I made a decision, I tried to be consistent—except in the case of Madame Nhu. In the chapters that depict her early years, I use the name her parents gave her: Tran Le Xuan. While women typically keep their family name after they marry, in the case of both Madame Nhu and her mother, Madame Chuong, I have chosen to refer to them the way that they are commonly spoken of in the United States, where this book was written and published.

Per the guidelines set out by the *Chicago Manual of Style,* 16th ed., I decided to abandon the use of diacritics in spelling Vietnamese names and places but to retain accents for French words. In Vietnamese, diacritics convey the language's seven tones, and words that may look the same on paper without marks may have very different meanings once assigned tones through diacritics. I apologize for any inadvertent offense stemming from my efforts to simplify these spellings for my readers.

Members of Madame Nhu's Family

Tran Van Chuong: Madame Nhu's father; also the South Vietnamese ambassador to the United States under President Ngo Dinh Diem

Nam Tran Tran Van Chuong (also Madame Chuong, Tran Thi Nam Tran): Madame Nhu's mother

Tran Thi Le Chi: Madame Nhu's sister

Tran Thi Le Xuan: Madame Nhu's childhood name

Tran Van Khiem: Madame Nhu's brother

Ngo Dinh Kha: Father of Ngo Dinh Nhu and Ngo Dinh Diem

Ngo Dinh Khoi: Eldest Ngo brother, killed by the Communists in 1945

Ngo Dinh Thuc: Nhu's older brother, archbishop of Hue

Ngo Dinh Diem: Nhu's older brother; president of the Republic of South Vietnam, 1955–1963

Ngo Dinh Nhu: Madame Nhu's husband and chief political advisor to Diem

Ngo Dinh Can: controller of Hue and surrounding areas during the presidency of his brother Diem

Ngo Dinh Luyen: youngest Ngo brother; served as ambassador to the United Kingdom

Ngo Dinh Le Thuy: Madame Nhu's oldest daughter

Ngo Dinh Trac: Madame Nhu's older son

Ngo Dinh Quynh: Madame Nhu's younger son

Ngo Dinh Le Quyen: Madame Nhu's youngest daughter

That hands like hers can touch the strings
That move who knows what men and things
That on her will their fates have hung,
*The woman with the serpent's tongue.**

*Last stanza of William Watson's poem "The Woman with the Serpent's Tongue." The poem was recited in its entirety in front of the US Congress by Ohio senator Stephen Young on October 3, 1963, in protest of Madame Nhu's upcoming visit to the United States. See *New Poems by William Watson* (Cambridge, UK: The University Press, 1909), 32–33.

CHAPTER 1

Paris, 2005

BY THE TIME I STARTED LOOKING for Madame Ngo Dinh Nhu, she had been living in exile for over forty years. In 1963, at the height of her fame, the *New York Times* named the thirty-nine-year-old First Lady of South Vietnam "the most powerful" woman in Asia and likened her to Lucrezia Borgia. But it was Madame Nhu's reputation as the Dragon Lady that brought her real distinction. When Buddhist monks were setting themselves on fire in the streets of Saigon, Madame Nhu's response was unspeakably cruel: "Let them burn, and we shall clap our hands," she had said with a smile. "If the Buddhists wish to have another barbecue, I will be glad to supply the gasoline and a match." The dangerous, dark-eyed beauty quickly became a symbol of everything wrong with American involvement in the Vietnam War.

Madame Nhu faded from public view after November 1963, when her husband, Ngo Dinh Nhu, and his brother, South Vietnamese president Ngo Dinh Diem, were killed in a coup sanctioned and supported by the US government. As President John F. Kennedy explained to his close friend, Paul "Red" Fay, the United States had to get rid of the Ngo brothers in no small part because of Madame Nhu. "That goddamn bitch," he said to his friend. "She's responsible. . . . That bitch stuck her nose in and boiled up the whole situation down there."

Plenty of books have dissected the events of November 1963 and established the overthrow of the Ngo brothers as pivotal in the American buildup to war in Vietnam. But the historical scholarship about the coup has largely overlooked Madame Nhu's role. How did a woman who was not even forty years old—and barely five feet tall in heels—come to command the full attention of a superpower like America and embroil the United States in a conflict that would last another decade and take millions of lives?

I was in Paris to find out—although, I had to admit, I was a little nervous. Pulitzer Prize–winning Associated Press reporter Malcolm Browne had written in his memoirs that he knew from "personal experience" that Madame Nhu "could be the most dangerous enemy a man could have." And that was exactly what was so intriguing. The Dragon Lady image was a Western fantasy of the Orient—sensual, decadent, and dangerous. The wicked stereotype had been applied to powerful Asian women before Madame Nhu, women like Chiang Kai-shek's wife Soong May-ling and the Chinese empress Xixi. The spectacular treason trial of Tokyo Rose, the voice behind Japanese propaganda during World War II, was still fresh in the American collective memory when Madame Nhu accused Americans in Vietnam of acting like "little soldiers of fortune." As a result, the public image of Madame Nhu as the Dragon Lady was one-dimensional, like the mustache-twisting villain in a bad Hollywood script, and a little too convenient.

Madame Nhu, whatever you thought about her, had had a direct hand in shaping history. But she had been silent for decades. Despite her reputation for outspokenness, the world had heard little from the woman herself. Madame Nhu had turned the last *New York Times* reporter who tried to gain access to her away from her doorstep in Italy for being too nosy. That was in 1986.

Although nearly twenty years had passed, there was no reason that I should have any more luck, I told myself as I stared at the building across the street. Just a few hundred meters behind me, the Eiffel Tower soared to its full height. I tried to look inconspicuous as I counted the building's stories. Tenacious old girl, I thought. As far as the rest of the world knew, including all the so-called experts I had interviewed, Madame Nhu was living in a rundown whitewashed villa somewhere on the outskirts of Rome. It had been anyone's guess as to whether she was even still alive.

But I had reason to believe that she was here, in Paris.

My search for Madame Nhu began with simple curiosity. I was born in 1976, some seventeen months after the end of the war and a universe apart. Like most kids I knew growing up during the 1980s, my early knowledge about Vietnam came from movies; grownups certainly didn't talk much about it. Vietnam wasn't a country; it was a cacophony of thumping helicopter blades, flaming thatched huts, and napalmed jungles. I held onto that perception until my junior year in college, when I enrolled for a semester abroad at Vietnam National University in Hanoi, which I'd thought of as something of a lark. A Communist country in the jungles of Southeast Asia sounded dangerous and exciting; adding to the drama, the State Department recommended getting typhoid, tetanus, and rabies vaccinations, as well as taking along antimalarial drugs and iodine pills. My father was stupefied: "I spent my twenties trying to stay out of Vietnam, and here you go, trying to get in!"

By 2003, I had a master's degree in Asian studies, had lived in Vietnam twice, and received a US Department of Education scholarship that gave me supreme confidence in my Vietnamese language skills—as long as I was talking about something simple, like a menu or the weather. When it came time to think about getting an actual job, I wished I had done more than pick up a cool CIA pen from the campus job fair.

Rather than face an uncertain future, I sought comfort where I always have—in books. I returned again and again to the second floor of Boston's Central Library, where the Vietnam books were kept. Four or five men roughly my father's age and dressed in ill-fitting coats and baggy pants would be sitting around the tables placed at the periphery of the stacks. The smell of stale coffee leeched into the air around them. It was hard for me to reconcile the Vietnam I knew from 2004, the friendly faces, overflowing markets, and modern cities, with the country—and the war—that had ruined so many lives. Who might these men have become if it hadn't been for Vietnam?

"Life is random," my father would say, like a mantra. He meant the words to be comforting. It was his way of soothing my naive sense of injustice, of making sense of the world. My father got his draft notice in the mail in 1966, just after his college graduation. He had already been accepted to graduate school and offered a stipend as a teaching assistant, but the draft board rejected his appeal for a deferment. My father's number all but guaranteed him infantry duty in Vietnam, so, like many in the same predicament, he applied to Officer Candidate School and was accepted into the army. He faced better odds as a volunteer officer candidate than as a draftee on foot patrol.

Just weeks before he was due to report to boot camp, my father was watching television in his parents' living room. President Lyndon Johnson appeared on the screen and publicly extended the draft deferment to include graduate student teachers. My dad leapt up from the couch and hugged his mother; in short order, he called his local draft board, got his deferment, and unpacked his bags.

He caught hell from the recruiting officers, who were anxious to make their quota, and from his friend Don. Don and my father had carpooled to the university every day for four years. They were from the same neighborhood, a working-class suburb of Seattle, and lived at home with their parents to save money on room and board. They had talked about how education was their ticket out of their families' poverty. Don had a spot in a graduate program too. He could have used the same deferment as my dad to avoid the draft.

But Don didn't see the point of deferring. He tried to talk my dad back into enlisting, "just to get it over with," he reasoned. They would do a quick tour of duty in Southeast Asia before starting the rest of their lives.

Don wasn't in Vietnam two weeks before his helicopter was shot down and he was killed.

As a little girl, I would stretch on tiptoe to pull the maroon-covered Time-Life book about the Vietnam War down from our living room bookshelves. The photographs were horrible and fascinating and raised more questions for me than the grownups could answer. There was the one of the South Vietnamese policeman shooting a man's brains out and the image of the little girl running down a road, naked and burning. It was a war I would never begin to understand, I thought, but instead of closing the book, I returned to it time and time again. My favorite was Larry Burrows' 1962 photo of Madame Nhu. With her piles of black hair and lacquered fingernails, she jumped out from the rest of the war's drab, olive-clad personalities. Wearing a traditional Vietnamese dress, the flowing *ao dai,* in virginal white, she was a tiny-waisted creature who could have been described as dainty, except for the heavy, black .38 caliber pistol that she held raised, aimed, and ready to fire. When her brother-in-law, President Ngo Dinh Diem, had once questioned the modesty of Madame Nhu's slim-fitting tunics, referring to their décolletage, she is said to have silenced him with a withering reply: "It's not your neck that sticks out, it's mine. So shut up."

My fascination as a little girl with Madame Nhu's glamour gradually evolved into recognition of a very contemporary problem. A female who dressed impeccably and took care to look good would always be accused of a lack of seriousness about changing social policies. Today, Michelle Obama is criticized for her biceps and bangs, but she is only the latest American First Lady to wrestle with questions of style and substance. Jacqueline Kennedy, Madame Nhu's contemporary in 1963, was an American icon of fashion, elegance, and grace. She believed, at the time, that women should simply stay out of politics because "they're just not suited to it." Jackie prided herself on her own "Asiatic" marriage and wholly disapproved of Madame Nhu, who had a "queer thing for power."

The lack of easy answers about Madame Nhu ensured that my intrigue lingered until I found myself in the library with plenty of underemployed time on my hands. Passing through the vacant gazes of the Vietnam veterans I shared the stacks with, I began to piece together the life of the woman everyone said had caused so much trouble.

I still had only the roughest outlines of Madame Nhu's story when I landed in Paris two years later. I had followed a flimsy trail based on an article on an obscure Vietnamese-language website written by someone I had never heard of. The author said that he had interviewed the famously reclusive Madame Nhu in her apartment three years before, in 2002. I would have dismissed the claim, but the author had been particularly precise about an eleventh-floor apartment with a view of the Eiffel Tower through the kitchen window. The description reminded me of something.

While poking around the papers of Clare Booth Luce at the Library of Congress a few months before, I had found a letter from Madame Nhu, postmarked in 1964. Luce had been an author, a playwright, a US senator, and, as a staunch supporter of ultraconservative Republican politics in Washington, something of a friend to Madame Nhu. The return address scrawled on the back of the envelope had provided my first glimpse of Madame Nhu's spidery handwriting. When I read about the Eiffel Tower view, I thought back to how carefully I had copied the curls of her script into my notebook: avenue Charles Floquet. It hadn't occurred to me that she might still be living there, but now I wondered, why not?

One glance and I knew I was wrong. The elegant building on avenue Charles Floquet where she had once lived looked like just the sort of place a deposed dictator might hide in until his money ran out. But it was only eight stories high. Even given the European penchant for designating the floor above the ground floor the first floor, this building was several short of the eleven I had been looking for.

I almost gave up on the spot. Even if the article was right and Madame Nhu was living in Paris, how many hundreds of buildings could boast a view of the Eiffel Tower? She could be a mile away and still see it. The tower was the only thing that stuck up in such a low-lying city. Just as I raised my gaze to the skyline to curse the aesthetics of the most beautiful city in the world, I had a crazy thought. I jumped onto a nearby bench and looked around. Such a low city simply did not have many eleven-story buildings—especially not this section of Paris. I just had to walk until I found one.

I had gone about a block when I saw them: three matching buildings, a mid-century mistake, near the Seine side of the avenue de Suffren. They were all concrete and right angles gone wrong. No matter—the sight of them dazzled me, for each stood a glorious twelve floors high. At the first one, I found a small bundle of a woman in a housecoat sweeping the steps. I approached her tentatively with an "excusez moi" and proceeded to ask, as tactfully as I could, whether there was an old Vietnamese lady who lived in her building on the eleventh floor. She paused just long enough to point to the building next door. "I think you are looking for the woman in number 24," she said with a little smile and a shake of her head. Maybe I was paranoid, but she seemed to be laughing at me.

She wouldn't have been the first to doubt me. When I confided to my graduate school advisor that I was thinking of pursuing the Dragon Lady, she had given me a patronizing smile—I assumed because, like everyone else, she thought Madame Nhu was simply too frivolous a topic. It took me longer to understand that my advisor, who had lived in Saigon through Madame Nhu's reign and seen school friends arrested by the South Vietnamese police, didn't think Madame Nhu was a subject worth revisiting.

But I was close now. Buoyed by something like confidence, or maybe naive optimism, I buzzed the concierge at 24 avenue de Suffren, and when she appeared, I grinned broadly at her. After she'd let me in, I slid a thin blue envelope inscribed with Madame Ngo Dinh Nhu's name across the front desk.

"Is she expecting something?" the concierge inquired dully. She was less than polite without being exactly rude, but I didn't care. She had confirmed that Madame Nhu lived upstairs.

"Please just make sure she gets this," I replied sweetly. Inside the envelope was a carefully worded note requesting an interview and one of the embossed calling cards I'd had made up in case I needed to make myself look professional. Tomorrow, Madame Nhu would know exactly who I was. As I walked back toward the Metro, I was already running through everything I would say when she called: how I would like to get her story right, how I hoped to fill in the gaps of history, and how I dared to think that we might redeem a little bit of the Dragon Lady's legacy. It never occurred to me that she might have plans of her own.

CHAPTER 2

Forgotten Graves

NO ONE HAD HEARD FROM Madame Nhu since the summer of 1986—the summer her parents, Tran Van Chuong and Tran Thi Nam Tran, had been murdered.

Madame Nhu's parents had been well known in diplomatic circles, even briefly famous when they publicly disowned their Dragon Lady daughter in 1963. In Vietnam, the Chuong couple had enjoyed an illustrious pedigree: Chuong was a large landowner and the first Vietnamese lawyer to get a French degree; his wife, Nam Tran, was related to the royal family and had been born a princess. They had lived a grand life in Vietnam before the war, with twenty servants waiting on them hand and foot. Madame Chuong clung to a sense of regal entitlement even in her role as a diplomat's wife in Washington, DC. When she hosted events, she asked that no one be allowed to wear the imperial color, yellow, except for her.

The Chuongs had lived in Washington since Chuong's appointment as the South Vietnamese ambassador in 1957. They returned to

Vietnam for brief visits in the 1960s, but never after the 1975 Communist victory. The Chuongs were long retired; Madame Nhu's father was eighty-eight and her mother seventy-six. They were just an elderly couple living out their last days in a quiet suburb of Washington, DC, when their only son killed them in their home. The murders brought the tragic and bizarre family history back into the spotlight.

Madame Nhu did not go to the funeral. By that time, she was growing old herself. She was a sixty-one-year-old recluse living in a shabby villa on the outskirts of Rome with her children. There had been rumors that Madame Nhu had emptied the South Vietnamese treasury before she left the country for the last time, but there was little outward sign of luxury anymore. Piece by piece she had sold off her property. A few straggly olive trees and some grazing sheep were all that separated the grandly named Villa of Serene Light from Rome's urban sprawl. Her only valuables had been those she managed to squirrel out of Saigon on her person, the jewelry and furs she was wearing and those tucked in her valise. Those were soon gone too. In 1971, Madame Nhu had been the victim of a jewelry heist: thieves made off with $32,000 in gold, jade, and gems.[1] Madame Nhu probably would not have been able to afford the trip to Washington, DC, to see her parents buried—at least not in a style that she would have considered fitting.

On Madame Nhu's last trip to the United States, in October 1963, her parents had left her standing on the doorstep of their Washington home with the door shut firmly in her face. Her father had called her "power mad" and said they "did not wish to know her" anymore. Her mother urged Americans to throw eggs and tomatoes at her.

Talking back would have broken the most sacred Confucian value: filial piety. A child should always respect her parents. The furthest Madame Nhu would go was to suggest that her parents must be "intoxicated." It was one of Madame Nhu's favorite lines—she used it against her parents, the international press, and even American president John F. Kennedy. But its meaning in English was not exactly what she intended. Intoxicated in French means poisoned. She meant to suggest that the Communists had poisoned the well of public opinion against her. She was trying to suggest that a desperate Communist tactic was at work—one intended to alienate her family from the Americans. But Madame Nhu didn't get her message across. Instead she sounded shrill, accusing those she didn't like of being drunk. After the 1963 coup in Saigon, the press reported that Madame Nhu had reconciled with her father. Chuong said of the rapprochement, "My heart was very near my daughter's."

To their neighbors, the Chuongs were just a sweet old couple, the kind who smile at children and puppies and wear sweaters even in the summer. Their home, at 5601 Western Avenue, was a two-story brick Georgian with white trim. The hedges were always neat, the walkway swept clear. Chuong's doctor described him as a pleasant gentleman, "very friendly," his wife, somewhat effervescent, always with a smile. It was inconceivable to think that this couple had survived three wars, evaded the colonial secret police, and outwitted the Communist guerrillas only to meet their end on a quiet July night in the seeming safety of their own home.

The police report had been graphic in detailing the discovery of the bodies. Madame Chuong lay on top of her husband. Her right arm was draped around him, as if she had died hugging him. They wore matching striped pajamas, but his were soaked with urine. Madame Chuong's upper lip was bruised, and she had a scratch under her chin. The red pinpoints on her eyeballs were from petechial hemorrhage, when blood leaks from the eye's tiny capillaries, a strong indication of death by strangulation or smothering—in this case, probably with a pillow.

All the evidence pointed to the Chuongs' only son, Tran Van Khiem. Khiem had been left behind in Vietnam in 1963 and had suffered badly. Until then, Khiem had been the scion of a once elite Vietnamese family to whom things had always been handed. When his sister was the First Lady, he was given a seat in the South Vietnamese government's National Assembly and diplomatic missions to foreign countries. Khiem skated along in typical playboy fashion, but he was fascinated with the inner workings of politics, especially the intrigue. Khiem started rumors that he was the head of a secret security force. He told Australian journalist Denis Warner that he had a hit list of American targets in Saigon that included embassy and military personnel. Madame Nhu's husband didn't like him much; he thought Khiem was immature and headstrong. So when Khiem came to the palace to visit his sister, Madame Nhu made sure to close the door to the sitting room or used the bedroom. Nhu and Diem weren't to know he was there. In fact, it didn't matter whether the Ngo brothers liked Khiem or not. He was family, and the regime's umbrella was broad enough to cover him. No real harm could come to him while the Ngos were in power.[2]

But afterwards, when Madame Nhu was in exile, Khiem was on his own in South Vietnam. The new military junta in Saigon arrested him. His mother tried to intercede from Washington. She called Roger Hilsman at the State Department, begging him to do something to save her only son. He would recall that Madame Chuong had been highly distraught, but even in her hysteria, unsentimental and pragmatic. Khiem was "only a stupid boy," Madame Chuong pleaded. He was harmless, just someone who had fallen "foolishly under the sway of his older sister," Madame Nhu.

Madame Chuong's pleas fell on deaf ears. The American ambassador, Henry Cabot Lodge, might have helped but he had no sympathy. He thought Khiem a "thoroughly reprehensible individual" and would not interfere with what he said, without a trace of irony, was the junta's "orderly administration of justice."[3] Khiem was locked in a cell in Saigon's old French prison. Looking back on his time there, he called what they did to him—using sleep deprivation and exhaustion to break his mind—"scientific torture."[4] At least he had been spared the firing squad. The new junta didn't like holdovers from the old regime that might threaten their power, but apparently they didn't think Khiem posed much of a threat. Or maybe he was more useful to them alive, an example of what happened to those loyal to the old regime. Madame Nhu's brother-in-law, Ngo Dinh Can, didn't fare as well. He was so paralyzed by diabetes left untreated during his incarceration at Chi Hoa Prison that he had to be carried to the courtyard, unable to stand for his own execution.

Khiem was subsequently shipped south to the prison island of Poulo Condor, assigned to hard labor until his broken body matched his fragile mind. Who knows what backroom negotiations got him out of Vietnam and to France, but by then forty-year-old Khiem had the body of an old man. He suffered from a heart condition and a kidney ailment. His other scars, the mental ones, were not immediately as visible.

Khiem couldn't find a job, and he had a wife and twelve-year-old son to support. His parents came up with an arrangement that was supposed to save face: they said they needed him to move in with them now that they were getting old. By allowing Khiem, his wife, and son to live with them in Washington, his parents were helping him just as much as he was, in theory, going to be helping them. But it never really worked out. Family dinners dissolved into shouting matches, political disagreements about history long past in a country that no longer existed.

The Chuongs had been working up the courage to kick him out when Khiem discovered their will. He had been disinherited. In a witnessed letter, Madame Chuong had written in a neat, tight script that her son had "behaved all his life like an exceptionally ungrateful and bad son and has been too often to his parents a great source of worries and deep sorrow. Such behavior cannot be forgotten and forgiven in a traditional Vietnamese family."

With all the evidence against him, the Chuong murders should have been an open-and-shut case, but it dragged on. At question was not whether Khiem killed his parents—that was clear. The problem was determining whether he had the mental capacity to stand trial for two premeditated murders. Khiem's legal team challenged the court order forcing him to take psychotropic drugs that would render him competent, but because of the lack of legal precedents, it took seven years' worth of appeals for a determination to stick. Khiem's bizarre behavior and courtroom theatrics, railing against the drugs' side effects, didn't speed the process.

Khiem's mental state didn't improve during his seven years as a forensic patient at St. Elizabeth's, a psychiatric hospital in southeastern Washington, DC. The institution was like a parody of an insane asylum: thousands of brains were preserved in formaldehyde, and an on-site incinerator fueled rumors about what happened to the victims of botched lobotomies and CIA-tested chemical cocktails like "truth serums." During Khiem's time there, the most basic facilities of the massive, red-turreted building evidenced years of neglect. Equipment failures and medicine shortages occurred frequently, and the heating system was broken for weeks at a time.[5] Khiem stayed at St. Elizabeth's until 1993. The Supreme Court rejected his appeal when it became clear that Khiem would never be competent enough to participate in his own defense. He was deported to France and has not been heard from since.[6] Whenever I asked Madame Nhu about her brother, I was met with silence. At most she would say, "Of course he is still alive!" but I never found any trace of him.

Years of prison and torture had twisted Khiem's brain. He believed he was at the center of a Zionist conspiracy—he wrote as much in a letter to Ronald Reagan, and that was before he tried to get the US president subpoenaed to testify in his defense. The thought of living on his own, cut off from his parents' wealth, snapped the fragile threads that connected Khiem to reality. Whatever wild thoughts had been running through his mind as he asphyxiated his frail and elderly parents with a pillow in their bedroom, Madame Nhu showed a kind of sympathy. Had she stayed in South Vietnam, who knows what she would have suffered? Her younger brother was in no way as notorious as she was; she would have fared much worse.

Madame Nhu stood up for her brother. She continued to claim that Khiem was framed for the murders and insisted that her parents had died of natural causes. Her brother was the real victim. "Agents provocateurs" were trying to silence him because he knew terrible secrets about the United States. "They [had] decided to finish him" by framing him for the murders and locking him up in an insane asylum, they being the unnamed but implied American government. You couldn't really blame Madame Nhu—the US government had certainly conspired against her in the past.

Like Khiem, Madame Nhu had been cut out of her parents' will. Her mother simply believed that her middle daughter "had no need of being provided for by me." Madame Nhu didn't agree. While Khiem's murder trial was bogged down in appeals, she hired Khiem's lawyer to represent both her and the mentally incompetent Khiem to reclaim part of their dead parents' estate. Madame Nhu's motives were opaque if not duplicitous: if Khiem lost his insanity plea and was found guilty, and if they managed to overturn the inheritance issue, Madame Nhu would get his share. The case was thrown out of the US court system because of the conflict of interest.

Soon after the murders, Madame Nhu stopped speaking to the press altogether. "This is a family affair," was her final statement. The family was indeed remarkable: one Dragon Lady daughter exiled to Rome, one murdering son locked up in a mental institution, and the oldest child, Le Chi Oggeri, living a seemingly normal life as a professor and artist in North Carolina, left to mourn the loss of her parents. "The end did not match the beginning," Le Chi wistfully told the reporters from the *Washington Post*. "For such beautiful lives, it should have been a beautiful end."

The Chuongs are buried less than five miles from the home they died in. Rock Creek Cemetery is a sprawling eighty-six acres of pastoral beauty in the northwest corner of metropolitan Washington, DC. A narrow paved road dips down and rises again; headstones dot the hills like masts bobbing in an undulating sea of green. They bear some illustrious names from the past—Roosevelts and Adamses—and some distinguished contemporary names, like Tim Russert and Gore Vidal. The Chuongs' double plot is in Section L, halfway up one of the smaller rises.

The twin headstones are of rose-colored granite, with a simply carved lotus below each of their names. Ambassador Tran Van Chuong. Princess Nam Tran Tran Van Chuong. The ground has shifted in the twenty-five years that they have lain together on that hill. Madame Chuong's grave is no longer perfectly straight but just slightly off kilter, as if she is leaning into her husband.

On the spring morning I visited the Chuongs, long grasses waved around the headstones and between the graves, making them look slightly unkempt. With my sister-in-law and infant niece sleeping in her portable car seat as company, I imagined that we were the first visitors the Chuongs had had in a while. I was suddenly self-conscious about having arrived to visit them empty handed.

"Should have brought flowers," I mumbled to myself.

My sister-in-law stepped forward and joined me at the gravesite. She placed the baby's carrier between the graves, dropped to her knees, and began to tug at the weeds. Together we made quick work of neatening up the site. As we pulled at the clumps of tall grasses crowding the headstones, the scent of wild onions bloomed in the air. The smell would linger on our fingertips for only a few hours, but the satisfaction of seeing and grooming the graves stayed with me. It was symbolic of the task at hand. To find out anything about the Dragon Lady, I would have to put her family life in order and place the Chuong family into the larger context of Vietnam's history. The important thing was to tell the story before it suffered the neglect of a forgotten grave.

Before leaving, I rested one hand on each headstone. The image of the Chuongs' kindly faces from the newspaper floated before me. I was so sorry for them; what a terrible way to go. The words of Le Chi, their oldest daughter, echoed in my head: "The more you tell about the glories of the past, the more horrible the end becomes."[7]

CHAPTER 3

A Distinguished Family

THE MORE I LEARNED ABOUT MADAME NHU'S early years, the less glorious her family's past seemed. It became hard to reconcile the smiling faces of the elderly couple pictured in a 1986 Washington newspaper with the darker portrait of the Chuongs that emerged. Madame Nhu's "miserable" memories of childhood fell into place when I understood that no one, certainly not her mother or her father, had any inclination to think that the little girl, born in a Hanoi hospital on August 22, 1924, might amount to anything significant.

A traditional birth would have taken place at home with a midwife, who would have said that this particular spirit was reluctant to be born because the baby was in a stubborn position, refusing to come down the birth canal. She would have disapproved of the forceps, shiny instruments and modern science, as interference with heaven's will. A midwife would have left this child, born blue, silent, and immobile, to return to whatever crossroads exist for unborn souls hovering somewhere between heaven and earth.

But no midwife was there that day. The child was going to be a boy. The mother was so sure of it that she had arranged to give birth in the hospital. She suffered through the terrible agony of the long labor, knowing it would be worth it—for a boy.

The French doctor may have feared that he would be blamed if anything happened. It was his first time delivering a Vietnamese baby since his arrival in Indochina, but this was a special case.

The young woman lying soaked in sweat and blood on his table was Madame Chuong, born Princess Nam Tran, a member of the imperial family. The fourteen-year-old's exquisite beauty was so rare that it later earned her a legion of French admirers, who nicknamed her "the Pearl of Asia."[1] Although schooled in the domestic arts of homemaking, as well as singing and sewing, she would never need to lift a porcelain finger, except to ring for a servant. Her most important duty as wife would be to bear her husband a male heir.

Her husband hailed from a family of powerful landowners. As the eldest son of an esteemed provincial governor in French Tonkin, Chuong had been given the very best of everything, from a Western education to a bride with royal lineage.[2] The Tran family was also related to the imperial throne, making Chuong a distant cousin to his bride.

The French doctor must have felt great pressure to save the pale form that finally came out in a great gush of blood and fluid. This was the doctor's chance to prove himself—and the superiority of Western medicine. He took a firm grip on the infant's ankles and laid a series of well-placed spankings on the tiny backside until the first cries rang out.

With that, the newborn came howling into the world.[3] It was a girl.

What did the fourteen-year-old Madame Chuong make of her newborn daughter, a scarlet-faced bundle, now screaming in her arms? When she came into the world, there was little reason to suppose her fate would differ much from that of centuries of Vietnamese women before her. In the East Asian Confucian tradition, boys were expected to provide care for their parents when they aged, and only males honored the ancestor cult of Vietnam. Traditional Vietnamese sayings capture the disappointment of a daughter's birth: "One boy, that's something; ten girls, that's nothing"; or "A hundred girls aren't worth a single testicle."[4] On their marriage, men brought into their families the most prized possession of all: a daughter-in-law, who would be released from her role as virtual servant to her husband's family, his mother in particular, only when she had produced a son of her own. It was a vicious cycle.

Madame Chuong had already given birth to a girl. Her first child, Le Chi, was born less than two years before, and Madame Chuong had convinced herself that this second child would be a boy. She was so certain that she had already bought baby-boy toys and baby-boy clothing.

A second daughter only postponed Madame Chuong's freedom. Until she gave birth to a boy, she was the lowest person in the hierarchy of her husband's family. What's more, her husband's mother had been making some ominous threats. She wanted her son, Chuong, to take a second wife if the second child wasn't a boy. Chuong, after all, was the firstborn son of the illustrious Tran family—he should be given every chance to sow the family's greatness with his seed. Polygamy had been part of the cultural tradition in Vietnam for centuries. Royal daughter-in-law or not, a woman who gave birth only to daughters wasn't worth very much. Failures should be written off quickly.

It was a dismal prospect for the fourteen-year-old Madame Chuong. If her husband took a second wife, and if that one succeeded where she had failed, in giving the family a boy, Madame Chuong and her girls would be fearfully trapped in submission to others for the rest of their lives. It wasn't long before she set her mind to the fact that she would just have to do it all over again—and again—until she had the son she expected. And the one expected of her.

The new baby girl was named Le Xuan, or Beautiful Spring. Except it wasn't spring. August in Hanoi typically marks the beginning of autumn, and that year was no exception. It seemed that the early days of autumn had turned the city a little cooler, providing a refreshing break from the long, hot summer. Willow branches hung down, kissing the surface of the lake, inviting the breeze to dance in their leaves and the city's residents out into the open air to enjoy the fleeting mild season before the cold winds from China swooped in.

Little Le Xuan and her mother were not to enjoy a moment of it. Vietnamese tradition required that the newborn and its mother remain practically bedridden in a dark room for at least three months after the baby's birth. The room was supposed to be a cocoon for mother and child. Even bathing routines were restricted. The custom evolved from practical concerns having to do with infant-mortality risks in the tropical delta, but in practice the postpartum gloom must have been stifling. Except for the necessary traditional-medicine practitioners and fortune-tellers, Madame Chuong's visitors were limited to her closest family members.

The family astrologer was one of the first people to see the new baby. His job was to determine the fate of this child by cross-referencing the birth date, zodiac season, and birth hour with the positions of the sun and moon and to take into account any passing comets. It seems very possible that the fortune-teller intended to boost the spirits of the miserable young mother he found trapped in a dark room for three more months with the baby girl she didn't want. He exclaimed over the baby's fate: "It defies imagination!" The child, he told the stricken Madame Chuong, would rise to great heights. "Her star is unsurpassable!" The little girl would grow up believing in her fortune and also that the shining prediction had made her mother profoundly jealous. The result was a lifetime of strained mother-daughter relations and endless suspicion.

Madame Chuong was by all accounts a young and ravishing beauty from Hue, the imperial capital in the center of Vietnam. Emperor Dong Khanh, who ruled briefly from 1885 to 1889, had been her grandfather. A succession of her cousins had sat on the throne ever since. As a member of the extended royal family, she was considered a princess, and she exemplified traditional loveliness with one exception: when she smiled, her teeth were pearly and white. She had resisted the customary practice of lacquering her teeth with calcium oxide to turn them black. To her elders, her white smile looked rotten, like a mouthful of bones. Long white teeth belonged to savages and wild animals;

blackening them warded off fears that an evil spirit lurked inside the person. A mouthful of glossy black teeth was a traditional sign of elegance and beauty.

But to Chuong, the white smile of his young bride made her the perfect image of a modern wife. Chuong had become accustomed to European pleasures when he was a student abroad; he had a taste for French poetry, wine, Western movies, and motorcycles. Stepping away from tradition himself, Chuong had cut the long hair worn in a bun and abandoned the practice of wrapping a turban around his head typical of other men of his class and education. Long hair was a Confucian ideal, the value of filial piety applied to the body, hair, and skin, all extensions of the life bestowed on children by their parents. But Western ways were taking hold. Chuong embodied progress with his short hair, suit, and position as a lawyer with the colonial administration. As such, he would never accept a girl with blackened teeth as his wife.

The couple married in 1912.[5] The date of birth on Madame Chuong's headstone, and the date given to the Metropolitan Police Department for the 1986 death report, was 1910. This would have made her only two years old at the time of her marriage.

It was not uncommon for girls in the countryside to be married off at a very young age, perhaps thirteen or fourteen, but rarely was a toddler given away as a bride. The fact that both families were members of the elite made even less sense; they could have afforded to wait. A plausible explanation is that Madame Chuong's birth date had been conveniently confused, allowing her to age gracefully in the United States, far from anyone who would contradict her version of the truth.

But age confers status to the Vietnamese. There would have been no reason to try to appear young. Maybe Madame Chuong really was a two-year-old bride. An uncharacteristically long time passed after the marriage before the royal cousins started a family. Their first child, daughter Le Chi, was born almost a decade after their wedding date. Maybe the baby bride needed to reach childbearing age.

Chuong was still a boy himself on their wedding day. He was born in 1898, making him only fourteen years old when he wed. Chuong was the eldest son of Tran Van Thong, a *thong doc,* or esteemed provincial governor, in French Tonkin. According to his dossier in the French colonial archives, Chuong left both Vietnam and his bride shortly after the wedding. He went to France and North Africa to continue his studies.

The teenaged Chuong's timing was impeccable. He left Indochina just before World War I broke out. Leaving even a year later would have been impossible in wartime. World events forced young Chuong to stay far away from his homeland for over ten years. He was able to take advantage of educational opportunities that were available in Europe but unheard of for a Vietnamese, even one of his social standing. Chuong attended schools in Algiers, Montpellier, and Paris, receiving his law doctorate in 1922.[6] He was the first Vietnamese to do so.

During the years that Chuong was studying abroad, colonial tension in Vietnam had escalated. French authorities had begun to recruit "volunteer" native Vietnamese for the European war front, forcing thousands of peasants and impoverished workers to report for duty. The French swiftly tamped down any hint of riot or rebellion and turned the countryside "upside down" in search of traitors.[7]

There was also a growing chorus of disapproval about the educational opportunities available to the Vietnamese. The first, and for a long time the only, French lycée, Chasseloup-Laubat in Saigon, catered to the sons of European administrators. But with war raging in Europe, a shortage of personnel loomed increasingly large. The colony realized it needed to recruit more French-trained natives into the civil service if it hoped to survive. The hope was that spreading French ideas among the Vietnamese would bind the natives more closely to the mother country. The result, however, was ironic: by schooling the Vietnamese in Western principles, including those of freedom and the history of the republic, the educational reforms helped to spark a quest for political empowerment that would prove impossible to extinguish.

When Chuong finally returned to Vietnam at age twenty-four, his years of Western scholarship were handsomely rewarded. He landed an exalted apprenticeship in the French colonial judiciary and was awarded French citizenship on September 16, 1924, less than a month after the birth of his second daughter.[8]

Not long after Madame Chuong and her baby girl emerged from their postpartum isolation, Madame Chuong became pregnant for the third and final time before her sixteenth birthday. In 1925, she bore the boy she had so hoped for, Tran Van Khiem. The birth of a son put a decisive end to her childbearing responsibilities. It also confirmed Le Xuan's lowly position in the family.

Chuong was promoted to a new job near the town of Ca Mau, near the southern tip of the country, hundreds of kilometers away from the urban luxury of Hanoi. It was a high-profile post within the French colonial administration. Although the promotion would mean moving away from the cosmopolitan pleasures of the capital in Hanoi, rising to such a high-level position was a professional coup for a native Vietnamese.

There was only one small casualty: the Chuongs' middle daughter, Le Xuan, would be left behind. Like a chit at a coat check, Le Xuan was a token of exchange between her father and her paternal grandmother. It was a kind of proof of his filial devotion and a sign of his intent to return, but really it was nothing more than a symbolic gesture to make his mother happy. If keeping the child honored her, it was a small price to pay.[9]

The cluster of well-appointed homes with red-tile roofs surrounding a courtyard that made up the Trans' family estate shouldn't have been a bad place for a girl to grow up. The patriarch, Le Xuan's grandfather, was a large landowner, and anyone in his household was like a local celebrity in the lush green countryside of northern Vietnam. Le Xuan's grandmother was highly educated, which was exceptional for a Vietnamese woman of her day and age. Even as she had aged, and even as her eyesight had failed, she continued to read passages from the Vietnamese classics, or had them read to her.

Vietnamese stories are filled with strong, intelligent, and decisive women, but theirs is not always a happy ending. Was it here that Le Xuan heard pieces of the beloved and often-recited Vietnamese epic poem *The Tale of Kieu*—the story of a talented young woman, wellborn and extraordinarily beautiful to boot? Jealous of the girl, fate forces her to abandon her true love and sell herself into prostitution to save her father from prison. Kieu struggles in an unjust world, but she remains a model of integrity and righteousness. More than just a tragic heroine, she symbolized the Vietnamese people, caught in the moral degradation of political change. Though the story was hundreds of years old, in 1924, the year Le Xuan was born, Kieu was formally honored as a national cultural hero. The woman-as-victim officially became the most beloved heroine.[10]

Le Xuan's grandmother certainly did not see herself as a victim of anything. She presided over a sprawling household that included herself and two other wives and all of their children. In addition to her first son, Chuong, she had given her husband three more sons and two daughters, after which she had considered her wifely duties fulfilled. To avoid any confusion about that fact, she simply installed a pillow bolster down the middle of their marital bed. She also introduced her husband to his second wife, who bore him seven more children. In order to prevent the second wife from gaining too much power, she introduced her husband to his third wife. Each one of the wives and their children held a distinct rank in the family hierarchy. The skill of the grandmother, the matriarch, showed in the fact that none of them ever obviously sabotaged each other.[11]

Le Xuan's paternal grandparents' home was the perfect place to observe the disjointed and conflicting roles that Vietnamese women, especially members of the elite, assumed. Certainly, there was a clear emphasis on the behavioral code of Confucianism. Wives and daughters-in-law were expected to be outwardly dutiful and compliant. But behind the villa's closed doors, another reality prevailed. Men were not expected to pay attention to domestic affairs. Practical matters, like the family budget, were left to the women. It was understood, if not discussed, that women held the real power inside the family. If the family were a country, the husband would be the nominal head of state, in charge of foreign relations. The wife would be the minister of the interior and in control of the treasury.[12]

At first, Le Xuan's daily upbringing was entrusted to the care of nurses. Even the domestic help understood the base position of their child charge, so they mostly ignored her. She was a nobody in the traditional order of things. The nurses handed Le Xuan off to the gardeners who played with her like a toy. It just so happened that the gardeners employed at her grandparents' home were local petty thieves and village thugs, men ordered by her grandfather's court to serve time for their wrongdoing by doing good for the community—or the community's chief, her grandfather. She followed the men around as they took care of the animals. Sometimes she was even bathed alongside the animals.

Within a year of her parents' departure, the little girl became deathly ill. Madame Nhu would always claim that her parents never cared for her, but she concedes that the Chuongs returned from their new post in the far south as soon as they heard. It couldn't have been an easy trip to make. There were no rail lines linking the country, and the provinces were too distant for road travel. The most obvious means of traveling from south to north would have been by steamer ship along the coast. For ten days and nights, Le Xuan hovered between life and death.

Once Le Xuan's mother returned, she did not let her little girl out of her arms. But this, at least as the little girl would come to understand it, wasn't out of love, or even concern, for her middle daughter. It was a reproach directed at the child's grandmother. In the wild arena of family politics, her sick child had just earned the young Madame Chuong an edge over her mother-in-law.

Le Xuan recovered her health. She would remain scrawny for the rest of her childhood, but what she lacked in strength, she made up for with sheer will. Le Xuan would need to be scrappy. The severity of the illness had made her mother more suspicious than ever of her middle daughter. When she had last seen her, Le Xuan had been a black-haired infant with round cheeks. The skinny, hollow-cheeked girl she came home to could easily have been the child of a household servant or local peasant woman. Suspicion that her child had been switched nagged at Madame Chuong for the rest of her life. Her two other children knew this and exploited it, teasing their middle sister about being the nurse's child. And Madame Chuong used it as an excuse to forgive herself for not loving her middle daughter like she loved the other children. As the little girl grew up, she would feel like "a bothersome reminder for her [mother], an object of morbid doubt [and] family infighting."[13]

Once Le Xuan was well enough to travel, the Chuong family made their way back down the coast, all together now. They settled into life in the remote province of Bac Lieu. Madame Chuong, not even twenty-years old, presided over a large home with servants and an outsized tract of land.

With the cosmopolitan diversions of Hanoi now far away, the Chuongs reverted to a more traditional Vietnamese family life, one with distinctly Confucian leanings.[14] Free of her mother-in-law and her oppressive judgments, Madame Chuong managed the homestead, as she had been raised to do. Still, after a taste of city life in Hanoi, with all its Westernized pleasures, the quiet of the countryside and the traditional duties she assumed must have seemed tediously old-fashioned. Madame Chuong had left behind the chance to participate in the new opportunities emerging for women in cosmopolitan society. The wife of a modern man in the city, aside from running her household and supervising her children's education, could stand beside her husband in a social setting. This must have seemed impossibly exotic to the young girl living the life of a traditional Vietnamese wife and mother, as women had for centuries before her.

Did she dare to hope for something different for her own daughters? Judging from the educational opportunities she pushed for her girls, the answer seems to be yes. And yet, on those occasions when their educations conflicted with family hierarchies, centuries of tradition won out. The ground rules of a proper, traditional lifestyle demanded loyalty to family and fidelity to an ancient culture. Women were expected to obey three submissions, first to their father, then to their husband, and finally to their sons. Women were also encouraged to display the four virtues: management of the household income, decorum, harmonious speech, and virtuous behavior.

The ideals of domestic femininity were spelled out clearly in classic Vietnamese texts, manuals in "family education in verse." Written to be read aloud in singsong for easy memorizing, they made expectations for household management and morality clear.

> Do not talk to a man who is not a relative;
> Do not say hello to him, so as not to arouse suspicion.
> Do not frequent women who are not virtuous;
> Do not alter your clothing without reason;

> When sewing, do not let your needle be idle;
> When alone, do not sing or declaim poetry;
> Do not look out the window with a pensive air.
> . . . Do not shrug, do not sigh;
> Do not laugh before you have even said a word;
> When laughing, do not show all your teeth;
> Do not gossip or talk crudely.[15]

Le Xuan learned early that she must defer to the established role of middle daughter. Her parents and elders were to be honored and obeyed, and so were her siblings. Le Xuan occupied the most menial position in the family. Her aggravation at being told what to do started at a young age. "It is something like a game my [brother] used to tease me with when I was a child. I would be sitting down, and he would say, 'Sit down.' So to show that I was not sitting because he ordered me to do it, I would stand up. But then he would say, 'Stand up.' It made me very angry."[16]

Another child might have reacted differently, becoming docile as she acclimated to the reality of her circumstances. But Madame Nhu remembered her childhood as an infuriating time. She craved attention and approval. To get it, she had to work a little harder, cry a little louder. Even as a little girl, she believed she was entitled to more.

Le Xuan's formal education started when an old, turbaned tutor with two fused fingers came to the family home to instruct her and her two siblings. At the exceptionally young age of five, she was sent off to boarding school in Saigon with her sister.

Young Le Xuan was studious and serious. Her younger brother envied her good grades and intelligence. When she was away, he missed his sister as a playmate, but when she returned, he often felt frustrated by their differences in ability. He didn't like being treated as the baby. One day he got so frustrated that he ripped her writing plume out of her hands and threw it at her head. The sharp tip stuck straight into her forehead. Le Xuan ran upstairs with the feather sticking out of her head and ink running down her face to show her mother. Her younger brother was not perfect, she wanted to scream.

Le Xuan's mother was angry—but not with her son. A girl with proper manners would never have shown such determination to humiliate the family heir. The girl was punished.[17]

CHAPTER 4

Portrait of a Young Lady

THE CHUONG FAMILY MOVED BACK TO Hanoi before Le Xuan's eighth birthday. Her father had been appointed to serve on the Hanoi Bar, the highest-profile job a Vietnamese lawyer could aim for in the colonial system. While an honor, it was also a reminder of the limited options available to even the best-educated Vietnamese.[1]

After seven years in the southern countryside, Hanoi was a foreign city to Le Xuan. The people spoke with an accent filled with industrious buzzing. They hit the low tones with hard clicking stops that southerners usually just rolled through. The food was less sweet. There were no more floating chunks of pineapple or mango in her *canh,* the soup served over rice at most meals. Every time Le Xuan took a bite of something, even something she thought she knew, she had to be careful. *Cha gio,* the crispy spring rolls of the south, were called *nem* in Hanoi, and their sauce had a different heat in the north, a black pepper that tickled her nose rather than the spreading warmth of the chili used down south.

Le Xuan felt oddly out of place in Hanoi for another reason: it was much harder in a dense city to avoid the complications of race. To some extent, the Chuong family's wealth and elite status cushioned the otherwise stark segregation of the colonial city. Their home, Number 71 on the boulevard Gambetta, was a grand manor, tall and narrow with a mansard roof, gabled rooms, and dormer windows. It looked like the others in their neighborhood, but most of those belonged to French families. In fact, the whole neighborhood was known as the French Quarter. At the end of the nineteenth century, colonial urban planners had filled in swampland and carved broad avenues shaded by tamarind trees. A British visitor to Hanoi described how it must have looked to Le Xuan in 1932: "The villas are pure French, making no concessions to climate, and were it not for palms, bougainvillea . . . they might be standing in some pleasant outskirt of Paris."[2]

Le Xuan would have seen how most urban Vietnamese lived only when she was driven through town—either from behind the windows of a chauffeured Mercedes or from the perch of a *cyclo-pousse,* a narrow, open-topped carriage pushed by a servant pedaling a bicycle. The jumble of thirty-six streets to the northwest of the Chuong home known as the Old Quarter was far easier to navigate by *pousse*. Traditional houses had clay walls and thatched roofs. Impossibly narrow alleyways linked the homes, creating a veritable labyrinth. Behind darkened doorways, artisans meticulously plied their crafts from dawn to dusk, weaving silk, pounding silver, or making parasols, many in exactly the same manner as their ancestors. Steam from curbside noodle shops and incense smoke from the pagodas perfumed the air.

Although less than a kilometer from where Le Xuan lived, the Old Quarter was separated by a chasm. The better-off could afford wooden frames and tiled roofs, but others with less-substantial shelter suffered through summer's torrential rains and winter's chill. The Great Depression had put an added strain on living conditions for Vietnamese in Hanoi. Peasants had fled the countryside looking for opportunity in the city, but found little, if any. Open sewers and shantytowns expanded the urban periphery. Violence simmered among the discontent.

Eight-year-old Le Xuan had a different experience with colonial injustice. She went to a French school with French children and spoke

French at home with her parents. The Chuongs and the few Vietnamese like them who could afford it took part in Western pastimes, like tennis and even the yo-yo. Women imitated the Paris fashions; boatneck blouses permitted a peek at the soft skin below the collarbone, and propriety no longer required women to bind their breasts so tightly. Rouge, lipstick, and perfume became the rage. The good life was a big party featuring French champagne and swing music. The quest for pleasure became the new preoccupation among the young and liberated generation of elite.

Le Xuan wanted to fit into her new surroundings, but how? There simply were not many Vietnamese families like hers. Le Xuan's best friend from childhood was an outsider too, a Japanese girl. Their shared misery forged a permanent bond, and they remained in touch for the rest of their lives. Most of the other Vietnamese that Le Xuan saw regularly worked on her family's staff of twenty servants, including cooks, drivers, maids, and gardeners. The little girl knew her French history well enough to know that her street, a main thoroughfare that ran east-west across the city, was named for Leon Gambetta, a nineteenth-century French statesman who believed that France's prestige in the world hinged on aggressive colonialism—on conquering people and places. The French had only been in Vietnam since the 1860s, and the seven decades of European presence were nothing compared to Vietnam's history of 1,000 years of Chinese occupation; all the same, colonial injustice was a fact of life for young Le Xuan.

Indeed, the French forbade the use of the word "Vietnam," which referred to the unification of the country. To keep their colonial power intact, the French had to keep the Vietnamese from getting too strong—so they conquered by dividing. The administration of the country was split into three parts: the north (Tonkin) and center (Annam) were nominally sovereign Vietnamese territories, or protectorates, of France. The resource-rich southern third of the country, Cochinchina, was governed by direct colonial rule. The colony was carved into large estates for the production of rice, rubber, and other valuable commodities. To fund the colonial administration, the French state depended on revenue from the monopolies it controlled: salt, alcohol, and particularly opium. The French knew just how dangerous opium was, but they also knew how profitable addiction could be. They opened opium-buying centers in every village. Villages that didn't meet their sales quota were punished.[3]

Colonial prosperity in Indochina had a dark underbelly. There were stories of village families forced to sell sons and daughters to pay onerous taxes. Working conditions at the French-run factories, in the mines, or on the rubber plantations were hell on earth for the Vietnamese laborers. Malaria and cholera were rampant, and there was barely enough rice to fuel the twelve-hour workdays. One worker at the Michelin plantation watched as his French manager called in soldiers to deal with seven men who had tried to escape; the manager "forced the escapees down on the ground and let the soldiers tramp on their ribs with their nail studded boots. Standing outside I could hear the sound of bones snapping."[4] Factory owners were said to provide dark cages for workers' children, who emerged to rejoin their parents at the end of the day covered in filth.

More than just the profit motive encouraged the French to believe that Indochina's natural resources were theirs for the taking. They believed that Vietnamese were biologically inferior.[5] The French term for the Vietnamese, regardless of which region they were from, was *Annamite.* The word had its origins in Chinese, but to the French it sounded very much like *une mite,* meaning insect or parasite. Another term they used to address any Vietnamese, regardless of class, was *nha que,* or peasant. An educated city dweller would have bristled at the characterization, but the careful ones and those like Le Xuan's father, who had the most to lose, didn't dare show their displeasure.

The Chuongs didn't participate in any overt anti-French activity—at least not at this point. Their lives were too comfortable to take the risk. But even they could see that the colonial system was fraying. The timing of the Chuong family's move back to Hanoi coincided with the aftermath of the Yen Bay uprising, the most serious rebellion the territory had seen in the French era. In February 1930, a group of Vietnamese nationalists (Viet Nam Quoc Dan Dang, or VNQDD) attacked a French garrison post in North Vietnam, killing the French officers stationed there and seizing an arms depot. To preserve their authority, the French responded with a show of strength intended to terrify the Vietnamese back into submission. The colonial government clamped down on suspected rebels, guillotined those they caught, and threw bombs into assembled crowds and suspect villages.[6]

The children's school in Hanoi was located next to the French governor-general's residence. The saffron-plastered building still stands today but houses the offices and reception rooms for the Central Committee of the Vietnamese Communist Party. In Le Xuan's day, the school was named after Albert Sarraut, the governor-general in Indochina from 1911 to 1913. Although Sarraut was celebrated for pushing education reform, his motivation was, at its base, another troubling example of the predominance of racism. He believed that the Vietnamese could not be civilized until their thinking, customs, and institutions mirrored those of the French. For Albert Sarraut, the self-proclaimed champion of native education reform, the Vietnamese would "deserve independence from French rule only when they no longer desired to be Vietnamese, but Frenchman in yellow skin."[7]

Le Xuan was taught to speak, read, write, and think like a good little French schoolgirl. She learned the order of the kings of France and the dates of all the French battles against the British. She could sing about forests and snow-capped mountains without ever having laid eyes on them. She was tested in French poetry and dictation but never about her own heritage. Le Xuan was supposed to forget that she was Vietnamese and encouraged to believe that she was destined to participate in another, superior culture.

Now that the family was back in Hanoi and the children were busy with school, the lady of the house, Madame Chuong, could enjoy a bit more liberty. Freed from the traditional countryside, the pressure to bear another child, and the meddling of her mother-in-law, Madame Chuong could explore what it meant to be a Vietnamese woman in an era of experimentation and even permissiveness. Unthinkable just one generation before, Vietnamese women now joined men in public social settings like restaurants and dance halls.

Because Madame Chuong didn't have to flatten her breasts with cloth under a tunic anymore, she could show off her figure. She could have dresses made to order, copying the latest fashions, such as dropped hems and flouncy skirts. Godard's Department Store on the corner of rue Paul Bert sold silk stockings, hats, and hairpins. The Chuongs' favor with the French gave them the economic means to pursue all of Hanoi's European pleasures. A chauffeured Mercedes squired them around the town; they ate in the city's most elegant Chinese restaurants and enjoyed the cinema showing American and French films. The Palace was the most modern and most expensive of the seven movie theaters in Hanoi, but even the poorest urban Vietnamese could see movies. There was the Trung Quoc across town, where people squatted together on wooden slats, craning their heads for a better view of the screen. An even cheaper ticket could be had for those willing to stand on the wrong side of the screen and watch the flickering images back to front.[8]

On Tuesday afternoons, Madame Chuong hosted a social gathering in her home. Her guests were Vietnamese and French—and after 1939, Japanese. Men and women mingled comfortably over canapés and cocktails in the parlor. Anyone who was anyone, or might be someday, attended. Laughter and conversation floated up past the crystal chandeliers and wound up the stairs to the landing where the children crouched, listening to the adults below.

Madame Chuong was adapting the tradition, dating back to the French Revolution, of elite women presiding over salons in their homes, where guests could engage in intellectual debate over art, literature, and even politics. Powerful men were always in attendance at Madame Chuong's gatherings, but feminism and women's rights became vehicles for arguing about another topic, one much too dangerous to address outright: Vietnamese freedom from French colonialism. There were spirited debates about the proper role of women, the value of education for women, and the balance between family hearth and public life, but at the root of all these questions was a much larger one: how could Vietnam become modern and free?

I had expected to find reams of information on Madame Chuong's Tuesday salons in the archives of the notorious French Sûreté, the secret police, but instead of intelligence on the dangerous people and ideas she hosted, I found a salacious account of the Chuongs' life as a couple.

Nothing in the French files supported the idea of the "glory" described in the Chuongs' obituary so many years later. In fact, the reality was quite the opposite. French army general Georges Aymé described Le Xuan's father, Chuong, as "a little runt," a limp character who couldn't keep his own wife satisfied. The most generous description I could find of Chuong in the archives characterized him as "intelligent, if subtle." It seemed a far cry from the portrait of the dignified diplomat presented at his death.

But the description of Madame Chuong shocked me most. "Chuong's WIFE is beautiful and very intriguing. In Annamite circles, it is known that she is the one in charge, she directs her husband." That wasn't so surprising. Even with greying temples, Madame Chuong always looked regal and in control in the pictures I had seen. But I had never seen a picture of her wild side—which was, according to the French secret police, "famous throughout Indochina." She was known as much for "her dogged ambition as for her *coucheries utilitaires*—sleeping around with people of influence from any and all nationalities."

French reports tallied her lovers, including the most prominent—and most threatening—one. Sometime after his arrival in 1939, the Japanese diplomat Yokoyama Masayuki betrayed his French wife for Madame Chuong; in return, she was described as more than his mistress.[9] Madame Chuong became the Japanese consul's "right arm" in Hanoi. To the French, it was an ominous sign that a woman as smart and ambitious as Madame Chuong would choose the Japanese over the French. She was doing what she could to help secure her family's good position in quickly shifting political sands.

The allegations were transmitted to Paris on faded onionskin sheets and archived, preserving the tittle-tattle of diplomats for posterity. According to one rumor that gained traction many years later as café gossip, among Madame Chuong's many lovers in Hanoi was a man by the name of Ngo Dinh Nhu.[10]

Nhu was approaching thirty when introduced to the fifteen-year-old Le Xuan in 1940. An eligible bachelor from a good family in Hue, he had the kind of handsomeness that would only improve with age and experience. They met in the garden of the Chuong house in Hanoi. Nhu was just back in Vietnam after having spent much of the last decade studying in France. First he had gotten a degree in literature. Then, while studying librarianship, he had earned a degree in paleography, the study of ancient handwriting, from the prestigious Parisian École Nationale des Chartes. Nhu was beginning a position at the archives in Hanoi when he met Le Xuan.[11] All of this might have seemed bookish and small to someone with more experience, but to Le Xuan, who was still in high school and had never left the country, Nhu's experiences abroad gave him an exotic appeal. A marriage would deliver her from the daily humiliations visited by her family. It seemed to Le Xuan that a man who preferred books to politics would be a relief from the duplicity and shifting loyalties she witnessed in her own parents' marriage. The fact that Nhu smiled more than he spoke seemed another good sign. Getting married was the next step for a girl of her breeding, and Le Xuan didn't think she would do better than Nhu.

The catch was that Nhu's family was strongly Catholic. Catholic families were a minority among the Vietnamese elite and somewhat of an oddity. Still, it was as good as a middle daughter should expect.

Nhu was the fourth boy in his family. His father, Ngo Dinh Kha, had once held an important position in the royal court in Hue, but by the time Nhu was born in 1910, the French had deposed the emperor whom Kha served. In solidarity with his sovereign, Kha quit his position and moved his family to the countryside to raise buffalo and cultivate rice, a notable—if noble—step down. Kha's rejection of the French intrusion into Vietnamese affairs reinforced the family's sense of honor and nationalist duty—traits duly passed along to all six sons.

Every morning, Kha's nine children attended a mass at 6:00 a.m. After that, school. Their father also expected them to work in the fields alongside the local peasants, getting their hands dirty. Although Kha himself wore the traditional silk robes of a scholar and grew his fingernails two inches long as a sign of his elite mandarin status, he continually admonished his boys that "a man must understand the life of a farmer."

Kha personally oversaw the education of his boys, in and out of the home. At school, he demanded that they follow the European curriculum. At home, he taught them the mandarin classics. In addition to its scholarly emphasis, Kha's home was a place to learn about anti-French nationalist politics.

By the time of Nhu and Le Xuan's first meeting, the older brothers in the Ngo family were already established in prominent careers. The eldest son was serving as a provincial governor. The second eldest was on his way to becoming one of the first Vietnamese bishops in the Catholic Church. The third brother, the family member who would have the most direct hand in shaping the country's future, was the future president of South Vietnam, Ngo Dinh Diem.

In later interviews with Western reporters, Madame Nhu would candidly admit that her marriage to Nhu was a practical matter, not a romantic one. "I never had a sweeping love." She confessed to Charlie Mohr of *Time* magazine. "I read about such things in books, but I do not believe that they really exist. Or perhaps only for a very few people."[12]

But young Le Xuan was a good actress, and she knew a good role when she saw one. In 1940, just before she met Nhu, the young ladies of Madame Parmentier's ballet school had put on *Snow White*. The other French and Vietnamese students had refused to play the terrible witch, but Le Xuan saw the potential in the role. She would never be cast as Snow White; that part would go to one of the fair-skinned French girls. So she might as well steal the show with a magnificent, if cruel, performance.

Le Xuan saw Nhu as an opportunity. Whether out of love, ambition, or mutual convenience, Le Xuan and Nhu were engaged shortly after their garden encounter. They were betrothed for three years, a Vietnamese tradition, although one not followed by Le Xuan's parents. But during that time, from 1940 to 1943, the universe as Le Xuan had always known it changed entirely.

World War II raged in Europe. The military defeat of France left Indochina all but cut off from the motherland. The Vichy government in

France granted the Japanese the right to transport troops across northern Vietnam to southern China, build airfields, requisition food supplies, and station 6,000 men in Tonkin.

Japanese diplomats, interpreters, intelligence specialists, and businessmen took the places of honor at the Chuongs' Tuesday salons, and the French colonials in Indochina took it badly. They simply couldn't, or wouldn't, believe that their surrender in Europe compromised their colonial rights to rule Indochina. So for a time, the French tried to live as normally as possible, retaining their servants, dressing formally for dinner, and gathering at cafés to talk about their weekend trips to the beach or the winner at the horse races. The French might have handed the deed to their colonial property in Indochina over to the Japanese, but for five more years, they would do their best to keep up appearances. The French flag continued to fly. *Boulangeries,* deprived of their customary 20,000 tons per year of imported wheat flour, also tried to make the illusion last, baking bread from corn and rice. Indochina was the only Southeast Asian area under Japanese control that had allowed white colonials to remain.

In 1942 ration tickets were issued to Europeans for rice, salt, sugar, cooking oil, soap, matches, "quality" cigarettes, and fuel. The French still enjoyed favored status when it came to meat and condensed milk: they were supplied first. All this was justified in the colonial mindset by the notion that the Annamites were accustomed to simple diets, whereas Europeans would become ill without variety.

Although the Chuong family did not exactly suffer, they were deprived of the luxury goods they were used to. But the Chuongs were masters of political maneuvering and managed just fine—at least for a while. The Japanese infiltration of the nominal French regime made for a rather confusing state of political affairs. Who was in power, the Westerners or the Asians? Who would be more sympathetic to the nationalist aspirations of the Vietnamese? The Chuongs tried to cultivate important friendships on both sides, but eventually they chose to cast their lot with the Japanese under a banner of "Yellow Brotherhood." The Japanese encouraged the Vietnamese to think of themselves as part of a greater

Asian Co-Prosperity Sphere—one led by Japan, of course. At least the Japanese wouldn't claim superiority based on the color of their skin.

Le Xuan's mother signed on for Japanese-language lessons, and her romance with Yokoyama, the Empire of the Rising Sun's envoy in Hanoi, was soon rewarded. In 1945, her lover Yokoyama was appointed resident of Annam, and Tran Van Chuong, her husband, was promoted to a cabinet position in the Japanese puppet government.

Le Xuan and Ngo Dinh Nhu were married in the first week of May 1943 at the Saint Joseph Cathedral of Hanoi, or as Hanoi residents called it, *Nha Tho Lon*, the big church. It was only Le Xuan's second time in the towering, neo-gothic style church. The first had been the day before, for the confirmation of her conversion to the Catholic faith. She had worn long gloves and a lace mantilla that draped over her dark hair and cascaded past her shoulders. The profession of faith, which Le Xuan read aloud, proclaimed her new belief in God, his son Jesus Christ, the Holy Spirit, and the church and all its sacraments. Three times—at the mention of the Father, the Son, and the Holy Spirit—the priest poured water on Le Xuan's forehead, signaling a washing away of her sins. Then Le Xuan received her baptismal name. They chose Lucy, after St. Lucia, the patron saint of the blind. A Christian among pagans, Lucy had chosen to remain a virgin and clawed her eyes out instead of marrying a pagan suitor. Le Xuan's most beautiful features, her liquid eyes, stayed open during the ceremony, newly vigilant to the senses she most had to guard against—sensuality, pride, and vanity.

Sometime before the ceremony and behind closed doors, the groom's family had paid a *thach cuoi,* a bride-price, to Le Xuan's family. Traditionally, the payment acknowledged the loss of the bride to her family and monetized the forfeit of her labor. The fact that the Chuongs were an urban, rich family changed nothing about the custom. The Ngos may have paid entirely in cash or included practical items: cloth, jewels, meat, and tea. The bride-price for Le Xuan was determined by the status of her family, and thanks to their shifting allegiances, the Chuongs' status was still very good indeed in Japanese-occupied Hanoi.

The Chuongs' garden was transformed into a lavish oasis for the wedding reception after the full mass. The early May air was fragrant, full of blooming lilies and aromatic frangipani. Women flaunted their rationed silk and cosmetics. Some might have pulled their formal attire from careful storage, preserved in tissue from the era of carefree parties—before the mess of war. Others dressed in obvious contraband: women who knew the right men sported the latest fashions.

Wartime privation had not yet stemmed the Chuongs' supply of French champagne. It flowed into the clinking goblets of the guests, who were, as Madame Nhu would recall wistfully, the "tout Hanoi"—all of Hanoi who mattered, that is.

All eyes were on the eighteen-year-old bride when she entered the garden. In Le Xuan's official bridal portrait, taken on her wedding day, her features are composed and serious. Her hands are clasped in front of her but hidden from the camera under the wide sleeves of a traditional robe. The expanse of red silk is embroidered with Chinese symbols of double happiness and dotted with exquisitely detailed blossoms. Bands of imperial yellow follow along the neck and sleeves, a style befitting the daughter of a royal princess. Around her neck hangs a heavy medallion of the finest jade; matching rosettes adorn her ears. A heavy black turban sits back on her head. Underneath, her hair is parted severely down the center and wound tightly around her head. Le Xuan's eyes are lightly kohled and her eyebrows painted on carefully. Her lips are stained, and her cheeks are powdered. She looks like a china doll that might crack if she dares to smile, but a powerful marital alliance of this kind was a serious matter. Le Xuan had assumed her new role impeccably. From now on, she would be Madame Nhu.

CHAPTER 5

Long-Distance Phone Call

MONTHS WENT BY. I HAD SENT MADAME NHU more polite letters, reintroducing myself and giving her my background. "I want to tell your story," I wrote. My mind churned through an endless list of possibilities to explain why she wasn't answering me. What if Madame Nhu was not as grateful as I assumed she would be for the attention? Maybe she didn't even know she was the Dragon Lady.

I daydreamed about what our first conversation would be like. I saw myself flying to France, sitting on her crushed-velvet divan, chatting over a porcelain cup of tea and sweet peppermint candies . . . but it was taking more and more energy to pin my hopes to the same starting place everyday. I really thought I had imagined every possible scenario for how and when Madame Nhu might choose to contact me, but I was wrong.

One Saturday morning in June 2005, when my husband was still asleep in bed, a deeply, unmistakably pink plus sign bloomed on the home-test stick. I was pregnant. It was something of a shock since my husband and I had been trying to get pregnant for over a year. Doctor's appointments and blood work and invasive ultrasounds and second opinions had left me with an ugly-sounding diagnosis of polycystic ovary syndrome. Without medical intervention, I was told, pregnancy would be nearly impossible. And yet, I was standing there, staring at the sodden stick in absolute shock, when the kitchen telephone rang.

"Bonjour," a gravelly voice said through the receiver. "Madame Demery?"

I barely managed to squeak out a *oui*. It was hard to swallow. My heart was exploding out of my chest. Could it possibly be who I thought it was? Who else would it be? I briefly wondered if I was dreaming.

"Is this, I mean, are you Madame Nhu?" There was no point at all in playing it cool. The Dragon Lady was on the phone. And I was pregnant. And yes, it was Madame Nhu. But her barrage of questions came at me so fast, they yanked me right out of any blissful dream state.

"Are you a government agent?"

No, no, I assured her.

"Your husband then? Perhaps your father, anyone in your family?"

I promised her that no government had ever employed anyone in my immediate family.

"Have you been hired by police, or perhaps the *New York Times?*"

An interrogation like this would have sounded certifiably mad coming from anyone else. But I took every question seriously. Eventually, Madame Nhu declared herself satisfied.

"Bon," she said definitively, "that is behind us. Good."

Then she laid out the ground rules. Madame Nhu would do the calling. She would not give me her telephone number. She would not speak to anyone else who picked up the phone; she would hang up. And she would absolutely not leave messages on my answering machine. I agreed to all the conditions easily.

"Bien sur. Of course, Madame."

"I will call you again in three days."

Madame Nhu and I began to talk by telephone on a fairly regular basis. I got to know it would be her when the caller ID on the telephone read "Unavailable." She tended to call in what was the late morning for me and the early evening for her, given the seven-hour time difference. She might start in with a tidbit of Vietnamese history that she thought I should know. Sometimes she repeated herself. She recounted the standard fare of Vietnamese fables—of Vietnamese heroines like the Trung sisters or Lady Trieu vanquishing Chinese invaders. I was pretty sure it was a pretext. She was testing me, getting to know me. Stories would give way to questions—about my family, my religion, and my knowledge of the Bible. None of my answers seemed very satisfactory.

I learned that it was better to let Madame Nhu talk. She would stay on the phone longer, and it would inevitably lead her back to the past. From there I could tease out little vignettes from her childhood and ask her what she remembered about the different eras of her life. But when I asked a question that Madame Nhu deemed too probing, she would shut me right down. It might be a frivolous question about life in the palace in Saigon—for example, I had heard a rumor that she had gold toilets. When I asked her about it, she called me a silly child. If I tried to ask about the regime shutting Buddhist monks and university students up in the infamously squalid tiger cages, she told me to be careful of my sources. The political opponents of her regime, she said with a serious edge in her voice, had been duped by the Communists.

I told Madame Nhu about my pregnancy after my husband and I had told our families but before we shared the news with many of our friends. I told her, almost shyly, about the amazing coincidence—about how she had called me on that same morning and about how it had been difficult to get pregnant at all.

Madame Nhu was effusive. "Mais, c'est merveilleux!" Maaaarvelous! She almost sang her praise. "It is exactly as I supposed," Madame Nhu spluttered. "It confirms what I suspected!" I wondered a little at all the emotion she was showering on me; it was a strange way to say congratulations, but what could I say other than, "Merci"?

The situation was awkward and quickly got more so. Madame Nhu said the next words slowly into the phone, like she was sharing a secret with me.

"You are an angel. You have been sent to help me finish the memoirs. And then everything will be revealed."

I wasn't naive. I took much of what Madame Nhu said with a heavy dose of skepticism. I was no angel—but memoirs? Finally, she held out the promise of personal details—where she met her husband for the first time, what their wedding was like, and what kinds of games she had played with her children. I fairly drooled at the thought. If she wanted to think that I had been sent by God, maybe it would encourage her to be more open with me.

The memoirs tantalized, especially when, as she proudly told me herself, they would "illuminate all the mysteries." Madame Nhu had been an eyewitness to history making and political intrigue at the very highest levels. I was a little in love with the idea that somehow I had been chosen, if not by God, then by Madame Nhu.

I was flattered. It was impossible for me to separate out whether I actually liked talking to Madame Nhu or just liked the idea of talking to her. The feeling was simply thrilling—like the early stages of a romance. She led me on, and I followed.

CHAPTER 6

The Crossing

I WAS THE PERFECT AUDIENCE FOR MADAME NHU. I was eager for her acceptance, I played by her rules, and I usually believed what she told me. Why should she lie? And her harsh judgment of her own early character made her all the more believable.

"I was still in the days of unconsciousness," Madame Nhu mused to me about the young woman she had been on a December day in 1946. At twenty-two, still a young bride, she was a brand-new mother. After her wedding in Hanoi in 1943, Madame Nhu had followed her husband to his home in the city of Hue. According to ancient legend, the city sprang from a lotus flower in the mud. History instead grants all the credit for the 1802 founding of the imperial capital of Vietnam to one of Madame Nhu's own ancestors, Emperor Gia Long. Seven kilometers southwest of the South China Sea in the center of the country, the city is Vietnam's intellectual and spiritual heart. The two-story villa the Nhus rented from a family member was well situated in Hue's modern section. It anchored a corner of what was known as the Triangle, a bustling residential and business community named for its irregular shape, bounded by a canal on one side and the Phac Lat stream on the other.

From her front windows, Madame Nhu had a perfect view of the ancient capital. To the north, the vista on that chilly December morning looked as it did on any other day. The flag tower soared. The walls of the ancient citadel remained firmly rooted. The city's nine cannons, symbolic of Hue's divine protection, were trained on nothing at all. Beads of dew gathered on their cold metal.

But the south side of the Clemenceau Bridge was strangely silent. The twisting alleyways were empty. By this time in the morning, there should have been a steady pulse of pushcarts and people. No boats were slipping up the An Cuu canal, no vendors sang out their wares, and no smoke from cooking fires puffed above the squat wooden houses that stretched to the city limits. Windows were shuttered and locked—for all the good that would do the people behind them.

Late the night before, the distant rumbling that had surrounded the city for days turned into distinctive, acute booms that rattled the windowpanes ferociously. Madame Nhu knew then that they had ignored city officials' orders to evacuate for too long. But as to who was out there fighting in the streets, "On l'ignorait"—no one knew.

The Vietnamese were still reeling from all the shocks their country had suffered during the last year of World War II. Ruthless in their demands for labor and unquenchable in their thirst for raw materials, the Japanese had imposed crop requisitions at two or three times the rate of the French, sapping the countryside of manpower and resources. Hungry peasants ate into their seed stocks, which meant they planted still fewer seeds. Rice yields fell due to a particularly nasty spell of weather, and a devastating famine struck northern Vietnam in 1944. In urban areas, people got ration cards; in the countryside, people were cut off and left to die. Lines of walking corpses streamed into the cities. First came the men; straggling behind them were withered women, then children with bloated bellies and the elderly on spindly legs. The fields they passed through were silent. Even the birds had succumbed—the famine upset the natural order of the food chain. The hungry foraged for bugs and crickets for extra protein. They ate grass and leaves and even pulled the bark from trees. Every day, hundreds of corpses, people who had died from hunger on the side of the road, were gathered up for disposal. Historians estimate the famine's death toll at over 2 million people.

The famine of 1944 and 1945 became the perfect proving ground for Communist thought and ideology. The Communists breathed life into a political and military organization named the Viet Minh, but they kept the group's identity cloaked in nationalism to try to reach the broadest base possible. Vietnamese who might initially have been put off by the close link to the Indochinese Communist Party were drawn to the Viet Minh. No one else—not the French, not the "independent" government propped up by Japan, and certainly not the Japanese themselves—did anything to alleviate the pain and suffering in the countryside. Madame Nhu had hardly noticed it from within her rarified cocoon. It was the Viet Minh who reached out with famine relief. Their network helped people find food, and their manpower helped farmers replant. They earned the devotion of the countryside for their actions.

The loyalty of the people would come in handy in the wake of the Japanese defeat at the end of World War II, when Vietnam suddenly found itself in a political vacuum. The French assumed that they could step right back in to retake their colony and that they would be welcomed with open arms, but they were wrong. Many families formerly under the French thumb, like the Chuongs, had collaborated with the Japanese. They didn't want to see the French return. The Japanese had dangled the promise of freedom in front of them, and not surprisingly they didn't want the nation to revert to a French colony. But rich families like the Chuongs didn't like the alternative the Viet Minh offered. Communist themes of class struggle and wealth redistribution threatened their comfort and safety. The leader of the Viet Minh, who also founded the Indochinese Communist Party, had finally stepped out of the shadows. On September 2, 1945, Ho Chi Minh proclaimed Vietnam independent. He was ready to fight the French for the country, and suddenly the postwar period in Indochina devolved into a political mess. Who was in charge of what region changed from day to day, province to province. The most practical concern for a bystander like Madame Nhu was survival.

On that chilly December morning in 1946, Madame Nhu didn't know who was fighting whom anymore, but the women and children gathered in her parlor stood well enough away from the windows for safety. They were five in all: Madame Nhu with her infant daughter, Le Thuy, her mother-in-law, her sister-in-law, and a niece. It was her sister-in-law Hoang's fault they were still there at all. It was her house, although she lived, not so happily, with her husband, Am, and his family across town. The house provided Hoang with a kind of insurance in case things didn't work out in her marriage. She had been unable to bring herself to abandon her only asset. For extra income she rented it to her brother and his new bride, and Madame Nhu's status in the family, as newest wife and youngest sister-in-law from an aristocratic family with a rather scandalous reputation, had obliged her to go along with the arrangement and keep her mouth shut.

Madame Nhu castigated herself for her naiveté, which she said had "bordered on idiocy." Despite the fact that she must have been absolutely terrified, when she told me about it by telephone more than sixty years later, she showed shockingly little mercy for herself. I wondered at the harsh edge that had crept into her voice as the memories of that day intensified.

Instead of taking shelter with the Jesuit priests down the road, Hoang convinced her elderly mother it was just as safe not to leave the house. The French might requisition it if they thought it had been abandoned, and even more harm might come to it in the Communists' hands. Madame Nhu couldn't defy her mother-in-law, so the women enlisted the gardener's help to push the heaviest furniture together in the center of the parlor and piled on blankets and cushions. They spent the night listening to the explosions get closer and closer from their makeshift refuge, folded in on each other and praying for safety. They were still huddled together, wondering what to do with themselves in the sudden stillness of the morning, when the men came through the door.

They were Viet Minh soldiers. No insignia distinguished them, but their uniforms pieced together from jute sacks gave them away. On their feet they wore nothing but bits of rubber lashed together to fashion a sandal. They carried machetes and long rifles, repurposed hand-me-downs from another war altogether. The French colonials had used the same arms against these soldiers' fathers and grandfathers to show the natives who was in charge.

The Viet Minh was more than just a nationalist movement, and Madame Nhu knew it. As the military arm of the Indochinese Communist Party, its members carried general insurrection to every corner of the country. Her brother-in-law and nephew had been two of their highest-profile victims: a local Viet Minh squad had taken Khoi and his son for questioning in August 1945, imprisoned them briefly, convicted them of being bourgeois traitors, and executed them. Madame Nhu's husband had hidden upstairs in Hoang's house when they came for him next. Madame Nhu herself had opened the door and lied coolly to the soldiers' faces. Then, surprising even herself with how brazen a bluff she could manage, she invited the leader to come in and wait for her husband. Nhu slipped out under cover of dark and stayed mostly in hiding after that. On one of the rare and clandestine visits Nhu had made to his wife during the previous year, their daughter, Le Thuy, had been conceived. Aside from those hurried moments of intimacy, Madame Nhu hadn't known where her husband was. By December 1946, she didn't even know if he was still alive.

Now they had come for her. Madame Nhu wished she could disappear. As the pampered daughter of a colonial puppet and imperial princess and the flashy new wife in the Ngo clan ensconced in the large house on the banks of the An Cuu canal, she represented everything the Communists were looking to take down. They wouldn't let a prize like that slip away. Madame Nhu had to know that a pretense of humility and timidity was her best defense. She held the baby tighter and kept her eyes down.

They looked like cavemen to Madame Nhu. Even their smell was primal—sweat, smoke, and wet earth. She could barely make out what they were saying to her, much less what they were saying to each other.

The toneless speech of commoners in the central region had continued to elude her, despite the three years she had been living in Hue. Distinct rising and falling tones distinguish words from one another in Vietnamese, and to the well-bred northerner, the flat, pounding noises these men lobbed across the room at each other sounded like savage grunts.

Madame Nhu's dog whimpered pitifully from another room. Quito, a German shepherd, was a magnificent and loyal animal. After her husband had left her all alone, the dog had kept her safe from the Chinese Kuomintang troops stationed in the city after September 1945. They had descended on the city like a swarm of locusts.[1] When a motley crew of them decided to settle in her garden, Madame Nhu, her cook, and the housekeeper had tried to scare them off by making a ruckus, banging ferociously on pots and pans and yelling. The men hadn't budged—they weren't field mice. They saw that Madame Nhu was pregnant, her husband was nowhere to be seen, and her only company in the big house by the river was two old maids. The ragged troops, sick of war and starved for food, warmth, and the comforts of home, began to think they would be more comfortable inside the house. Madame Nhu looked vulnerable enough standing alone at the window, clutching at something behind her rounded belly, but then they saw what it was. She was holding a dog loosely by the collar. He performed well, baring his teeth and laying his ears flat against his head. The threat worked, and after that the men had left her mostly alone, a blessing for which she couldn't help but thank her darling, snarling beast.

He had had no chance to come to her defense this morning. She had locked the dog up in another room for the night. It was a foolish mistake.

The Viet Minh soldiers turned their attention to the piano. It was a fine instrument that Madame Nhu had tried to have transported out of the house, along with the few valuable heirlooms of lacquer and silver, which she had asked the Jesuits to store in their monastery in case something like this should happen. But the piano had jammed in the doorway. The men encircled it, running their hands over the glossy wood, but not out of any particular admiration. Human skin oils leave a rainbow residue in their wake, dust and grime can scratch a prime paint job, and touching the strings, given the difficulty of keeping them in tune in the tropics, during wartime no less, would ordinarily have constituted an unspeakable trespass. The callused fingers were seeking something as they probed under the hood and around the insides. The men were looking for hidden communication devices. They seemed to think the piano, with all its strings, was some sort of telegraph.

Finally, the Communists decided to detonate the piano. "Imbeciles," Madame Nhu had fumed. "They didn't even know what a grand piano was!" But Madame Nhu didn't actually watch as they packed the cavity with gunpowder. Perhaps the Communists had known exactly what the piano was all along, and blowing it up was their revenge for the bourgeois decadence on display. But it is possible that something else caused it to explode. The cast-iron harp of the grand piano might have suffered during the hasty attempt to move it. If the harp had cracked or the frame had been weakened, the tons of pressure holding the strings taught might have released in a cataclysmic boom. Whatever the cause, the eruption blasted an enormous hole through the main section of the house.

Amid the wreckage, Madame Nhu set to gathering up what she could for baby Le Thuy: blankets and diapers, a change of clothes, and a large basket to carry it all. Then, before she was forced out of her home, she put on a coat, a wool redingote, a bit like a coatdress that fastened narrowly at the waist with darts and tucks. It had been fashioned in Europe, an unimaginable luxury during the last years of war and privation. It was the warmest piece of clothing she owned. Tropical conditions ruled her corner of Southeast Asia ten months out of the year, but December in central Vietnam was predictably damp and cool—conditions that would only get worse the farther she got from home.

She was herded out of the city under a gunmetal sky, part of a human stream pouring down the road, heading inland away from Hue. They were mostly women, children, and the elderly. Baskets bobbed along like flotsam, carried across the shoulders of women using the traditional *dong ganh,* long poles balancing a basket on either end. Much was made of the fact that their shape resembled the long and narrow contours of the country itself. The full baskets on either end represented the fertile deltas, the Red River of Tonkin to the north and the Mekong of Cochinchina in the south. The area in the middle, the long hard yoke that rubbed the skin off the back of the novice, was the rocky and relatively infertile region in the center of the country, the area that the refugees now tramped through.

The roads cut like a red gash through flooded fields. They were awash with clay and scented with manure from the water buffalo in the fields. The road itself got too dangerous as soon as the concrete towers came into sight. The French army had constructed these watchtowers along the country roads to keep watch for Viet Minh troop movements, so the captives cut through the rice paddies instead. They were corralled single file on narrow dikes. To avoid soaking the only pair of shoes she had with her, Madame Nhu had to measure each step minutely. It was exhausting work, carrying her daughter in one arm and the baby's things in the other. She tried to keep pace with her sister-in-law and her niece; her mother-in-law, a tiny, fragile thing, was carried on the gardener's back and hung back a little farther. Around them, the rice grasses rippled like waves. The vast sea of emerald was broken by white marble gravestones—ancestral burial plots that served as a constant reminder that death could lurk nearby.

Where the paddy ended, the procession of women and their guards had to return to the road. They were approaching a bridge when a loud blast shattered the air. "Nằm xuống!" Get down! The guards crouched at the edge of the road. Pebbles scattered as the quickest women scurried down an embankment. Others followed, heads tucked low, elbows around their ears, their baskets abandoned on the road. The road to the bridge was suddenly deserted except for Madame Nhu and the baby she clutched in her arms.

Madame Nhu knew that decomposing bodies would have washed up against the pilings and abutments. She had been close to bridges like this one before and had heard others graphically describe the scene. From where she stood, she thought she could smell the putrefaction. Whether killed by the Viet Minh or caught in some crossfire, what did it matter? They were the bodies of fallen fighters too poor or too far from home for a proper burial. The swollen corpses of those anonymous unfortunates were rotting and leaking their fluids into the very same shallows where she was being told to take cover.

Madame Nhu simply couldn't go. It was too awful. It had begun raining, but she planted her feet in the center of the red-clay road and held on even tighter to the baby. She would not take refuge like the other women among the dead; she'd rather join them as a corpse herself. It was the first time Madame Nhu had seen, at first hand, the grim reality that had gripped her country for the last few years, the same years that she had spent as a newlywed, then a young wife and new mother, far removed from political intrigues. She'd moved into Hoang's fine house. She had servants, including a cook, a gardener, and a nanny for the baby, to tend to the business of homemaking for her. In her spare time, Madame Nhu had taken up the *don trang,* a delicate instrument that resembled a lute. She was also content to be pushed around town in her *pousse,* which she had actually had brought to Hue by train after her wedding. She boasted that its northern comforts were so envied that people would stop and stare at her daily passage along the banks of the An Cuu canal to dine with her mother-in-law. But she could never be entirely sure if they stared out of admiration or with some more sinister intent. Now all such luxuries were gone.

To Madame Nhu, standing there in the rain, death leered at her from every angle. It was a grim kaleidoscope. Yet, she insisted, it was liberating. If she stayed on the road to cross the bridge, she wondered, who would come to get her? Her captors or whoever was shooting at them? She doubted either of them would be brave, or foolish, enough to risk it. Madame Nhu felt free. How tired she was of adhering to pointless expectations. Her shoulders fairly ached from all the slouching toward whatever it was she thought she was supposed to do. She straightened and looked ahead into the mist. What would come next she didn't know, but she would look it in the face, and she would make her own way. Madame Nhu believed that in that moment in the rain, surrounded by desolation but strangely untouched by it, she began to understand things. She would not step down into the filth and decay; she would hold her place on the high ground.

Madame Nhu flipped up the hem of her coat. It was long enough to fold over the baby's head, making a sort of shield from the rain, which was falling hard and cold. Le Thuy thought it was a game of hide-and-seek and pushed her face out, giggling with delight. When Madame Nhu insisted and tried to position the coat again, the baby only laughed more. Peels of high laughter escaped from the woolen folds of Madame Nhu's coat. The joyful sound rolled over the battleground as mother and daughter set off across the shaky wooden beams of the bridge.

As fantastic an image as it must have been, Madame Nhu wasn't the first woman to cross a battleground with a baby. The Vietnamese have a rich mythical history featuring noble and heroic mothers. One of the fabled Vietnamese kings, Le Loi, is said to have hidden from the Chinese Ming invaders in the skirts of his mother. The mother myth is tied to the creation story of the Vietnamese people, and the mother's affection and devotion are credited with the remarkable feats of Vietnamese heroines. The Communists would be the most effective at conflating maternal sacrifice and patriotism in their revolutionary propaganda, but Madame Nhu would also try, during her years in power, to use motherhood as an image of righteousness. So, I had to wonder, did the Vietnamese emphasis on Quoc Mau, or National Mothers, influence Madame Nhu's version of herself in the story? Whatever the case, her perceived invincibility became her reality. Madame Nhu's audacious bridge crossing boosted her confidence that she would survive this trial and whatever else might come.

Madame Nhu met up with the group again on the other side. As the other women had waited for the firing to stop, then followed their guards by wading farther downstream to cross, Madame Nhu had time to rest before she continued on the march. Presumably she hadn't thought to run away because there was nowhere for her to go. Flooded alluvial fields gave way to rocky terrain. At around 5 p.m., the soldiers halted the flow of staggering women and children. The shadows had finally grown too deep to navigate the winding paths through the thickening trees. There was no shelter except for the overhanging branches. Each captive was given one ball of cold cooked rice, no more than a handful. It had been an impossibly long day. If they had taken the main roads, Madame Nhu was certain they could have covered the same ground in half the time. But they had travelled into a new world. Madame Nhu had woken up to witness the end of the only lifestyle she had ever known and tramped through an interminable dusk only to get halfway to the unknown.

And yet, that very night, Madame Nhu found her spirits bolstered again. The prisoners were ordered to arrange themselves in a neat row; their heads were counted, and they were finally granted permission to lie down. The coat Madame Nhu was wearing was the only thing between herself and the cold, wet ground. She made do as best she could. She probably laid the coat sideways, using the extra length to roll herself and the baby into a woolen embrace. Mother and daughter dropped into an uncomfortable sleep.

Rough hands shook the captives awake a few hours later, and a gruff voice told them to stand. As Madame Nhu came to her feet, there was much stomping and yelling. Someone had escaped! The alert was shouted through the night sky. Torches were lit, the prisoners lined up again. A group of armed soldiers was dispatched to search the forest while the captives counted off one by one. "Mot, hai, ba . . . " Madame Nhu spoke her number and then another, adding one on behalf of the infant in her arms. Maybe it dawned on her right away, or maybe she realized it only later: no one was in fact missing. The guards had made the simple mistake of overlooking the sleeping baby wrapped in Madame Nhu's arms. It took them a while to sort out the error. Madame Nhu enjoyed watching the soldiers go through their emergency measures. The bumbling, half-asleep Viet Minh tripped over themselves looking for an escapee who was right in front of their eyes. All the fuss over a fugitive, and it was just a baby. It was hard to be afraid of people if you were laughing at them.

Things looked better in the morning. The day wasn't as wet. There was some comfort in knowing that the march would come to an end before the day was over. And the incompetence of those self-important soldiers was a morale boost that fortified Madame Nhu.

The marchers arrived in the afternoon at a modest farmhouse. Madame Nhu took note of a vegetable patch and well-tended garden. A

Viet Minh leader appeared, wearing fashionable, Western-style clothes, a tennis sweater tied around his shoulders. His name was Bay, the Vietnamese word for the number seven. It was common for large Vietnamese families to name children according to their birth order. One of the first things he did was to seek out the young bride from Hue among the arriving captives. The instruction was a significant insult to the older women Madame Nhu was traveling with: he should have addressed her husband's mother or her sister-in-law first. Instead, Madame Nhu recalled, he bowed and assured her that he would do everything he could to make their stay a pleasant one.

What did Hoang, Madame Nhu's sister-in-law, make of the breach of etiquette? Did she think back to the rumors she had heard? Madame Nhu's mother's liaisons, so clearly relayed in French diplomatic cables, must have taken on salacious detail in the gossipy versions traded over tea or betel nut. In a memoir written decades later, a friend of the family recreated a dialogue among the Ngo family to make sense of the internal conflict regarding Nhu's choice of a bride.

The matriarch, Mrs. Kha, warned her son with an old proverb: When you want to buy a pig, you look at the sow first. When you buy a wife, you look at her family.

"Telle mere, telle fille," brother Can had said. "She will not be different from her mother."

If Hoang harbored any suspicion of Madame Nhu, it was confirmed when the Viet Minh leader Bay greeted her first and when Hoang witnessed the easy charm her sister-in-law used to get more rations for their group. Hoang's anxiety was assuaged, however, once she saw the room they were assigned to. There was one big bed for the five women to share. Madame Nhu wouldn't be able to sneak around easily.

When she talked about Bay, Madame Nhu used the French slang term for Communists, calling him a *coco*. It almost sounded like an endearment coming from her, and Madame Nhu remembered Bay warmly as one of the few civilized *cocos* she had ever met. He made the captives—Madame Nhu, her daughter, and her in-laws—as comfortable as he could, given the meager means available. The women received three bowls of rice a day and little to eat besides that, except when Bay arranged for sardines and milk. The five of them stayed on the farm, sharing one room and one bed, for nearly three months. When the French bombs began to drop too close to the farm, and he could no longer guarantee their safety, Bay arranged for the release of Madame Nhu and her family, personally signing the pass granting them safe passage to a convent. And many years later, when Bay rose to become the highest-ranking Communist in the central region, he would make polite conversation and remember to ask after Madame Nhu's health when negotiations put him in touch with anyone from the Ngo regime.

Almost overnight, Madame Nhu had gone from pampered princess to starving waif, but if anything she had more confidence in herself than ever before. She had been defiant and brave and borne witness to the ineptness of her captors. In the end, even their leader seemed to defer to her. She knew in her heart that she would survive.

The effort of recounting the events of so many years past tired Madame Nhu. By the end of the story, I could hear fatigue in her voice, in the way the last sentences rattled through the receiver like dried stalks of bamboo. But I wasn't quite ready to close down the conversation. I wanted to preserve the moment, and the spirit of sharing confidences, a little longer if I could. I offered some platitude. I don't remember what it was now because I was so busy trying to keep up, scribbling notes on the unprecedented account she had just given me.

I was hoping for a *Gone with the Wind*–style crescendo to mark the end of the story—like when Scarlett crumples to the red earth, shakes her fist at the sky, and vows never to be hungry again. Madame Nhu reminded me a lot of Scarlett O'Hara: both had been taught to defer to men, to look nice, and to stay sweet, and both had indomitable spunk. They were feisty and stubborn. They had a solid core underneath the fancy layers. Women like that could turn on the charm and turn it off. They did what they felt they had to do to get through the rough patches; they could be conniving and manipulative.

But instead of coming up with some grand "Tomorrow is another day" epithet, Madame Nhu returned to her characteristic brusqueness.

On my end of the phone, I could only shake my head silently as she prepared to deliver the usual send-off.

"Bon. Alors. C'est tout." Good. So. That's all. And just before the click, Madame Nhu said, "I would never wear such a wasp-waisted coat again."

CHAPTER 7

A Mountain Retreat

"YOUR TOMMY LOOKS VERY HAPPY and very healthy," Madame Nhu cooed over the phone. She had called to congratulate me after receiving the "It's a Boy" announcement in the mail. We had sent it out to our close friends and family—and at the last minute I had mailed one to Paris. It featured a picture of Tommy tacked onto heavy card stock. She remarked right away on the card's red color and declared the baby's future "very auspicious." The voice she used with me had changed. It was softer, higher in tone. The abrupt and awkward pauses of our early phone calls had eased into a more conversational patter.

We talked about the birth, the baby's sleep schedule and feeding, and, to my surprise, breastfeeding. Madame Nhu was an unlikely champion. From what I understood, most Vietnamese women of a certain class from her era had used nursemaids—and I could understand why. In those first few weeks nursing the baby, I was constantly in various stages of undress and dishevelment, a cause and consequence of feeding on demand. I had nursing bras and baby slings and elaborate wraps. The *ao dais* in Madame Nhu's wardrobe were made of silk and fastened with a row of hook-and-eye clasps, making it impossible to do a hasty feeding. One splash, one leak, one messy drool from the baby would have ruined the garment forever. And yet, she boasted, "I breast-fed each one at least six months." It was hard to picture the Dragon Lady with an infant on her breast, let alone four times over. I must have sounded surprised because she laughed a little as she confessed that it wasn't really her idea. Rather her husband and his family had wanted it that way. But in all, Madame Nhu said, she had enjoyed it. All that reminiscing left her sighing into the receiver, "I so love babies."

Le Thuy had been born in early 1946 amid the chaos of the postwar period. The chaos had morphed into a full-blown war by the time Madame Nhu gave birth to her next two children, boys Ngo Dinh Trac in 1949 and Ngo Dinh Quynh in 1952. Madame Nhu became a mother just as the world she knew was turned upside down and given a good shake.

But at least Madame Nhu and her husband had been reunited. While his wife, daughter, mother, and sister were being forced out of Hue with bayonets, Nhu was working in the shadows, establishing a network of other non-Communist political figures. Despite his discretion, he eventually aroused the suspicion of the Viet Minh in Hanoi, and Nhu had taken shelter in Phat Diem, a Catholic town in Ninh Binh province.

Nhu crossed paths with his wife's parents in Phat Diem. The Chuongs had sought refuge there—making a characteristically dramatic arrival by throwing themselves on the steps of the Catholic church with Viet Minh soldiers just a few steps behind them. Chuong had tried to buy his way into the good graces of the Viet Minh by making "enormous" donations to the government of Ho Chi Minh, and he and his wife were apparently quite put out by the fact that the Viet Minh couldn't be "more flexible" when it came to dealing with them. The Catholic priest of Phat Diem granted Madame Nhu's parents shelter in his church, despite the fact that they were Buddhists.

From Phat Diem, a network of Catholics gave Nhu, and eventually the Chuongs as well, safe passage to Saigon—with Chuong disguised as a monk and his wife dressed as a peasant woman.[1]

Madame Nhu had been at her sister's home in Saigon when she received an urgent message from a Redemptorist priest to come to the rectory quickly. Instead of receiving bad news—she still feared Nhu might be dead—she was led to a room where a visitor awaited her: her husband. The reunion with her parents would come later; for now, the Nhus had to find a way out of Saigon. The French were suspicious of Nhu's activities, and the Chuongs' wartime collaboration with the Japanese cast a long shadow over the entire family.[2]

The Nhus moved to Dalat, a picturesque village nestled among pine forests and mountains in Vietnam's central highlands. And despite the war, Madame Nhu came to call those years her "happiest times."

Dalat had been carved out of nothing, specifically for happy times. The French had decided at the beginning of the twentieth century to build a resort town up in the mountains as a retreat from the heat and the squalor of the cities. It was designed to be very segregated, which the founders believed would make the Dalat experience all the more enjoyable. The French were creating a spot to make them forget they were in Indochina at all—a "white island" in the tropics.[3] They built their houses like ski chalets, and the train station looked like the one in Deauville, a seaside town in Normandy. They planted crops for the foods they missed. To this day Dalat's markets are full of ingredients to make a proper French soup: leeks, celery, carrots, onions, greens, and potatoes.

Madame Nhu's family had been going to Dalat "forever." They loved it for the same reasons the French did. It put them above the reeking mess of humanity in the overcrowded and hot cities. There were fancy hotels, golf courses, and French and Chinese restaurants. There were also nightclubs and theaters and jazz music. Madame Nhu's cousin, the Vietnamese emperor Bao Dai, had a palace in Dalat, as did the French governor-general.

Dalat still has a reputation for leisure and luxury; it is now *the* honeymoon destination for Vietnamese newlyweds. Dalat reminds me of

Niagara Falls with slightly less neon lighting and infinitely more karaoke. Stenciled pink hearts and red roses are stamped everywhere—even on the ubiquitous party slogans displayed on bright yellow banners hanging over the main streets. Christmas lights flicker up the trees all year long. Swan-shaped pedalos are for rent along the lakefront. They churn up the placid water of the man-made lake in the center of town, making the water silty and soupy. Famed for its flowers, the town feels more like the Valentine's aisle at CVS in mid-February. The state's rush to plan and manage the lucrative industry of romance tourism has trounced Dalat's natural beauty.

When the Nhus arrived in the spring of 1947, Dalat was no longer as Madame Nhu remembered from her youth. The mountain's jungle brush had reclaimed large swaths of the city. The worldwide depression that hit Vietnam in the early 1930s had set the budget for tourism well back. By the time war came to Europe in 1939, Dalat had been badly neglected. The tennis courts were cracked and choked with weeds. The casinos were shuttered. Nightclubs and cinemas had been shut down, and the boardwalks along the lake were empty. During the war, the Japanese had rounded up and interned anyone who tried to stay. The Palace Hotel had no visitors—the once majestic staircase had collapsed, and there was no one to pay for renovation. Wild boars and jungle cats encroached on the borders of the city.

The Nhus stayed in a borrowed house at 10 rue des Roses. It belonged to a doctor friend of Madame Nhu's father, and although it wasn't a large villa, Madame Nhu's parents came to stay, as did Nhu's older brother, Ngo Dinh Diem.[4] French writer on the Far East Lucien Bodard said the place was "tawdry"; Madame Nhu would only say that "you wouldn't want to cross the garden to get to the kitchen after dark because you wouldn't want to run into a tiger."[5] But sacrifices were only to be expected—a war was on.

The new war would become known as the First Indochina War, but back before anyone knew there would be a second one, it had other names. To the Vietnamese, it was the War of Resistance; to the French it was the Guerre d'Indochine; either way, it began just as soon as World

War II was officially over. The war in Europe had left France badly battered—the economy was broken, as was basic infrastructure—and Vietnam's vast natural resources glittered. They had been France's for the taking once; why not again? Recolonizing Vietnam would reconfirm the old colonial notions about French superiority. It was a cause the whole country could rally around—never mind what the Vietnamese themselves wanted.

The French ran headlong into the Viet Minh. France had a modern army and state-of-the-art weapons, as well as ever-increasing American funding. The Viet Minh relied instead on the ingenuity of recruits, surprise guerrilla tactics, and the sheer determination of people brought in from the villages, fields, and cities who had had enough of foreign domination. The war would rage for eight years. Estimates vary, but historians put the casualty count for the Viet Minh side somewhere between 250,000 and 500,000 dead. French casualties would exceed 75,000—more dead than the United States would incur in the next war fought on Vietnamese soil.

The war's decisive battle took place on May 7, 1954, in a far northwestern valley of Vietnam called Dien Bien Phu. The French were outsmarted. The Viet Minh had managed to surround them with heavy artillery and men. The French lost their will to fight. After a hundred years, they finally packed up and went home. It was an early lesson in how futile any attempt to exert long-term foreign control over Vietnam would be. If only the Americans had been paying better attention.

The war's front lines were very far away from the Nhus' mountain retreat. Madame Nhu called it *une guerre bizardouille,* a weird little war. She described her life in Dalat as safe and simple and left politics out completely. Madame Nhu tended to her growing family, had babies, took care of chores around the house, and cooked family meals. The same woman who had grown up with twenty servants rode her bike to do the daily shopping in the market and accompanied her daughter to school. All the while, her husband Nhu was indulging in his orchid-raising hobby.[6]

But nothing in Dalat was ever quite what it seemed. The very premise of the place as a white island of healthy rest and repose was one big deception. For one thing, it was never isolated from the Vietnamese. The place was built on the sweat and blood of forced labor. Despite the endless supply of human capital and the emphasis on luxury, the colonial builders had run out of money. Ironically, the resort built as a getaway where people could go to get healthy was a breeding ground for malarial mosquitoes because of the man-made lakes. Dalat was not a sleepy hideaway from the war either. It became the de facto headquarters for French political and military ambitions in Indochina. Moreover, Nhu was not nearly as interested in orchids as he appeared. He was cultivating something much more dangerous.

During the Dalat years, from 1947 to 1954, Ngo Dinh Nhu was planting the seeds of a political party, one he called the Can Lao—the Personalist Labor Party. It recruited members into a shadowy network of cells in which no one knew more than a handful of fellow members. All that intrigue would eventually bear fruit, generating a political apparatus with tens of thousands of enlistees. It would support and sustain the presidency of Ngo Dinh Diem for nine years, but the organization would never shake off the secrecy of its founding years. It would earn itself and its creator, Nhu, a nefarious reputation.

"Personalism's" most basic tenet was that a "person" was the antidote to an individual. It was a totally bewildering notion. Nhu had picked up on the obscure Catholic philosophy as a student in the 1930s in France. His attempts to explain how a French Catholic philosophy could apply to building an independent Vietnam would always be long-winded and confusing. His belief, however, was fervent. Nhu was building a real alternative to both the French and the Viet Minh. He was building a network of supporters for his brother Diem.

"I was alone most of the time," Madame Nhu wrote about her marriage during that time. While Nhu was building his political base, his wife didn't know where he was. "My husband would simply disappear without a word." Madame Nhu may not have known exactly where her husband was, but she had a rough idea of what he was working on. The honeymoon location could not disguise the fact that theirs had become a marriage of pragmatism and plotting with little time left for romance.

Madame Nhu wasn't altogether isolated when her husband took off on his secret missions. She had her cousin in Dalat, His Majesty the Emperor Bao Dai, who was good company. Technically he was her mother's cousin, and technically he was no longer the emperor. Bao Dai had never really ruled anyway. Under the French colonial system, his power had always been mostly symbolic. Bao Dai had been crowned emperor in 1925, when he was twelve years old. He had rushed home from school in France to see his father, Emperor Khai Dinh, buried, but then returned to France. The throne sat empty for the next seven years, during which the French resident superior was in total command. By the time Bao Dai returned to Vietnam in 1932, he had been groomed as a perfect little Frenchman, perfectly happy to do whatever the colonial powers told him to.

Bao Dai's life was one of pampered ease. He was married, but that didn't stop him from living like a playboy. Chasing wildlife and young women were his two passions. His actions during World War II and its aftermath demolished any reputation Bao Dai may have clung to as a leader through the colonial years. First he had capitulated to the Japanese; then he turned his crown over to the Communists before going right back to working with the French in their mission to reestablish control in Indochina by the late 1940s. Bao Dai should have ruled from Saigon, but he frankly preferred life in Dalat. He was wise enough to know that he wasn't doing anything anyway. Bao Dai was fully aware of, and resigned to, his pathetic fate. When he overheard one of his lady companions being teased for being a prostitute, the emperor protested. "She is only plying her trade," Bao Dai said. "I am the real whore."[7]

Bao Dai was presumably just as confounded as Madame Nhu by the *guerre bizardouille,* the strange conflict they were not a part of. The cousins, estranged from the rest of the country at war, could barely conceive the extent to which the world had tilted. At least in Dalat, the royal cousins were in a familiar Europeanized milieu. Madame Nhu accompanied her cousin on fishing trips and partnered with him for bridge. When her husband wasn't home, they went on picnics and swam in waterfalls. From behind the ochre walls of the emperor's art deco palace on the hill, Madame Nhu and her cousin could look down on the valley while remaining ensconced in their world.

She said her husband knew all about "those nighttime soirees and the daytime excursions." He probably encouraged them. As discredited as Bao Dai was, the monarch's stamp still meant something politically. If Nhu wanted to build a movement to oppose the French and oppose the Communists, he needed any help he could get. A nod from the emperor would give at least a facade of legitimacy.

If his wife's palling around with her cousin the emperor was convenient, it would also prove temporary. Bao Dai was one of the first political casualties of the Ngo regime. He spent the rest of his life in a run-down chateau in the South of France near Cannes. In Madame Nhu's memoirs, she refers to her cousin bitterly. There is no lingering family warmth: Bao Dai is "that French puppet."

The former emperor's palace is now a major tourist attraction in Dalat for the honeymooners. The state has preserved it, not out of any nostalgia for Bao Dai but rather to showcase the indulgent luxuries of a playboy. It had been built for the Vietnamese emperor in 1933 in the exact same style as the French governor-general's house—even using the same granite. Both houses had geometric angles, roof terraces, and circular bay windows. Maybe the twin homes were intended to show some kind of equality, but they really demonstrated that the emperor was as foreign as the Frenchman.[8]

Even when Madame Nhu became First Lady, she and her family continued to use the mountain retreat of Dalat as a special place to come together. It was where the children attended boarding school, and the family gathered there for holidays and breaks from palace life. By then, the Nhus used the French governor's home as their weekend home.

In 1962, Madame Nhu invited Time-Life photographer Larry Burrows for a weekend trip to Dalat. She wanted him to see and capture what a very special place it was to the Nhu family. Madame Nhu insisted that the family show their guest how normal they were. She traded her usual palace attire, the fitted silk *ao dai* and tightly coiled updo, for weekend wear. She sported a sweater loosely belted over capri pants and let her long hair tumble out of a half ponytail. The style made the thirty-eight-year-old First Lady look more like her younger self, the twenty-three-year-old she had been when she had first lived in Dalat. Madame Nhu clasped her hands inside the crook of her husband's elbow and drew herself close to him. With the children scampering around on the lawn, they could have been in a New Jersey suburb—until Madame Nhu got down on one knee and showed her two-year-old daughter how to properly aim a pistol and fire at a target.

The Nhus often said that when they retired, they would move back to Dalat full-time.[9] But Madame Nhu didn't intend to stay in the French governor's house forever. She commissioned construction of a cluster of houses at 2 Yet Kieu Street overlooking a beautiful mountain valley. She was building one for herself, one for her father, and one for guests. The houses would gather around a courtyard with a heated swimming pool, a Japanese garden, and a lotus lake. When the lake was filled with water, an image of a map of Vietnam was supposed to appear. Her villa was to be named Lam Ngoc, Forest Jewel, and guarded appropriately. A huge grey guard tower for a private security force loomed at the entrance. Even while the home was under construction, people said that if a stray bird flew into the garden, it would be shot immediately. The house would have five fireplaces and be decorated with the hides and heads of the wild animals felled by her husband. It would have a stainless steel kitchen with modern amenities and even an infrared broiler. All the main rooms were to be equipped with secret trap doors, which would lead to escape tunnels that ran under the swimming pool and emptied into a nearby safe house. A secret ladder under her bed would take Madame Nhu down to an underground room and a huge vault lined with enough reinforced iron to withstand firepower.[10]

Madame Nhu didn't think of the "little villa" she was building in Dalat as lavish, but traditional Vietnamese homes in the countryside still functioned with an outhouse on stilts, the hole positioned above a pond teeming with hungry carp. The amount Madame Nhu was spending just to build herself a porcelain-tiled and hygienically plumbed bathroom was beyond what most people earned in an entire lifetime.

The house took five years to complete. She had the front door rebuilt eight times. The corner window had to be remade ten times before it pleased her. One of her fifty gardeners, Pham Van My, said Madame Nhu was "a difficult lady" to work for. He said she shouted her orders and threatened the workmen but was scared of worms. The woman he described had expensive and fickle tastes. The construction was initiated by a woman just coming into her own, but Madame Nhu told me she never set foot in the place once it was done. By the time Madame Nhu's dream house was finally finished, so was she.

"We should meet," Madame Nhu said on the phone shortly after Tommy's birth. It was the first time she had expressed any willingness to meet me face to face. She must have reasoned that I couldn't possibly be conspiring to hurt her if I was with a baby, so she insisted that I bring Tommy. Would Paris be alright?

"Of course, Madame. I would be honored."

I really was. I was planning a September trip to introduce the baby to my French relatives. A stop in Paris would be on the way. I didn't tell Madame Nhu that I was also planning to visit the French colonial archives in the South of France to see what other history I could pull up. By this time, I knew how firmly Madame Nhu believed that her version of the truth should be adequate and reported unchallenged—even when it had obvious cracks.

She planned the time and place. Our meeting was to take place in the Église Saint-Leon, a Catholic church not far from her apartment in the fifteenth arrondissement. We would meet in the nave, in front of Saint Joseph's statue at 10:00 a.m. "Then we can go to the park across the street," she said. "To talk. It will be very discreet."

When I got inside the church, the vault-like doors closed behind me, shutting out the bright autumn sun. I thought, belatedly, that perhaps I should be worried. I reminded myself that I was just introducing Tommy to a little old lady. What could happen? Sure, she had been the Dragon Lady. She had run a militia of armed women and had her husband's henchmen at her disposal, but she had also been a mother four times over. I forced myself to focus on that aspect, but I was ill at ease. I told myself I was just nervous about making a good impression.

I wore a dark blouse tucked into a belted red skirt—the lucky color. I had smoothed my hair into a low bun and wore small pearls in my ears. I wanted to show Madame Nhu that I was professional without being too formal. I told myself I was glad she had insisted that I bring Tommy. He was sleeping sweetly, tucked into a polka-dotted stroller with his teddy bear and blanket, thumb inserted into his perfect bow-shaped mouth. He played his part beautifully. It was up to me to strike the right tone: respectful, smart, capable. I had control over nothing else.

What, I wondered, would the Dragon Lady look like at eighty-one years old? I had spent so much time poring over pictures of her as a young woman, but the voice I had gotten to know over the phone conjured up another image. In my head, I imagined her with the same hairstyle, swept high above her head, except wintery with age. Her cheekbones, I thought, would be smooth but powdery, like rice paper. Did she still wear red lipstick? I suddenly couldn't picture her as anything other than a stooped and sad old woman who refused to stop wearing caked red lipstick—lipstick that bled slightly outside the imperfect lines of her upper and lower lips.

My imagination was running away. I had arrived early, and now she was late. I was spending too much time alone in a dim church, and scenarios flooded into my mind. Had she been watching me the whole time? From a darkened pew, waiting for the right moment to approach? I made a loop around the church, the stroller wheels clacking over the stone and tiled floors, but all the rows were empty.

After an hour, I heard the door creak open. My stomach flipped over, but it was not Madame Nhu. I was so nervous that the disappointment that washed over me felt more like a flood of relief. Tommy woke up, and his happy little squawks eventually turned into cries that echoed off the stone floors and up into the rafters. I wrestled his stroller up the side aisle, out the thick double doors, and fled to the discreet park to feed him. When I got back to my aunt's apartment in Paris, I found a message on the answering machine from Madame Nhu. She had broken her own rules by leaving a message saying that she hadn't come because she wasn't feeling well. Her foot hurt, she sighed, and she was taking that as a sign that we should postpone our meeting.

When we spoke next, she didn't actually apologize, not in so many words. But her voice sounded contrite enough, and of course I forgave her. The next time we would meet in her apartment, she said. I believed her. I waited an hour, in the lobby this time, but she didn't let me up the elevator. I forgave her again. She told me a woeful story: she wasn't sure she could trust anyone again. I would have to prove myself. The Dragon Lady was keeping herself tantalizingly out of reach.

CHAPTER 8

The Miracle Man of Vietnam

THE DOOR OPENED BEFORE I could knock, and John Pham stepped out onto his doorstep. He was the father of my friend's sister-in-law. I had met his daughter exactly once, but John greeted me like a long-lost family member. He wore the standard uniform of the Midwestern grandfather, a checked shirt tucked into belted chinos. His big grin pushed his cheeks into taut-skinned apples. "Welcome to my home," he beamed, then took my hand to shake it, pumping it up and down, as if he were bringing water up from a well. The seventy-one-year-old's handshake was still strong. Back when he was a young man, John had been the presidential family's personal security guard in Saigon from 1954 to 1963. Now he lived in a split-level ranch on the Kansas side of Kansas City.

The house had been John's home since the late 1970s. He had escaped Vietnam on a fishing boat from Da Nang, the place US soldiers had called China Beach, only three hours before the city fell to the Communists in 1975. John arrived in the United States with his wife and ten children and no money. A friendly sergeant had advised him to take his family away from California—too crowded, he said. So John looked at the map and picked Kansas because it was right in the middle of the country.

The horns and tin whistles of a television show filtered down from the den. I got a timid hello from a grandchild passing through, and John smiled at the boy on his reluctant march into the kitchen. "Please," John said showing me to the faded peach sofa, "sit. Let's talk together."

John was slightly shorter than me, so even though I was sitting, I could still see the top of his head. The white of his scalp showed through the comb marks in his silver hair. It made him seem vulnerable. I tried to imagine him as a twenty-year-old kid, wiry and quick. He must have been a good shot to have been stationed as a guard inside the palaces. But it was hard to reconcile the smiling and kindly grandfather across from me with the hard-faced youth he had been. John had worked for the same notorious state security apparatus as the secret police squads that threw people into tiger cages—the cramped prison cells on Con Son Island where thousands were tortured, starved, and killed during the war. John's bosses, the president and his brother, lived just down the hall from John's post. He had spent nearly nine years working alongside Ngo Dinh Nhu and his wife, Madame Nhu.

I was settling into my position on the sofa when I noticed the decor on the wall in front of me. Jesus hung on a golden cross, and right next to him, a portrait of President Ngo Dinh Diem. A yellow-and-red-striped flag hung in the corner. The president had been dead for more than forty years, South Vietnam had been lost for thirty, but in this house, the past was still very much alive.

I stayed talking with John well into the afternoon. The smell of lemongrass, vinegar, and seared meat wafted from the kitchen. John's wife came in, her hands on her apron, to ask if we would like a bowl of soup. She had made *bun bo hue,* a spicy beef stew from the central region of Vietnam. As I slurped up an endless tangle of rice noodles, John continued to talk about life in Diem's palaces, nostalgia for the country of his youth filling his voice.

In this house, Jesus and Diem were both saviors and survivors.

Born in central Vietnam in 1901, Ngo Dinh Diem had been a good student as a boy, but instead of following his brothers to France or into the seminary, he got into local politics. Diem entered provincial administration under the French as a district chief when he was twenty years old. Public officials in Vietnam were scholar-bureaucrats called mandarins; they were products of rigorous training and had to pass imperial examinations in writing, literature, history, and mathematics. In just a few years, Diem had risen to administrative supervisor; he was tax collector, sheriff, and judge for an entire region. His position entitled him to use a rickshaw, but Diem preferred riding his own horse to being ferried around by a coolie. He recommended bold reforms to his higher-ups, including more autonomy from the French and better education, but was ignored. Appointed governor of Phan Thiet in southeastern Vietnam in 1929, Diem earned a reputation for fairness and unshakeable integrity. He was so righteous that when the French continued to deny Diem his recommended reforms, he handed back all his titles and decorations and walked off the job. It was all or nothing.[1]

Diem brusquely retired from public view in 1933 but did not fade away. He carried on working behind the scenes until 1954, when he reemerged as a public figure.

The Nhus and their three children arrived at Saigon's Tan Son Nhut Airport early in the afternoon of June 25, 1954, only to find that the incoming plane from Europe had been delayed. Along with the Nhus, a crowd of several hundred people waited for the plane to arrive, including a senior general in the French colonial army, members of the imperial family, foreign diplomats, and officials in the South Vietnamese Armed Forces.[2] Madame Nhu's husband insisted that she and the children join this mix of some of the most important people in all Indochina to await the return of Nhu's older brother. After all, Ngo Dinh Diem had just been appointed the new prime minister of South Vietnam at a peace conference in Geneva, Switzerland. In what would become known as the Geneva Accords, the participants—the United States, Great Britain, France, the Soviet Union, and China—put an end to the war between the Viet Minh and the French by agreeing to split Vietnam into two countries along the seventeenth parallel. Ho Chi Minh would serve as president of the Communist north from his headquarters in Hanoi. Bao Dai, the former emperor, would be the nominal head of the non-Communist new state to the south, but he stayed in France. The real powers of the government would go to the still relatively unknown prime minister the Americans were championing, the man on John Pham's wall and Madame Nhu's brother-in-law: Ngo Dinh Diem.

Under Diem, the southern half of Vietnam would be "free"—free from colonialism, free from communism, but exactly what else was free about it was unclear. In theory, in two years, 1956, the country would hold elections. The Vietnamese would decide for themselves what they wanted, but until then, Communist North Vietnam was above the seventeenth parallel, and something entirely new would be created below.[3]

Waiting for Diem to arrive at the airport, Madame Nhu took the youngest boy, Quynh, in her arms to keep him calm. She tried bouncing him against her hip in the shade of the hangar and shifting from side to side in her high-heeled sandals. There was no containing the other two; after watching them squirm and pull at the collars of their nice clothes, Madame Nhu gave the eight-year-old and her five-year-old brother a nod, and they were off, tearing across the otherwise clear tarmac in a game of tag. The children didn't need to be called back when the airplane appeared. It was just a black dot against the bright sky, but it represented something huge and a little scary because it was unknown: freedom. Le Thuy and Trac came to stand by their parents, and together the family of five faced the roar of the incoming engines with their hands over their ears.

A fifty-three-year-old man stepped out of the plane and waved over their heads. Diem was squinting—had he grown unaccustomed to the brilliant tropical sun during his time away? Could he even see them there, waiting for him? After all this time, Diem still didn't look like the one of whom so much was expected. He had a moon-shaped face and a head that sat almost directly on top of his shoulders. Diem's black hair, slicked back like the bristles of a wet animal, accentuated the general penguin effect of his big belly, characteristic white-sharkskin suit, and open-toed walk. He might have grown even rounder during his travels.

Madame Nhu had not seen Diem for four years, since his departure from Vietnam. Except for his brief stay with the Nhus in Dalat in the late 1940s, Nhu's older brother had always seemed a remote figure to her. He was almost the same age as her father, and before the First Indochina War, Diem had been too busy building a secret political party under the name Dai Viet Phu Hung Hoi, the Association for the Restoration of Great Vietnam, to pay much attention to his little brother's young wife. When the French had caught onto him in 1944, Diem had had to flee. He escaped with the help of the Japanese consul, who smuggled him out of the city by disguising him as a Japanese officer. Diem resettled in Saigon while the Nhus remained in Hue. He was safe there until after the Japanese surrender at the end of World War II. Diem was eventually captured—although not by the French. Like Madame Nhu, Diem was taken prisoner in 1946 by the Communists. He was stopped while riding a train back to Hue, taken to a remote mountain hut, and held there for three months before being brought to Hanoi. The leader of the Viet Minh, Ho Chi Minh, had requested a face-to-face meeting.

Ho Chi Minh and Ngo Dinh Diem had a few things in common. Both were from central Vietnam, and both of their fathers had instilled an anti-French, anticolonial, and nationalist ethos in their sons. Ho had even studied at the school in Hue founded by Diem's father. Like Diem, Ho Chi Minh hoped that the Americans would help the Vietnamese in the anti-French struggle. He had reason to think that they might. The Office of Strategic Services (OSS), precursor to the CIA, had intervened on Ho's behalf when he was a captive in Nationalist China. Ho had recited part of the American Declaration of Independence when he proclaimed Vietnam independent in August 1945, and his Viet Minh had joined US missions against the Japanese. At the same time, Ho Chi Minh was very much a Communist, a follower of Karl Marx and believer in the proletarian revolution. He wanted to build an independent, socialist Vietnam, but he also knew that he had the best chance of getting Vietnam to that independence by making common cause with capitalists, landowners, and the bourgeoisie, at least for a while.

He tried to convince Ngo Dinh Diem that they had the same goal: Vietnamese independence. Ho offered Diem a position in the government he was building, but by then Diem had heard about the murder of his older brother, Ngo Dinh Khoi, and nephew by the Communists in Hue. As Diem would tell the story, he threw Ho's offer back in his face. He had looked the wispy leader of the Indochinese Communist Party in the eye and replied, "I don't believe you understand the kind of man I am. Look at me in the face. Am I a man who fears?" Ho, Diem said, had been forced to look away. It is a stretch to believe that the hardened leader of the Viet Minh couldn't bring himself to meet Diem's eye, but Diem would maintain that Ho shook his head and replied almost shamefully that no, Diem was not a man who feared. The next morning, Ho Chi Minh let Ngo Dinh Diem walk out the open doors, a free man.[4]

Considering that they would be at war with each other barely a decade later, it is not surprising that Diem would never publicly acknowledge staying in touch with the Viet Minh leaders. But recent research into Diem's activities around that time shows that in fact he did. Diem was interested in keeping his options open for as long as possible. He was waiting to see if a third way, neither French nor Communist, would be viable. Not until 1949 did Diem finally jump off the fence. He spurned the Viet Minh and at the same time declared the former emperor Bao Dai's collaboration with the French unacceptable. Standing alone was risky, but Diem was tired of half measures. "I advocate social reforms that are sweeping and bold, with the condition that the dignity of man will always be respected and will be free to flourish."[5] Diem published a treatise to this effect under his name on June 16, 1949, hoping, according to scholar Edward Miller, to rally people to his cause. "The statement was widely read and noted within Vietnam, but it did not produce a new upsurge of popularity for Diem. . . . Its most immediate effect was to exhaust the patience of both the French and the Viet Minh." Diem was breaking with everyone in order to start something new.

After his short stay with the Nhus in Dalat, Diem headed out of the country looking for new allies, first, to no avail, to Japan and then to the United States. Diem figured he could turn the Americans' historical antipathy toward colonialism to his advantage. He couldn't have arrived at a better time. It was the height of the Red Scare; Americans were building bomb shelters and training their children to hide from Russian nuclear fallout under their school desks. The McCarthy era was the perfect time for Diem to pitch his anti-Communist credentials. He was incredibly successful in finding influential people who were sympathetic to his cause. The powerful Catholic cardinal Francis Spellman, along with academics, a dozen members of Congress, including the young senator from Massachusetts, John F. Kennedy, and even Wild Bill Donovan, founder of the OSS, all expressed their admiration for Diem.

Moral support and encouragement were well and good, but the critical work was happening in Vietnam, as Madame Nhu knew all too well. Her husband, Diem's younger brother, was the one laying the groundwork for Diem's return. It wasn't enough to be anti-Communist; an actual political philosophy was needed. Nhu adapted the Catholic philosophy of personalism to fit Vietnam's particular situation, a massive project more impressive for its audacity than for its outcome. The Can Lao—the Personalist Labor Party—was poised to become the practical foundation for a political movement. Nhu had established alliances with labor activists, supported the creation of worker and farmer cooperatives, and published a political journal called *Xa Hoi-Society,* which backed unions.

Madame Nhu left Dalat in 1953 when Nhu requested that she and their children move to Saigon to support Diem and his climb to power. They rented five adjoining rooms attached to the Clinique St. Pierre. Two housed the printing press of Nhu's weekly journal, and the other three were converted into living quarters for the family of five. Madame Nhu furnished their bedroom with an antique furniture set she had found at a local flea market. The ornate carving on the wood furniture pleased her; the pieces were fine enough to imagine that some well-placed colonial family had left them behind when they had fled back to France. It was some consolation for the otherwise "fly-specked" union headquarters they lived in.

Madame Nhu described her early days in Saigon as banal enough to make her cry. The French writer Lucien Bodard had seen her tawdry surroundings in Dalat. He described her situation in Saigon as even worse. "The first time I went there, I crossed a dusty yard where the washing was hung out to dry. Out of a passage covered with corrugated metal came a young woman in a white tunic and green pants. She was shabbily dressed. Children clung to her. She was so depressed by disappointment I did not recognize her." This wasn't the marriage or the life she had been groomed for. "All she had to do was wash clothes, cook meals and wipe her children."[6]

One afternoon, Madame Nhu awoke from a nap to loud thumps coming from the printing room for her husband's journal, located just next door. The children were still sleeping so she slipped silently inside. She saw the backs of eight men, dressed identically in white suits and straw hats, clustered together around something on the ground. Her view obscured, she couldn't quite make out what was in front of them. Instead of feeling fear, Madame Nhu was incensed at the thought that strange men had intruded into her family's space. She was going to figure out what was going on. She shook off one of her sandals, a soft-soled espadrille that she wore to pad around the house. But now she wielded it with purpose. She slapped the shoe across the back of the man closest to her.

"What is going on in here?" she demanded.

The seven others stopped what they were doing and stepped back enough to reveal a man crouching on the floor. He straightened and lowered his arms from his head, and that was when Madame Nhu saw that they were beating the man her husband had hired to run the press. He scrambled to his feet, blood running down his face. Instead of uttering thanks or gratitude, he raised his shoulders in a shrug and gave Madame Nhu an awkward smile.

"Oh, it's nothing," he said with as much nonchalance as he could muster and busied himself by shaking a cigarette out of his rumpled pack.

Madame Nhu looked around, but no one else in the room moved. The man clearly didn't want her assistance, so she stepped back. What could she do? Full of wounded pride and frustration, Madame Nhu turned on her heel and strode out of the room.

She barricaded herself in her quarters until her husband came home. She flew into his arms, asking what had happened. Who had those men been? But Nhu didn't respond. She found herself wondering at the man she had married. Hadn't she delivered his employee from harm? What if Nhu had been in the office, instead of conspiring as usual in some anonymous coffeehouse. Would they have hurt him?

Madame Nhu's distress finally provoked a response, but not the one she was hoping for. Nhu held his wife at arm's length and gave her his usual grin. "Mind your own business and don't go getting involved," he said, and despite the smile on his face, she knew it was a warning. As for the man who worked at the press, the one whose life Madame Nhu was sure she had saved that day, he continued to work next door. And every time she saw him, Madame Nhu was reminded again of how very far removed she was from whatever her husband was up to.

Diem, the new premier, faced all sorts of problems upon his return to Vietnam in 1954, starting with the fact that he had inherited a broken system. The official treasury was empty. The French had not trained competent Vietnamese administrators. South Vietnam was totally paralyzed militarily and politically. Gangsters ruled the cities. The black market thrived. The driving economic forces were drugs, gambling, and prostitution. The influx of refugees from the north just made everything worse. There was no place for all the refugees to live and work. They swarmed around Saigon; families bunked together in empty cement construction tubes.

After splitting the country in two, the Geneva Accords had made a provision for people to move both ways across the border, but any migration would have to take place within the strict limit of one year. The French army and the US navy provided logistical transport for northerners heading south, with the United States supplying nearly all the funds. The CIA also sent a team to persuade as many northerners as possible to leave for South Vietnam, creating evidence that people were "voting with their feet" for the Americans' man, Diem, and the promise of a free Vietnam.[7] But no one had imagined that so many people would actually go. An exodus of about 1 million people from the Communist north poured into the south. For all the Viet Minh had done, appealing to the nationalist instinct in many Vietnamese and succeeding in getting the French out of Vietnam, people were still too scared of communism to stick around and see it in action. There were whispers of what was to come: class purges, land reform, and the intrusion of the state into local matters—not to mention religion. The Catholics especially left in droves.

The reverse flow was barely a trickle. The highest-profile Communist cadres in the south went north, and Ho Chi Minh's government recalled the most visible People's Army units but encouraged the rest of the people with demonstrated Communist sympathies to stay put: "To go north means victory, to remain in the south is to bring success."[8] Southern supporters for the Viet Minh went clandestine. They would come in handy when the struggle for reunification was launched.

The immediate population pressure on South Vietnam threatened to break the new regime. Even the US Army's assessment of the situation Diem was stepping into was grim. The problems the new premier faced were so numerous and so difficult, the report concluded, they were probably "insurmountable."[9]

Not long after Diem's return, Madame Nhu realized with horror that his installation to govern South Vietnam had been an elaborate setup. Whoever faced this mess was sure to fail—and the French hated Diem enough to try to ruin him. Her brother-in-law had blatantly showed his independent streak and ingratitude for the French civilizing mission. If Diem failed, the French could reasonably argue for his replacement with someone more amenable to their influence.

Madame Nhu was not imagining things. The French really were trying to get rid of Diem, as confirmed by Edward Lansdale. Lansdale had joined the US Army after Pearl Harbor and was recruited into military intelligence, then later the OSS, by Wild Bill Donovan. He distinguished himself with success in counterinsurgency campaigns and was sent to Vietnam in 1954 to run the Saigon Military Mission. Lansdale took a shine to Diem. When other American officials tried to convey doubts about the South Vietnamese leader to President Dwight D. Eisenhower and the State Department in Washington, Lansdale adeptly sidestepped and countered it, establishing a pattern of reaffirming American support of the leader in Saigon. Some say that Graham Greene based the swashbuckling and dangerously naive Alden Pyle character in *The Quiet American* on Lansdale, but plenty of Americans thought he was a hero of the anti-Communist cause. John F. Kennedy was among those who considered Lansdale a mustachioed James Bond from his side of the pond. Whatever else he may have been, Lansdale was an eyewitness to French interference with Diem's power. In Lansdale's opinion, the French felt that Diem "was sort of rubbing salt into the sore wound of theirs." The French loss of Indochina at the hands of a Communist army was bad enough, and now that Diem was in power, a century of French colonial pride was at stake. He was renaming streets after Vietnamese patriots, nationalizing French industries, and making the remaining French in Vietnam feel as unwelcome as possible. The French felt that in order to defend themselves and their long-term strategic interest in Indochina, they needed to get rid of Diem.

Others had caught on quicker. From the very start, Madame Nhu's husband had been "obviously extremely worried" that his older brother "was not fully aware of the extreme seriousness of [the] situation in Vietnam" when he accepted the premiership from Emperor Bao Dai in 1954. Diem developed a "blind hatred for the French" and for the man who had bestowed the poisoned honor of premiership on him. The US State Department recommended that "Bao Dai should never return to Vietnam as his life would be in danger."[10] Once the implications sank in, Madame Nhu took the plot very personally. After all those hours with her cousin in Dalat, soothing his pride and burnishing his ego, she felt betrayed. She had dared to think that because of her, Bao Dai was giving Diem a shot at greatness. She could take pride in that when there wasn't much else. Now she saw that her cousin had used her and her family. She would not forgive him or the French either.

In 1954 and 1955, the Nhus cozied up to the Americans, and Madame Nhu became close to a woman her own age named Virginia Spence. Spence was a contract CIA employee who, because she spoke French fluently, was sent to Saigon without operations training. The CIA characterized her friendship with Madame Nhu as "genuine," but Nhu would certainly have encouraged his wife to pursue it. Due to their camaraderie, Nhu himself emerged in Spence's eyes as "the most promising of an unimpressive lot." Her description of him was skeptical: he was a "born schemer," and the covert nature of his role in the Diem government seems to have borne up her early analysis. She also described him as a naive country bumpkin who could get in over his head quickly. "Anything a friend tells him he swallows whole. He does have a certain political stature and a great flair for making nothing look like something." So Nhu was a tactician with some presence, and as far as Spence could see, there was nobody else to rival Nhu as an effective political operator.

The Nhus' other American friends in Saigon, Mr. and Mrs. Paul Harwood, were also CIA. The Harwoods sponsored the confirmation of Nhu's oldest daughter, Le Thuy. The CIA agents and the Nhus enjoyed a close enough relationship that they could joke about most things. Nhu teased his wife in front of their American friends by calling her a pagan for her relatively recent conversion to Catholicism, and Madame Nhu kidded right back about how stiff Nhu's older brothers were. Madame Nhu enjoyed the company of the Americans arriving in Saigon: they were "genuine people," "with whom one [could] easily get along," without the colonial baggage and pretensions of the French. Like her Japanese friend from childhood, Madame Nhu's new friends were outsiders too, which made her feel comfortable around them. Madame Nhu liked sharing one joke about her son, Quynh, whom she called "Quang Quang." The story made it into the CIA cables back to headquarters. "The child once wandered into a Cabinet meeting looking for his Uncle Diem. Someone pointed to a bathroom door at the end of the conference room and Quang Quang opened it, revealing the seated Prime Minister. Mimicking official protocol, Quang Quang executed a hand salute and began singing the national anthem."[11]

Instead of Diem in Saigon, the French really wanted General Nguyen Van Hinh in charge. He was thirty-eight years old with no political experience except for having watched the crumbling career of his father, Nguyen Van Tam, an ineffectual premier who served the French for two years in 1952 and 1953. Hinh was an army man, trained in

France, and had fought alongside the French against the Italians and Germans in World War II. During the First Indochina War, Hinh led the Armée Nationale Vietnamenne, the Vietnamese force fighting on the French side against the Viet Minh—and against the Viet Minh version of independence. The French believed that if their man Hinh were in charge, he would keep things running smoothly, whereas they were certain Diem would try to cut off ties with them. Hinh would continue using the established channels for trade—French companies—and provide kickbacks to the right people. Hinh and the French found an anti-Diem ally in the Binh Xuyen, a band of river pirates who ran gambling, prostitution, and security in Saigon. Together, they began conspiring to bring Diem down. They all knew which side their baguette was buttered on.

Saigon was still a small town in many ways. Only a few cafés and restaurants catered to Europeanized tastes. Most high-end businesses were located along what was still known as the rue Catinat, although Diem had renamed it Tu Do (Freedom) Street after the French were defeated and began leaving the country. The Cercle Sportif, a swimming and tennis club, stayed in business by shifting its membership to the Vietnamese business and political community. Madame Nhu was learning enough about General Hinh around town to make her mad. She knew that he was being bolstered by the French and that her cousin, Bao Dai, would give Hinh more real support than he had ever shown Diem. The army general was openly boasting to his friends that he would bring Diem down and dared to add that he planned to keep Madame Nhu as his concubine. As was inevitable in the small world of Saigon, Madame Nhu and General Hinh came face to face at a party. She drew herself up to her full five feet in heels and spat her contempt in the startled general's face. "You are never going to overthrow this government because you don't have the guts." Barely containing the shake in her voice, Madame Nhu continued, "And if you do overthrow it, you will never have me because I will claw your throat out first." She had publicly joined the fight.[12]

The public perceived Diem as an honest man with high morals who wouldn't be corrupted easily and wouldn't condone graft. If he had a fault, it was that he lacked street smarts—he didn't know enough about the situation he was walking into. To make matters worse, in addition to the external crosses the newly returned Diem had to bear—one French-sponsored, coup-plotting general, a million homeless refugees, two powerful religious sects, a gangster-run police force, and untold bleak economic woes—he was a miserable politician. He simply could not connect with the people he was trying so hard to represent. Lansdale noticed from day one how carelessly the Vietnamese mandarin squandered his political capital.

Lansdale had arrived in Saigon just before Diem, and he was looking forward to meeting the new prime minister. But on the day Diem was due to return to Saigon, Lansdale spontaneously decided to watch the prime minister's return to the city with the Vietnamese people rather than joining the diplomatic circle at the airport. The streets were mobbed. Emotions ran high; people hoisted their children onto their shoulders to catch a glimpse of the new future of Vietnam. "And we waited and waited and waited for something to happen . . . and suddenly past us at about sixty miles an hour came a motorcycle escort and a closed car. You couldn't see anybody in it." There was a genuine disappointment among the Vietnamese, who had been unable even to catch a quick look at Diem. "Here was a tremendously enthusiastic friendly crowd of people who didn't get to see the show that they wanted to, or to cheer the man." Lansdale thought it was as though Diem didn't want to get close to the people at all.[13]

In fact, Lansdale missed what was intended to be the real show. Nhu had gone to great lengths to mark the occasion of his brother's return to Saigon. In Diem's honor, civil servants were released from work early to attend, along with hundreds of others, a gathering in front of Independence Palace. Nhu's planning came off without a hitch; when Diem arrived at the palace, even the loudspeakers were placed perfectly. Diem's remarks hit all the right notes. He received a vibrant ovation from the crowd, but it went unremarked by diplomats and officials, who hadn't been on hand to see it. Instead, they left the airport with the impression that Diem was unremarkable at best; some, like Lansdale, thought the new premier was a cold fish.[14] Miscalculations and misunderstandings between the Ngo brothers and the foreigners would persist through the rest of Diem's time in power.

Instead of worrying about diplomatic protocol or dreaming up other ways to court his constituency, Diem spent his time personally signing all visas for entry into and exit from the country. His unwillingness to delegate even the smallest tasks meant that he worked sixteen or seventeen hours a day. When he could no longer keep his eyes open at his desk, he would take a pile of paperwork with him to bed. Diem was a terrible administrator partly because he didn't trust the bureaucrats he had inherited. The French had trained their Vietnamese subordinates to be passive and more concerned with self-preservation than the preservation of the state. Diem's empty treasury and inability to pay government workers reinforced the broken system. His brothers, however, he knew he could count on.

The new premier didn't inspire much hope in General J. Lawton Collins, the special US representative in Vietnam. Collins found Diem "completely intractable, unwilling to accept suggestions and using such poor judgment that his government will eventually fail." Instead of making things better, in Collins's view, the brothers "hover[ed] over the leader, pulling and tugging all the time," and he warned that the family's growing choke hold on power in South Vietnam would make a bad situation even worse.[15]

Madame Nhu launched herself into the political vacuum created by a distant pen-pushing prime minister and his furtive brother. The brothers had no flair, no sense of theater, and perhaps no stomach for the fight. Madame Nhu possessed all three—with some to spare.

Her first burst of political creativity came at a restaurant in Cholon, the Chinese part of town. The dinner was being hosted by Diem's new vice premier, who was also his minister of defense and Madame Nhu's cousin on her father's side—a man named Nguyen Van Xuan. With Madame Nhu and her husband and other Vietnamese from the Diem regime, the dinner guests included two counselors from high positions in the French embassy. Madame Nhu used the social occasion to press the Frenchmen. She knew very well that they couldn't admit the French wanted to oust Diem—not at a dinner hosted by his vice premier and not to Diem's sister-in-law. But Madame Nhu's social smile masked a sharp political mind. Why, she asked sweetly, hadn't they forced General Hinh to go to France? One of the French consuls proposed a schoolgirl's challenge: if she could get five signatures proving Hinh was unwanted, they would personally see Hinh removed. Madame Nhu dropped the niceties and leveled her gaze at the men. "You will have a million," she told them. The Frenchmen might still have thought the exchange nothing more than flirtatious dinner conversation when they exclaimed over their half-eaten entrées, "But you are dangerous, Madame!"

The challenge would have daunted anyone else, but Madame Nhu had a mission. Within a few hours of the dinner, she also met with a helpful coincidence. Her husband Nhu had stayed silent throughout the evening. If he had any thoughts on his wife's exchange with the Frenchmen, he kept them to himself. After leaving the restaurant, he and his wife parted ways. Nhu went to the palace to see his brother, and Madame Nhu went home, alone as usual. At her door she saw two disheveled looking men. They bowed and scraped, introducing themselves as Quang and Ho. They were waiting for her husband, they explained. "We represent the million refugees who came when we heard Diem received the *pleins pouvoirs* from Bao Dai. But the reality of the situation here is untenable because the Binh Xuyen police harass us. Even if we wanted to go back, we couldn't! What should we do?"

Here was a means to get the million signatures she had promised at dinner. "Do nothing for the moment," Madame Nhu coolly replied. But when the time comes, "You listen to me and do exactly what I say."

For the next month, Madame Nhu worked in secret. She got banners printed and worked to synchronize the swarm of northern refugees into networks of participants. She was planning a massive demonstration in Diem's favor; participants would march up the boulevard Hui Bon Hoa, turn on the old rue Chasseloup-Laubat, and arrive dramatically in front of Independence Palace. Not even the French could deny such an obvious display of will by the people.

But by the time Madame Nhu arrived at the appointed meeting spot on the morning of September 21, 1954, police were already there. They were Hinh's men, hired guns paid for by the Binh Xuyen gangsters. They were trying to disperse a crowd of 4,000, pointing bayonets and screaming at quaking refugees. The French army report of the situation described gunshots, a number of wounded, and at least one dead.[16]

Madame Nhu wove her car, a little light-green Panhard, through a sea of *cyclo* wheels and the bobbing conical hats of women on their way to market. She swerved to avoid the vendors and their pushcarts, but it was pandemonium.

Madame Nhu got out of her car but left the motor running. Taking strides as long as the slit of her *ao dai* would allow, she marched right up to the armed men. She couldn't let thugs derail her demonstration and had to think quickly. She did what she did best: she made a scene. Madame Nhu began berating the men, shouting at the top of her lungs, "What kind of police are you? What are you trying to do to these poor, defenseless people? Are you afraid of me?"

Suddenly, a hostile crowd of Binh Xuyen surrounded her. As they closed in on her with their weapons drawn, she jumped into her car, cried, "Arrest me, if you can!" and drove through the ring of tommy gun–toting thugs.

Madame Nhu's theatrics distracted the men long enough to allow her rally to continue. The people marched from the cathedral to the palace waving banners that read "Unification and Independence for Viet Nam," and "Put Down the Saboteurs of National Independence." The crowd chanted for Diem. Diem looked like a hero for helping out refugees, and General Hinh was backed into a corner. From far away in France, Emperor Bao Dai could not publicly support Hinh without looking like a heartless monarch and losing the last shred of respect that clung to him. Soon afterwards, Hinh was sent away to France and never came back. Madame Nhu got all the credit for having masterminded the rally, and then some for coming to its daring rescue in defiance of the gangster henchmen.[17]

Madame Nhu's dinner partners from the French embassy protested. This woman, they said, was causing trouble! Holding a rally in an already overheated political atmosphere was absolutely irresponsible. The French complained to the Americans, who talked to Diem, who in the end agreed to send Madame Nhu away for a few months. She was angry about her dismissal, but it was just to keep the peace, and just long enough for Nhu to get Diem stabilized; at least, that was how they rationalized it to her.

Madame Nhu was sent to Hong Kong to "convalesce" for three months at an Italian convent, the Couvent Italien de Chanoinesses de Canossa. Her children and her husband stayed behind. Instead of looking at it as punishment, Madame Nhu began to view their sending her away as confirmation of her potential power. If she didn't matter, they would have let her stay home. Clearly she was too dangerous to ignore.

Madame Nhu's rally marked the beginning of a new chapter for her brother-in-law. Over the next few months, Diem's government would continue working to establish control over Saigon and the South. No one expected the principled Catholic South Vietnamese premier to make it. Diem's most formidable foe was vice. The Grand Monde gambling establishment earned $10,000 a day. The mirrored cubicles of the elegant bordello Paradise (Dai La Thien) reflected three hundred girls scantily clad in silk—and enjoyed a long list of satisfied customers. Diplomats and generals shared a pipe at opium parlors before going to nightclubs.

So everyone was surprised when Ngo Dinh Diem emerged victorious. He proved ruthless. His police closed five hundred opium dens and confiscated thousands of bamboo pipes, a pile of which were burned in a huge bonfire kindled by pages torn out of pornographic magazines. Diem issued an order to close Saigon's nightclubs at 2 a.m. and layered so many regulations on the city's striptease industry that it collapsed. Some 2,000 licensed prostitutes simply vanished, breaking the back of the Saigon racket. Diem had the mirrored Paradise brothel turned into a rehabilitation institute for hookers, where they were taught sewing and nursing. He stopped short of shutting down brothels in the countryside where the army was stationed: Diem knew he needed the cops and the military on his side.

Most surprising of all was Diem's refusal to negotiate. He would not concede to any power-sharing agreement. This stance went against the instructions of the emperor, his theoretical boss; it also went against French advice. It was in Diem's political interest to boldly oppose the French and Bao Dai, but in this case, he also showed that he could withstand pressure from the American State Department.

The Binh Xuyen originated as a band of river pirates from a small village south of Cholon, Saigon's Chinatown. Their leader, a man named Bay Vien, had collaborated with the Japanese during the period of their occupation. The Binh Xuyen's anti-French stance made them allies of the Viet Minh, but the gangster-Communist alliance didn't last long. The political rift was too great. Bay Vien turned back to the French in 1945, as soon as doing so looked profitable. He bought the police concession in Saigon for 40 million piasters and then the opium factory that supplied the very same dens those police were supposed to shut down. In addition to casinos and brothels, Bay's Binh Xuyen group also owned the best department store in town on the fashionable rue Catinat. The gangsters had a fleet of riverboats, twenty houses, and one hundred shops throughout the city. A crocodile-filled moat surrounded Bay Vien's home and the Binh Xuyen headquarters. He kept a full-grown leopard chained to a guard post outside his bedroom, and inside, a tigress in a cage. Rumor had it that Bay Vien would feed the tigress any of the 15,000 men serving him who dared displease him.

Bay Vien's reach was so great and his pockets so deep that only someone as hardheaded and as scrupulous as Diem would think to bring him down. Diem was intransigent on the subject of the Binh Xuyen. The Americans tried to offer the gangster's foot soldiers 12,000 piasters, and the officers 28,000 piasters, to join with Diem, and they tried to get Diem to see that facts were facts: the Binh Xuyen were an unfortunate reality of life in Saigon. But Diem would not compromise.[18] The final showdown came on April 27, 1955, the day after Diem appointed a police chief who was not in Bay Vien's pocket. Binh Xuyen forces began shelling the palace. Inside, Diem showed firm resolve. "Fire back," he said. All told, 4,000 mortar rounds hurled toward the residence of the Binh Xuyen's leader, Bay Vien, and their command post. It was a furious barrage even before the airborne troops got involved. Eight hundred civilians died, and 20,000 homes were destroyed. Diem's forces and the thugs, gangsters, and policemen backed by the Binh Xuyen and, less overtly, the French waged hand-to-hand combat on Saigon's streets.

The battle against the Binh Xuyen showed Diem's mettle. The scrupulous leader bet on righteousness and won. It also showed Diem, once and for all, that he didn't need even the emperor's most tenuous support. A few months after crushing the Binh Xuyen, in the summer of 1955, Diem ousted Bao Dai and emerged as the sole leader of South Vietnam. No longer limited to the title of prime minister, Diem proclaimed himself head of state, the president of South Vietnam.

All of these developments went to show the Americans, or Lansdale at least, just how "damn wrong" the French had been in underestimating the new premier of South Vietnam.[19] A State Department telegram to John Foster Dulles provides perhaps the best summary of the situation Diem found himself in. "Diem is inexperienced and finds it difficult to compromise." What's more he "insists on building a government free of corruption and dedicated to achieving genuine national independence." American policy makers might find the man's personal shortcomings, like his stubbornness, frustrating, but ironically, "only a government of the kind Diem envisions, and it would be worthy of our support—has much chance for survival." American aid to South Vietnam in the fiscal year 1955 amounted to $77,500,000. Some of that money went to help refugees; some went to technical assistance in education, health, and public administration. But the bulk of it went to helping Diem win widespread public support for a governmental system that was not Communist. The sums would only go up from there. The little round-faced premier was about to become the man *Life* magazine would hail as the "Tough Miracle Man of Vietnam."[20]

CHAPTER 9

A First Lady in Independence Palace

THE NHU FAMILY MOVED into the presidential palace in April 1955, but without Madame Nhu, who was still in Hong Kong. Madame Nhu was comfortable enough. She was given a room in a Catholic convent and plenty of time for imposed contemplation and English lessons. The hybrid setting was familiar to her. Hong Kong was Chinese and British, and though she was used to a different cultural mix, Vietnamese and French, the East-West mélange felt familiar and soothing. The nuns were nice, as were the well-mannered schoolchildren who filed obediently in and out of classrooms with a shy smile at the elegant visitor in their midst. Madame Nhu spent her mornings taking English lessons and winding walks around the oval flower beds in the convent garden. Her afternoons, spent napping and reading, ticked by more slowly. Madame Nhu used the quiet hours away from her family to marvel at her doings over the last six months. What a course she had managed to chart! The rally had snowballed into an outpouring of real support for Diem. The audacious display was something Madame Nhu had known she was capable of, but to the others, it was a surprise. Although perhaps intended as a reprimand, to Madame Nhu's mind, this banishment in Hong Kong demonstrated that her influence was being recognized.

Maybe Nhu moved himself and their three children into the palace during his wife's absence because he wanted to be closer to his brother, or maybe he hoped that the move would keep his family safe. If so, he was mistaken. During one of their first nights in their new home, a midnight Binh Xuyen attack on the palace dislodged a pair of massive drapes from the floor-to-ceiling windows on the second floor. A crush of cotton, silk, wood, and plaster fell ten feet onto Quynh, the Nhu's three-year-old son. He nearly suffocated before he was rescued and revived.

Madame Nhu was terrified when she received the news. But far from taking the nearly fatal accident as an omen of the misfortune still to come, she viewed her family's relocation to the palace as a promotion. They had moved from the Clinique St. Pierre's barred windows and tin roof that clattered when it rained into a suite of rooms down the hall from the president of the Republic of South Vietnam.

Until Diem moved in and renamed it Dinh Doc Lap, or Independence Palace, the yellow stucco building had been known as the Palais Norodom, named for the monarch in neighboring Cambodia and built on a boulevard of the same name. The palace had served as the office and residence of the French gouverneur général for all of Indochina—a sort of French colonial White House. Conceived by French architect Achille Antoine Hermitte, who had built Hong Kong's regal city hall, its grandeur was intended to show the natives the full power and wealth of France. The palace's granite foundation had been imported from France, as had the smooth white stone for the carvings that festooned the facade. The only marble floors were in the central pavilion; the rest were tiled, a concession to Saigon's tropical climate. The palace was T-shaped, with two rows of graceful arched windows along the front, facing the city. On the first floor were offices and official reception rooms; the second floor housed the president's and the Nhu family's rooms. The reception hall and adjoining ballrooms occupied the leg of the *T* and jutted deep into the lushly planted grounds.

When Madame Nhu returned, she found a room that should have been very much to her liking: the heavy drapes had been reinstalled and her bed dressed in silk duvets and shams with a large canopy; fine rugs covered the floor. The furniture was highly polished. As soon as it was smudged, a retinue of household staff was on hand to buff it again. Madame Nhu could open the French doors to the balcony wide in the early morning to catch a quiet breeze. Pungent food smells no longer drifted through the window at all hours as had at their street-level apartment. The odors of frying oil and ginger, meat and garlic stayed in the kitchen, released only from heaving platters served in the dining room at mealtimes. Madame Nhu understood that this move was a sort of nod from her brother-in-law Diem, acknowledging her contributions and those of her husband.

But Madame Nhu found no happiness in the palace. At least, not at first. She was searching for real meaning in her life, and it would take her some time to find her stride.

During their first few years in the palace, Ngo Dinh Diem and his family regime accomplished a great deal. One million refugees were resettled in the South. Rice production increased from 2.8 to 4.6 million metric tons. Rubber production went from 66,000 to 79,000 million metric tons. Farm-credit programs and land reform broke up the colonial-era plantations and helped people invest in their own fields and try crop diversification. Three major highways were completed, two new universities were established, and the doubled production of electric power sped up reconstruction needed after the nine-year War of Independence. Fifty-one new manufacturing firms were established in South Vietnam, the largest in textiles, something the French had always controlled. South Vietnam's import costs were reduced by over $40 million a year, a significant amount in what was still a very poor country. But all these accomplishments were achieved in the shadow of US assistance—which amounted to $150 million a year for the five years between 1955 and 1960. The figure sounds small in today's dollars, but was close to 15 percent of the foreign aid budgeted by the United States for all foreign economic and technical development.[1]

The news out of Saigon was especially rosy when compared to the dismal information that could be gathered about living conditions under the Reds in the north, which endured floods and famine. The Viet Minh's nationalist rhetoric had taken a sharp turn leftward after the Geneva Accords, in part because Hanoi was accepting help from Mao's China. But how much was this shift due to pressure from China and how much to the Viet Minh leadership's ability finally to shake off any pretense that it was anything other than Communist at heart? To strengthen their hold, the Communists had to break down the traditional power of the elites. "Speak bitterness" campaigns purged the ranks of the Viet Minh of any "wrong" (i.e., high-class) elements. People were expected to denounce neighbors and even family members, and the situation was easily manipulated to settle old scores. There were trials and executions and a deeply disruptive land-redistribution program. Unlike the huge parcels of land in the south, the holdings in the north were already relatively small. Land was measured in something called a *mau*—someone had to own fifty *mau* in the south to be considered a landowner and only five in the north. The margin of difference between people in one category or another was very small, which made the redistribution of land painful even for small-scale farmers. It also pitted neighbor against neighbor; people of similar means worked against each other for the smallest of gains.

The Ngo regime in the south set itself up as the antidote to the oppression in the Communist north. President Diem denounced communism not only on his own moral grounds, underpinned by his religious convictions and family history, but also because, in his view, communism was just another "foreign ideology." If the Communists took over all of Vietnam, he insisted, "our beloved country will disappear and it will only be mentioned as a southern province of Communist China. Moreover the Vietnamese people will eternally live under the yoke of a dictatorship inspired by Moscow and denying religion, fatherland and family."[2]

But for all his impassioned speeches, Diem wasn't leading a free country either. Anything resembling real democracy was simply window dressing. Under the terms of the 1954 Geneva Accords, the separation of North and South Vietnam into two countries with capitals in Hanoi and Saigon was temporary. A referendum was supposed to have taken place in 1956 in both parts of the country to unite them again under one chosen president. But the South Vietnamese government of Ngo Dinh Diem refused to hold a vote on the grounds that the South Vietnamese had not actually signed the Geneva Accords; they had only been granted observer status. The Diem regime also accused the Communists of being unable to participate in an honest vote. It wasn't just the northerners living under communism who posed the problem; the south was still home to armed guerrilla fighters, former Viet Minh, who were loyal Communists and had gone underground, waiting for the time to rise again. The southern regime had one more good reason not to hold a vote: Diem would lose. There was no way he could win out over the man who had led the Vietnamese army to victory over the French and to independence. Ho Chi Minh would win any popularity contest.

The Communists weren't the only ones rigging elections. In October 1955, Nhu helped organize a referendum within South Vietnam for his older brother Diem to unseat former emperor Bao Dai once and for all. In a landslide victory, Diem shrugged off his mantle as Bao Dai's appointed prime minister and became South Vietnam's official chief of state and first president. The margin was overwhelming—nearly 6 million to 63,000. Reports coming out of the polling centers told of intimidation tactics and coercion. Red envelopes, indicating a vote for Diem, were being stuffed into the ballot boxes under the watchful eye of Nhu's men, and those who disobeyed risked a beating. Diem got 98 percent of the vote, but his margins in Saigon were even better: his 605,025 votes surpassed the city's number of registered voters by more than one-third.[3]

Madame Nhu was elected to the National Assembly on March 4, 1956. She joined 122 other members, almost all male, in the legislative branch of the new government. Madame Nhu denied that it was her idea to run for office, insisting that an anonymous person had proposed her name to represent the northern refugees whom she had championed so "heroically," and she scoffed at the notion that anything less than real admiration had motivated her election.[4] Still, a distinct pattern was evident. The people in control of South Vietnam were either Ngo family members or related to them by marriage.

Madame Nhu's father, Tran Van Chuong, was put in charge of economy and finance; shortly afterwards he and his wife were appointed diplomats and sent to the United States. Chuong was to be the Diem regime's South Vietnamese ambassador, while Madame Chuong was made the South Vietnamese observer at the United Nations. Madame Nhu's uncle was in charge of foreign affairs, her father's cousin was Diem's vice president, and her sister's husband, Nguyen Huu Chau, was, for a short time, one of Diem's most trusted advisors. Madame Nhu's new prestige had even secured a spot for her little brother, Khiem. Her younger brother had been pampered, petted, and spoiled throughout his childhood, and perhaps because of that, he made for a miserable student overseas. He attended a school in Paris for a while but left without an advanced degree, then failed to complete correspondence classes in law studies. As the French were leaving Vietnam in 1954, Khiem was living a barefoot bohemian lifestyle by the seaside in Algeria with a German wife. What a twist: the boy the Chuongs had always cherished was turning into such a disappointment, and his middle sister might be the one to turn things around by calling him back to Vietnam and appointing him palace spokesman. When the new First Lady of South Vietnam beckoned, Khiem came quickly, leaving his wife behind. It must have given Madame Nhu great satisfaction to manage something her mother had not been able to.

In addition to its nepotism, the Ngo regime discriminated against non-Catholics. The bias could be rationalized in the context of those early years—the Catholic community provided Diem and Nhu with a ready pool of anti-Communist support—but the Ngo brothers took it to an extreme. There were stories of people converting to the Catholic faith just to win political favor and promotions. Surrounding itself with family members and like-minded fellow Catholics meant the regime was isolating itself from people who had real differences in opinion. But politics in Vietnam had always been that way to some extent. Centuries of Vietnamese monarchy and French colonial rule bequeathed a political legacy that valued conformity, and under Diem, that adherence to a single mind-set was reinforced. There was an entrenched sense among politicians that disagreements or deviations from the status quo, even taking initiative, entailed career risk. The American advisors in South Vietnam pressured Diem to open up his government and make a showcase of political diversity, but Diem resisted. There was too much at stake. The march toward democracy would be a forced march—and a silent one. The regime said it needed stability before it could build a strong state. Madame Nhu rationalized the Ngos' insular tendencies to Australian reporter Denis Warner, explaining, "If we open the window, not only the sunlight, but many bad things fly in also."

A real dissonance soon emerged between the image of Diem as a moral and good man and the climate of fear that began to pervade Saigon. Those who didn't cooperate with the regime were silenced in one way or another. They might be sent to distant, Communist-friendly outlying areas, where they might be killed. They might be taken away by the secret police and beaten or imprisoned until they learned their lesson. Rumors of torture and imprisonment ran rampant. Carried on every whisper was the name of Diem's younger brother: Ngo Dinh Nhu.

John Pham, Diem's bodyguard, confirmed many of the saintly traits attributed to Diem in biographies. The president led a monkish, austere life. His private rooms on the second floor of the old French palace had bare wood floors, and his bed was a straw mat. His sleeping space adjoined his office, where he spent most of his waking hours. Furnishings included a round wooden coffee table and a worn leather chair. Diem ate at his desk while he worked through breakfast, lunch, and dinner. In the morning he drank coffee with sugar and usually ate *chao* (rice porridge) with *ca kho* (small fish).[5] His lunches and dinners were simple too, consisting of rice and *rau cai,* fried pork lardons, or some kind of fish. For dessert, he took two cobs of corn with sugar. Diem had simple tastes; he ate nearly the same menu every day with only the type of fish varying. He drank no wine or whiskey, just hot tea, but he was a chain smoker, lighting a fresh cigarette off the dying ember of the previous. Diem took small puffs and waited until the ash was long before tapping it into the ashtray. He smoked so much that his fingers were stained yellow.

Diem ate alone most of the time; his meals and sleep were erratic because of his work schedule. Sometimes he didn't dine until 4 a.m. He could push a buzzer in his quarters to ring the kitchen. Two or three valets were assigned to him around the clock, but he was always very generous with the people who worked for him. John told me that Diem even gave his own salary to refugees from the north to help them get established.

As devoted as Diem was to his country, he had no time for personal relationships outside his family. He was a bachelor, but that term implies a freewheeling lifestyle that would have been entirely out of character for the South Vietnamese president. His only personal attachment was to the garden. After work, Diem would stroll through the palace grounds. When foreign dignitaries visited, bringing fruit and food delicacies as a gift from their own countries, Diem gave the goods to his bodyguards; he asked only that they return the seeds to him so he could plant them in his garden.

The only woman the president saw on a regular basis lived just a few doors down: his brother's wife, Madame Nhu. There was a rumor that as a young man, Diem had been engaged to a girl from his hometown of Hue but had ended things when he decided to pursue politics instead of settling into marriage. Politics was a dangerous game under the French, but that still seems like a feeble excuse not to get married. Diem's chief of staff thought that the president had never had sexual relations, and a 1955 profile of Diem in *Time* magazine reports that he had been "long pledged to chastity." Diem's characterization as "shy" and "uncomfortable" around women may have prompted his chief of staff to confide that the president liked to keep "good looking men around him" instead of women.[6]

The fact remained that Diem needed a hostess to help him with his social obligations, someone with social graces and a pretty smile. Diem could have chosen one of his own sisters or the wife of another of his brothers. But he chose Madame Nhu.

She was well connected, pretty, and smart, but most of all, she was already there. Perhaps Nhu had always intended this outcome.

Since Nhu's family lived in the palace, it seemed just as smart to keep his brother's wife busy. The chief of staff who had noted that Diem liked to have handsome men working for him described Diem's relationship with Madame Nhu as comfortable: "She is charming, talks to him, relieves his tension, argues with him, needles him and, like a Vietnamese wife, she is dominant in the household." He likened President Diem's relationship with Madame Nhu to that of Hitler and Eva Braun.[7]

John Pham, the bodyguard, disagreed. He told me that Diem did not altogether like Madame Nhu. He thought his sister-in-law "look like a hot lady, talk too big." Everything about her showy personality went against Diem's quiet nature, but he put up with her. He recognized that he was indebted to his little brother Nhu for his political practicality—for doing things that needed to get done but might have compromised Diem's strict ethics. In John Pham's opinion, Diem didn't speak out against Madame Nhu because he didn't want to cause trouble for his younger brother.

John remembered with a smile the one time he saw Diem unable to hold back. It was October 1956. A picture was going to be taken in front of the palace with all the members of the government. The photographer took a long time to get his subjects organized, as the placement of people around the president was a political negotiation in and of itself. Everything about the situation that day was tense. Madame Nhu saw that everyone was distracted and took advantage of the moment. She snuck up onto the second floor of the palace and stood in one of the windows, managing to get herself included in the picture. When the photograph was developed and shown to the president, Diem was furious.

When I asked if she hadn't deserved to be included, John looked perplexed. "She always wanted too much too fast," he said with a shake of his head.

Although still beleaguered by political infighting and challenges from the Binh Xuyen and religious sects, Diem and his new regime were the darlings of the free anti-Communist world. As such, they had a high diplomatic profile to maintain. There were endless dinner parties and receptions, including elaborate state welcoming parties for visiting diplomats. The gardens of the park behind the palace would be lit up with garlands of light, and the walkways were illuminated with paper lanterns. After they made their way up the double ramp into the palace pavilion, Madame Nhu greeted invitees with one of her lovely smiles and offered a slim, gloved hand. Traditional Vietnamese music and clinking glasses accompanied her as she wove Diem around the room, mingling among members of the diplomatic corps and stopping strategically to chat with guests of honor before taking the prestigious and highly visible hostess's seat at the elegantly laid dining table.

She took right away to the duties of the First Lady, such as inaugurating new elementary schools, organizing flower exhibits, and visiting orphanages around the south. Madame Nhu arranged a huge reception at the palace for over 1,000 schoolchildren and traveled around the world on diplomatic missions. At a dinner for the Nhus in Rangoon given by the Burmese prime minister, she chatted with the leader's wife, Mrs. U Nu, about their shared passion for flowers. When the Nhus got ready to depart Rangoon on a special Vietnamese air force plane for the flight back to Saigon, they found a special gift onboard from their hostess: a Burmese variety of white blooming bougainvillea for Madame Nhu to plant in her own garden.[8] In Portugal, Spain, France, and Austria, delegations of women's clubs greeted her. Madame Nhu even found a way to make conversation with the Russian delegate to the Interparliamentary Union when they found themselves seated next to each other in Brazil. The Russian, Mrs. Lebedeva, was a thickly set woman known for her brusque manners, but Madame Nhu engaged her in a conversational debate in French about the economic need for foreign investment. And in Washington, DC, on a semiofficial visit with her husband in March 1957, Madame Nhu was invited to have lunch in the Senate chambers. She watched the senators scramble for a good seat at the table and remarked to someone at her elbow how shockingly childish this lunchtime ritual seemed. The statesman who caught her remark, and laughed it off, was a young senator from Massachusetts, John F. Kennedy. The Nhus' CIA escort, their old friend Paul Harwood, would recall that Madame Nhu caused the only blip in an otherwise highly successful trip. She had "reveled" in the attention paid to her by Allen Dulles and notables from the Departments of

State and Defense at a dinner held at the Alibi Club, a three-story brick townhouse a few blocks from the White House. Membership is still limited to the most elite—fifty of Washington's most powerful men—and new members are only admitted after an incumbent dies. Maybe Madame Nhu let the prestige go to her head, because her husband had been unhappy with her. He didn't enjoy his wife's flaunting her good looks, charm, and command of English. She had been the star of the evening—and Nhu must have taken it personally. In Harwood's view she had been "not a problem, but a sensation."[9]

Nhu sounded like he was taking a line from his wife's critics. Those who didn't like Madame Nhu said that she was exploiting Diem's unfamiliarity with women. Why else would he listen to her? She could make her chest heave with emotion. She could bat her lashes. Her body language was more effective on the president, they said, than an arsenal of weapons. She had other tactics at her disposal that he didn't know how to deal with, like tantrums and mood swings. At the same time that they accused her of wielding her femininity like a sword, they said she could also use it as a shield to deflect allegations that she was the real man in the family.

Madame Nhu learned to shrug off the carping. She had better things to do than worry about what people thought of her. She was intent on carving out a role for herself in the administration, one that went beyond serving as a pretty hostess.

The Communists in Vietnam had managed to arouse women's political consciousness, promising them that they had a purpose and reminding them how the old feudal society, not to mention the colonial one, had exploited them. They also gave women real work to do. The Communist cause valued their contribution and extended the promise of equality—a gaping hole in the Ngo brothers' revolutionary rhetoric. Female cadres enlisted in the Communist cause moved easily in and out of villages, spreading propaganda in the marketplace as if they were simply gossiping with friends or gathering produce for the family meal. In fact they were activating a network of foot soldiers. These women were the supply chain of what would become the National Liberation Front.

Vietnam scholar Douglas Pike meant all the respect in the world when he called these women the "water buffalo of the Revolution."[10]

Madame Nhu took it upon herself to match the progressive strides the Communists were making with women. If they were liberating women, she would too. Madame Nhu had only one reason to consider herself an expert on the subject: she too was a woman. She would call others like herself to arms. But therein lay her problem. Madame Nhu was never a typical Vietnamese woman. She spoke French at the dinner table and rode around town in a chauffeured car. Her forced march by the Communists through the countryside had been, for her, a great hardship, but she simply couldn't share in the experiences of women who had suffered so much injustice under the colonial system and so much hardship in the previous decade of famine and war.

Madame Nhu tried anyway. She used her position as a deputy in the National Assembly to promise her "sisters" that she would look out for them. She would make their voices heard and protect them. In October 1957, Madame Nhu presented the Family Code legislation. When enacted in June 1958, it outlawed polygamy and concubinage. It also gave women the right to control their own finances after marriage; they could open their own bank accounts, own property, and inherit wealth. Grumbling from some of Madame Nhu's male co-senators was to be expected. They said these new rights for women were too much too soon. There was "prolonged picking" at the various provisions of the bill. Madame Nhu suggested that those of her male colleagues who resisted the legislation did so because they wanted to keep concubines, and the rumor went around that she had called the leader of the assembly "a pig." At one point a motion was made to table the proposed law, but no one could afford to oppose Madame Nhu for long. When she appealed to Diem, he applied presidential pressure on the legislature, and the Family Code was approved with only one deputy dissenting.[11] It seemed that the majority of the Vietnamese people welcomed legislation reforming the status of women in the Family Code—except for one thing. Madame Nhu's law also banned divorce. That line item condemned the rest of the code to widespread criticism because, as even the most casual listener to Saigon gossip knew, Madame Nhu had a very personal stake in the matter.

Madame Nhu's older sister, Le Chi, was in a loveless marriage. Her parents had handpicked her husband, Nguyen Huu Chau, a rising young lawyer who had worked for Chuong in Hanoi. The young couple married at seventeen. But Chuong's collaboration with the Japanese had put his new son-in-law's career at great risk; to survive professionally he had to slip into obscurity. Did Le Chi resent the fact that her younger sister had married better? Nhu, the one-time librarian, now effectively ran the country. Madame Nhu had made sure all her kin had positions in the new government. Chau now toiled away drafting legislation for the regime, taking orders from Le Chi's younger sister. Instead of being grateful for her husband's inclusion, Le Chi felt indignant that she had been eclipsed. Maybe that was why she put so little effort into keeping her extramarital affair a secret.

Le Chi's lover was a Frenchman, a big-game hunter named Etienne Oggeri who killed elephants in the Vietnamese highlands for their ivory tusks, as well as tigers and guar, a horned bovine native to Southeast Asia. As soon as she started seeing the Westerner, Le Chi changed her look. She took to wearing light, brightly colored lipstick and white eyeshadow to make her eyes look bigger. And instead of setting her hair in the fashion of other ladies in Saigon society, she began wearing it down—straight, silky, and long. It was an embarrassment and, Madame Nhu decided, unacceptable behavior on the part of someone so close to the palace.

Radio Catinat picked up on the story right away. It was not a real station but the nickname for the chatter that zipped through the air in Saigon. Rumors crackled to life in the restaurants and bars on the old rue Catinat; they passed in a blink to other ears, other lips, as gossipers moved from bar stool to bar stool. Madame Nhu and her family were a favorite topic. It seemed everyone had an opinion on whether Madame Nhu was sleeping with Diem. Some suggested she was more like her mother, seducing the Americans who suddenly seemed to be everywhere. They pointed to aid money pouring into South Vietnamese coffers as proof that her sexual favors were being reimbursed. There was a even a story that a young army general had been one of Madame

Nhu's lovers until his wife found out and shot Madame Nhu in both arms. No one seemed to care that Madame Nhu wasn't wearing any bandages.

At first the palace tried to stop the gossip. They took out advertisements in newspapers and publicly denied charges of everything from corruption to love triangles.[12] But Madame Nhu couldn't staunch the rumors. She sighed about it to Charlie Mohr of *Time* magazine: "If any man is promoted and he is not too ugly, it is immediately said, 'A protégé of Madame Nhu's.'" But addressing each rumor explicitly seemed to fan the flames, so the Nhus stopped. Madame Nhu told herself she didn't care.

But the mess with Le Chi was a real problem for Madame Nhu. She might have cared a little less if her sister hadn't claimed Etienne Oggeri was more than just a fling. Le Chi declared he was the love of her life. Her husband, once a respected member of the government's inner circle, lost all prestige and self-respect; deprived of all influence, he was reduced to a simple civil servant.[13] Now he wanted a divorce, and that posed a threat—Chau knew too much about the workings of Nhu's political party, how it operated, and how it got financed. The gossipy conjecture was that Madame Nhu wanted to outlaw divorce to prevent Chau from speaking out against the family.

The public didn't know, however, that Madame Nhu's own marriage was coming apart. To the outside, the Nhus presented a formidable power couple, but Madame Nhu's private despair soaked through the pages of a diary she began to keep in 1959.

The diary came to my attention in August 2012, when James van Thach, a retired US Army captain, got in touch with me. He was my age, lived in the Bronx, and had found me through a Google search. Like me, James was interested in the history of the Vietnam War, particularly the story of Madame Nhu.

I was skeptical when James told me he had Madame Nhu's diary. That a fifty-year-old journal would surface now, in the hands of a thirty-six-year-old retired US Army captain in New York, seemed, well, far-fetched. Besides, she had never mentioned it.

I went to James's parents' house in Queens anyway. It was a flat-faced townhouse with a stucco exterior in an unlikely shade of brown. Hurricane Sandy had swept through the neighborhood two weeks before but had damaged only the trees here. Crews were still out clearing debris. James's father stayed out of sight when I came to the door. A former American soldier, now in his eighties, he had done two tours in Vietnam, where he had met James's mother. She was younger, just past sixty. She fairly skipped down the front steps to meet me but shivered when the air came through the cutouts in her sheer sweater. She was a full head taller than most Vietnamese women, with long black hair that she wore loose down her back. Her nails were lacquered, and she had rounded, squishy lips that echoed the curves under her sweater. As a teenager, she had been on the South Vietnamese Olympic team, a high jumper, before she left Vietnam in 1974. She was just in time. The south fell to the north less than a year after her departure, and it would take a decade of paperwork before she could sponsor the other members of her family and get them out.

James wouldn't, or couldn't, explain much about how he came to possess the diary, but it had something to do with family members who had served in the South Vietnamese police force in 1963. James shook his head, refusing to tell me anything more precise than "I came of age, and I got the diary." I couldn't tell if he feared getting into trouble for telling me where he had gotten the diary or if it was just nerves. James had already told me that having it in his possession made him nervous: "It's like I have a target on my back." He couldn't read it—it was in French—but he hoped I would tell him what the pages said.

It was hard for me to imagine James afraid of anything. He had a strong military frame, six feet, two inches tall and bulging with muscles, but injuries from his service in Iraq and Afghanistan had left him permanently disabled. He suffered migraines and short-term memory loss from brain trauma, nerve damage, and posttraumatic stress disorder. In spite of that, James seemed sanguine about the future. Payments from his retirement pension and disability would continue to arrive monthly and he got by just fine. James drove a big white Mercedes truck and carried a Louis Vuitton briefcase in the hand that didn't hold his cane. He took his mother to get one-hour massages at the mall nearby and spoke with a blush about an upcoming trip to Vietnam with his aunt to meet a distant cousin: she was only seventeen, but that's how these things are done in the traditional Vietnamese way, he explained.

James allowed me to look through the diary at a Starbucks on Jamaica Avenue. It was roughly five by seven inches, the perfect size to slip into a dressing table drawer after recording a day's entry and small enough to tuck into the waistband of a uniform to smuggle out of the palace. Time-mottled cardboard formed the front and back covers, bound by a fabric tape that threatened to lose its grip with every turn of the page. Right-leaning cursive filled some three hundred pages in brown fountain pen ink, blue ballpoint pen, and sometimes pencil. A few entries looked to have been written with a red wax crayon, the kind my mother uses to mark her sewing. But all the entries matched Madame Nhu's handwriting exactly. Just to be sure, I cross-checked certain dates, places I knew she had been, things and people I knew she had seen. Nhu, Diem, and the children were the main characters in Madame Nhu's story from January 1959 until her last entry in June 1963. The diary was hers, I was sure.

Once upon a time, this diary would have been the one place Madame Nhu could turn to without facing judgment or the pressure of living up to expectations. She would have been in her prime when she started the diary as First Lady. A glamorous and beautiful young mother of three children, she found comfort in the most ordinary things. Madame Nhu loved Hollywood movies and Russian novels. She liked to vacation with her children at the beach and in the mountains. She was afraid of getting old; she feared life passing her by. And in her scrawled pages, she revealed the misery of living as the wife of Nhu.

Madame Nhu had expected their marital troubles to get better once they lived together in the palace. For the first time in their marriage, she could expect her husband to be home. He had worked hard to get his brother into the palace, and Madame Nhu felt she had proved her worth with her seat on the National Assembly and as Diem's hostess. She expected everything else to flow from that: emotional support, physical love, that Nhu would quit smoking and be nice to her. When those things didn't happen, there were violent quarrels and slammed doors. Madame Nhu was tired of being at Nhu's beck and call, she said—because he never called. She couldn't understand why at first. She was still young and beautiful. Nhu must be getting too old to enjoy it, she wrote. At first, she seemed to pity him; his lack of interest in sex was a casualty of aging. But in other entries, Madame Nhu expressed sorrow only for herself; she was stuck with an impotent old man and had to devise ways to divert herself from her otherwise all-consuming "rising desire." There is biological proof that Nhu gave in to her at least once, because Madame Nhu got pregnant again in 1959, but that seems to have been an exception in her otherwise frustratingly lonely life. When Madame Nhu was seven months pregnant with their fourth child, she learned that Nhu was still capable of being sexually aroused after all, but by someone else.

Madame Nhu wrote a detailed account of their argument when she confronted Nhu with his cheating. She raged against him, less for cheating than for doing it with someone so "vulgar" and "dirty." Madame Nhu never wrote the girl's name in the diary, referring to her only as that "creature."

Nhu defended himself and his lover: the girl was sweet and nice, and "not dirty—just poor," and to her credit, she was nothing like his wife, because "you scare me," he said. The ensuing fight was vicious, but it ended, days later, on a chilly note. Madame Nhu and her husband agreed that their marriage had been much better when they spent more time apart.

Madame Nhu found herself lying awake in bed, blinking back tears. Who was this strange man sleeping next to her? Love like in the movies, love like she read about in the books, would never happen for her. To survive this marriage, she would have to stop pretending it would ever be more than it was. Madame Nhu had thought she could bind Nhu to her with her youth, beauty, social graces, or even the fact that she was the mother of their children, but she was all but invisible to him in the palace. There was no real danger that he would leave her—he was too religious—and she wouldn't leave him. His position behind the throne insured her security, and that of her children and extended family. Without him, what would she be?

In context, Madame Nhu's divorce ban seems sad. She didn't want her older sister getting out of an unhappy marriage if she was going to be stuck in one herself. A story leaked that after Le Chi heard about the law she had driven to the palace with her wrists slit. Madame Nhu refused to see her; what was done was done, she said. Le Chi went running through the palace, dripping blood all over the tiled floors. Madame Nhu had the palace guards take her sister to the hospital and imprison her there.

Madame Nhu didn't write about the suicide attempt in her diary, but she did claim that she had done what she had to in order to protect her sister. Le Chi was disgracing the family and herself. The president of the country couldn't be connected to such a scandal. Later, Madame Nhu's sister would tell reporters her own version of the events. Five secret policemen dressed as hospital guards had been posted outside her door day and night. She had written a cablegram to her mother and convinced a sympathetic nurse to smuggle it out of the hospital. Her mother had arrived from the United States to rescue Le Chi and used the fact that she was Madame Nhu's mother to overrule the First Lady's wishes that Le Chi remain locked in her room. It seems the guards were sufficiently impressed, or maybe just confused enough, to let the patient slip out the hospital door.

Whatever the facts behind the story, the Saigon rumor mill was working overtime but still missed the signs of an unhappy marriage inside the palace. Instead people speculated about whether Le Chi was in jail or in a hospital? Had Madame Chuong flown back from Washington to smuggle her oldest daughter out of the country? Had Madame Nhu really told her sister, whose wrists were still covered in bandages, "I have only one regret—that you didn't succeed at death"?

The palace tried to make it all go away. Despite having been a good advisor in Diem's inner circle, Le Chi's husband was also sent away, to Paris. Etienne Oggeri would publish a memoir years later claiming that Madame Nhu had ordered someone to inject him with the cholera virus. Maybe that was what Madame Nhu meant when she wrote that she did what she had to do.

Oggeri spent some time in a South Vietnamese prison before being extradited back to France, and from there he followed Madame Nhu's sister to the United States. In 1963, President Diem would still be complaining about Le Chi; he feared she was "acting like a prostitute in Washington," "scandalizing Georgetown," and "even jumping on priests." But he was ignorant of her genuine love. Le Chi married her Frenchman, and despite the horrible end that befell the rest of her family, she and her husband were still living together contentedly in North Carolina at the time of this writing.[14]

With Chau shipped off to Paris and Le Chi nursing her wounds in America, the divorce scandal eventually simmered down, and the Family Code stayed in place. In the eyes of the law, women in South Vietnam had the same rights as men. Wives had parity with their husbands, fathers, and brothers. But not in the palace. Madame Nhu was still deeply unhappy. The rooms were loud—people were constantly running in and out, and the high ceilings and grand scale amplified noises. There was little peace inside, but for Madame Nhu, stepping outside in Saigon was increasingly difficult. She couldn't just throw on a bathing suit and go for a swim at the Cercle Sportif with the other political wives; she couldn't play cards or gossip with her friends.

Edward Lansdale, the American intelligence officer who developed such a good relationship with Diem and Nhu, found Madame Nhu's situation in the palace tragic:

> She knew all of the social graces of a hostess in a household of wealth and culture so that her training was to be the gracious lady who invites people and knew how to make conversation at the dinner table, could entertain at the grand piano and live a life of quiet charm. She married a man who looked as though this was going to be his life. . . . She would come in to [a room in the palace where people were gathered and] ask if anybody would like to hear her play the piano in the salon. Her husband was busy with his brother, there was some terrible problem taking place, there might be military types come running in with their problems and there might be an alarm that the palace was about to

> be bombed or something very unladylike taking place, something very unsocial. And the men would say no, just leave us alone now. So she couldn't act her true role that she was trained for in life.[15]

It was easier for Madame Nhu when she was away from the palace altogether. Whenever she could, she escaped back to the mountains in Dalat and dreamed of the jewel of a house she would build there, a place where she could swim in her own pool, walk in her own forests, take refuge, and find solitude when she needed it. While that dream was still under construction and years away, Madame Nhu made use of a French villa by the sea in Nha Trang. The children could run without shoes on the beach, play in the waves, and learn how to fish. When they ran in from their fun to give their mother a hug, she inhaled their scent. They smelled of sea brine and sweat and something sweet, maybe the pineapples on the beach, or maybe it was just the smell of childhood. It was something their lives in Saigon didn't let them taste very often.

The one thing that Madame Nhu and her husband could agree on was their shared concern for the children. Growing up in the palace, "with too many servants and no playmates," was an odd childhood, one they worried would have lasting effects.[16]

Le Thuy was bright but so serious. It made her seem wiser, sadder, than a thirteen-year-old girl should be. Her brothers were a puzzle. Trac was withdrawn and sullen at school; at home he pinched his little brother Quynh and made him cry. But Quynh, Madame Nhu remarked, stayed sweet, chasing after his brother and begging for attention, even if it came in the form of a physical punishment. She tried to talk to the boys, tried to discipline Trac, and tried to get Quynh to stick up for himself, but what the boys needed was more time with their father.

They didn't even know they were missing him. Nhu had been gone much of the time after the boys were born in Dalat. He was away again when the family first lived in Saigon. And he was always absent now, traveling in the countryside, visiting his brothers, or working in his office. For relaxation, he went away again—to hunt or to visit his lover, the "creature." Soon there would be another baby, a fourth child, to care for and worry about. A little part of Madame Nhu hoped that this last child, born at such a momentous time in their nation's history—and in their family's history—might change things. And maybe once this pregnancy was done, Madame Nhu would try a different way to attract her husband's attention, one that relied less on her beauty than her brains.

In July 1959, Madame Nhu gave birth to her last child. It was another girl, and this one, Le Quyen, looked very much like her father. They had the same downward tilt of the eyes and the same off-center smile. Madame Nhu kept her youngest daughter dressed in shorts and styled in a pageboy haircut. The little tomboy outfits were certainly easier to manage than frilly dresses and hair bows, and they emphasized the child's resemblance to her father. Nhu still didn't seem to notice. Most nights, he simply said, "I have to work," and pushed his chair away from the dinner table, leaving his chopsticks leaning against the rim of his rice bowl above the half-eaten morsels.

Nhu would descend one level on the spiral staircase and spend hours in his office with the door closed. It was packed floor to ceiling with books and papers. Sometimes he would confer with his brother, but Nhu didn't go down there just to work—he went to smoke cigarettes. Madame Nhu had been after him to quit for years. She hated the smell of stale smoke. It fouled his breath, his hair, and the air around him. Even his fingers were stained yellow. She had tried soft encouragement, then gentle teasing. When they moved into the palace, she had put her tiny foot down. The palace was big enough that he could find somewhere else to indulge his habit. She would not let him smoke upstairs in their private living quarters. Nhu complied but didn't quit. He snuck around just enough so that Madame Nhu couldn't very well be angry with him for breaking her rules, but he still made it clear that her rules were not going to change his habits. At the end of his evenings in the office, Nhu would tip the full ashtray into an envelope and hand it to the guards to get rid of. There wasn't much Madame Nhu could do about it.

It was 3 a.m. on November 11, 1960, when distant pops of artillery woke Madame Nhu up. The sound was strangely celebratory, like fireworks or champagne corks, but that was because it was still far away. Three hours later, the sharp crack of rifle fire shredded the illusion that this was anything but deadly serious. Then word came through to the palace that two of the Ngo nephews, their sister's sons, had been shot dead. The streets just outside the gates were chaos. Madame Nhu took the children and hid in the basement of the palace.

Diem and Nhu were apprised of the situation. Three battalions of on-duty paratroopers had gone rogue, led by a small group of military men and civilians who had grown deeply resentful of the regime. They were tired of the nepotism. They were sick of the ruling family's always distrusting them. The paratroopers had already seized key government centers in Saigon and were now planning to attack the palace.

The brothers were badly shaken. They conferred in Diem's office, still wearing their pajamas. Only the South Vietnamese navy in Saigon had stayed loyal; many of the key military points were in rebel hands. Twenty-eight civilians had already been killed. A group of mostly young men and boys gathered outside the gates at daybreak. They had no particular sympathy for either side; they were simply curious about what was going on and who would win. The police were staying neutral too, just redirecting the eerily normal traffic out of the line of fire. Most infuriating to the brothers under siege was the lack of response on the United States' part. Allies were not supposed to be neutral. Diem and Nhu were considering backing down.

Periodically, one of the servants would dash upstairs for an update, coming back to where Madame Nhu and the children huddled in the basement to report on the current situation. The president was now taking a meeting with General Nguyen Khanh, they said. Madame Nhu's eyes flashed. She wondered whose side he was on that night. Madame Nhu knew Khanh far too well to trust him. His mother had run a nightclub in Dalat that catered to the French. His father had been a wealthy landowner in the south whose mistress was a well-known singer and actress. Khanh had joined up with the Viet Minh before switching sides to the French, probably because there were more perks to being a soldier in the French army. He went to a military academy in France and came back to fight on the French side during the First Indochina War. He liked to boast that he had served under the famous French general Jean de Lattre de Tassigny, who had worn uniforms tailored by Lanvin, a prominent Parisian fashion designer, to battle. Some of the French general's grandiosity had rubbed off: Khanh grew a goatee and swaggered around Saigon like a bandy-legged rooster circling the henhouse. It had been nearly a decade since Khanh had accompanied Madame Nhu and Bao Dai on their afternoon picnics in Dalat. Madame Nhu recalled that on their first outing together, Khanh had paid close attention to what she selected from the picnic basket and quizzed her on the activities she enjoyed. The next time they were together, he brought the things that Madame Nhu had liked best and made a show of entertaining her. Instead of considering those touches endearing, Madame Nhu had found Khanh conniving.

That Khanh would show up at the palace in the middle of a firefight made Madame Nhu suspicious. She very much doubted he would risk harm to his own precious hide. He must have the coup plotters' protection, she reasoned. So Madame Nhu entrusted the children's care to the Chinese nurse hiding with them in the basement and made her way alone through the quiet halls in search of Nhu.

In the rising light of the morning, she saw a dead deer on the palace lawn. It had been shot through the head and somehow landed flat on its belly, its four legs sprawling horribly akimbo. The sight of death so close to the palace was jarring, much more so than all the abstract warnings of danger delivered to her while she was cowering in the basement. The dead animal triggered a primal instinct, which clicked into place as soon as she found her husband and Diem in the office on the first floor, contemplating their next move.

Diem had already started negotiating terms with the coup plotters. He had promised them a new and different government, and by the time Madame Nhu arrived in his office, he had even gone on the radio to proclaim it. "The president is much too softhearted," she realized; someone was going to have to take charge. Conciliation was a sign of weakness. Just like when Diem had stood strong in the face of the Binh Xuyen mobsters, he needed to stand firm now.

Madame Nhu strode over to Diem. She did not hide her frustration. In later interviews, she would say that when the president behaved like a child, she wanted to slap him. In her diary, she accused Diem of acting like a baby. She also wrote, "I am disgusted with him; he has no confidence in himself and has lowered himself by talking with the rebels." One published account of the confrontation that morning maintains that Madame Nhu actually did slap the president, hard and across the face, before grabbing him by his sloping shoulders and shaking him in a fury. But that sounds like the kind of story that was embroidered on its way through the café gossip circuit before it landed in the *St. Louis Post-Dispatch* three years later.

Even if Madame Nhu didn't slap Diem, her words had a lasting impact. "Keep only the necessary men here to defend the palace," she instructed. "Send the rest of them to retake the radio."

The military units that had remained loyal to Diem were moving in as fast as they could from their countryside positions, but they calculated that it would still take twelve hours to mount a full counterattack on the coup plotters. "What is the state of mind there?" a loyal soldier radioed in to ask the captain in charge of palace security.

"Mrs. Nhu is very tough," the captain answered. "She wants to fight even if she dies. Mr. Nhu is quiet. He doesn't seem to know what to do."[17]

But Nhu figured it out quickly enough and convinced the president that his wife was right. They needed to hold firm against the rebels. The brothers followed Madame Nhu's instructions to the letter. A few hours later, just as Madame Nhu had predicted, Diem's men retook the key city centers. The unsuspecting rebels, caught off guard as they celebrated the president's announced plans to capitulate, were crushed.

Madame Nhu had saved the brothers at a crucial moment. Every time Diem received congratulations, he nodded at his sister-in-law and graciously acknowledged her: "C'est grâce à madame."

Looking around her at the jumble of papers cascading off the desk and at the wall of books cluttering her husband's office, Madame Nhu realized that she did have a place in this regime. The brothers' expressions of gratitude confirmed it. She was much more than just a pretty face in the palace. Without her, the Ngo brothers were too unworldly, too intellectual and removed from reality. They were the insecure ones after all. It would fall to her, she felt, to be the steel in the spike of the regime. It was the strangest conviction, but she was sure of it. "Up until then," she told *New York Times* journalist David Halberstam in 1963, "they had not taken me that seriously. But then they began to notice me."[18]

CHAPTER 10

Tiger Skins

AT THE BEGINNING, I HAD BEEN a little starstruck when talking to Madame Nhu. She had been so powerful, so notorious, and so glamorous. It took nearly two years of telephone conversations for me to get up the courage to prod for something more. I was interested in the quotidian details that had slipped through the cracks. In all the press coverage of the powerful woman she had once been, there wasn't much about life in the palace, what she ate and what she wore. I hoped these details would tell me something more about the woman behind the glossy photographs and the Dragon Lady image. But for Madame Nhu, those were the hardest to recall. It had been almost half a century ago and half a world away. Memories were all Madame Nhu had left, but even those were starting to fade. When I urged her to remember the particulars of life in Independence Palace, Madame Nhu's voice thinned out on the line, and I had to press the phone hard against my head, squishing my ear to catch her words. She sounded a million miles away. "I can't seem to remember how the room looked—I mean I can't remember it exactly . . . "

She could tell me that she usually woke at 7:30 a.m., took a light breakfast of tea and rice or bread, then dressed for the day. She devoted the rest of the morning to work. If she wasn't drafting letters with her secretary in her study, she was out visiting her constituents, but she was almost always back by noon. Lunch was the main meal of the day, eaten under the massive chandeliers with linens and formal china. Although the president usually ate simple meals in his office, when there were guests, or once or twice a week on his own, he might dine more formally with his brother and sister-in-law in their dining room on the second floor. Semiofficial evenings were also hosted in the Nhus' dining room; it was spacious and elegant but more personal, without the ceremonial pomp of the official presidential dining room on the first floor. Madame Nhu wished the family's five rooms in the palace were just a little bigger. They had a spacious parlor, two large bedrooms, and two other sitting rooms with balconies, but Madame Nhu wanted a kitchen a little closer. By the time the food made it to the dining room from the kitchen on the first floor at the back of the palace, it was cold.

After lunch, Madame Nhu usually went to lie down in her bedroom. It was too mind-numbingly hot to do anything else. This was the time of day when she was most nostalgic for the seasons in Hanoi. She missed the lakes and wide boulevards and having a place to stroll. In Saigon, she felt like she stared from behind the palace's massive gates at life passing her by. She thought about how different things would be if she were just living a normal life. What would she do if she weren't trapped? Madame Nhu imagined that she would be content to live in a small house as long as it had a big garden for the children to play in; she would cook simple meals for her family and spend her days writing children's stories.

In response to her daydream, I suppose I must have clucked sympathetically into the telephone as she was speaking. But the eighty-three-year-old wasn't after sympathy. Her life as First Lady in the palace might not have been the one she would have chosen, but it was the life chosen for her by God. As such, she required not compassion but determination. "How else can I explain my powerful drive? My agenda

FIGURE 1. Portrait of Tran Thi Le Xuan as a bride circa 1943

Figure 2. Portrait of Ngo Dinh Nhu circa 1963 (*above*)

Figure 3. Portrait of Tran Thi Le Chi, Madame Nhu's sister (*right*)

FIGURE 4. The South Vietnamese presidential family

FIGURE 5. Ngo Dinh Nhu and wife, Tran Thi Le Xuan

FIGURE 6. Madame Nhu playing with two-year-old daughter Le Quyen (*above*)

FIGURE 7. Portrait of daughter Le Thuy circa 1963 (*left*)

FIGURE 8. Malcolm Browne, Saigon correspondent, in front of his photo

Figure 9. Madame Nhu showing Lady Bird Johnson and Mrs. Jean Kennedy Smith her collection of tiger skins

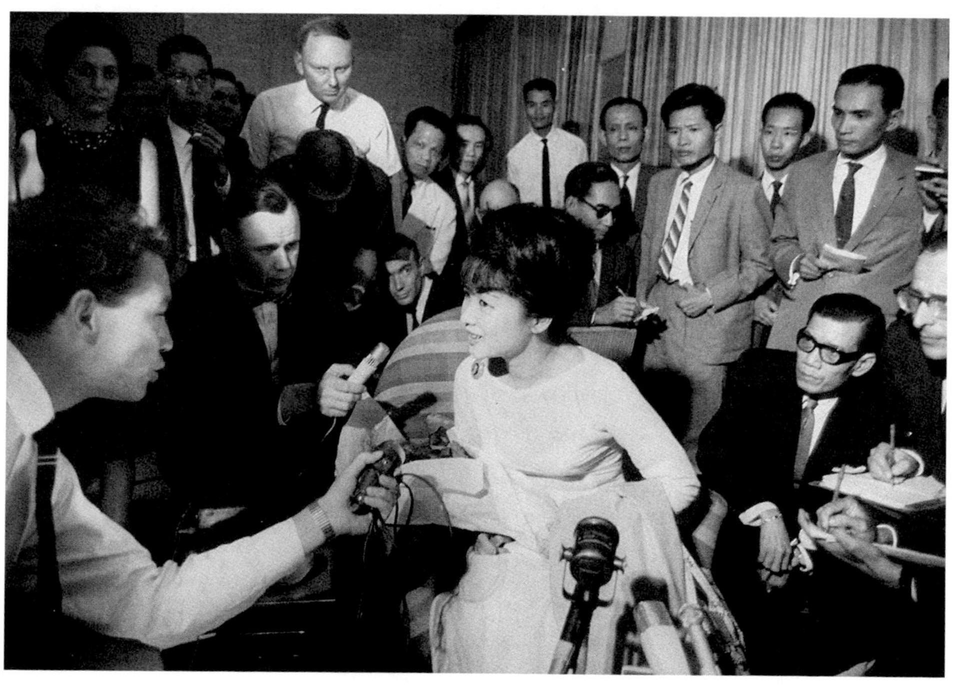

Figure 10. Madame Nhu talking to the press at the airport as she is leaving Vietnam in 1963

FIGURE 11. Barefooted Vietnamese youth about to come down on the head of the Trung sister statue

to change the lives of women? I, myself, would have been content with a peaceful life! I have told you that over and over. But God had different plans for me. It was my duty to see it through."

Madame Nhu had another test for me. "I want to see it again. If you can help me, find pictures of my rooms in the palace for me, then you really are sent by God." The mission was perfectly clear: find photographs of the rooms circa 1961. Get them to Madame Nhu, make an old lady happy, and get her memoirs. Easy enough. Except Madame Nhu's quarters had taken a direct hit when Independence Palace had been destroyed in the bombing of 1962. Anything retrieved from the rubble was lost again eighteen months later.

"I never showed my bedroom to anyone. No visitors were ever allowed in my private quarters." Madame Nhu let a wry laugh escape. "But there was one time, I really wanted to make an impression on my guests. It was so spontaneous for me."

The guests that she had wanted to impress so badly had been part of the American vice presidential delegation. Lyndon Johnson and a diplomatic entourage had come to South Vietnam in May 1961.

"Ooh, they were so surprised!" Madame Nhu's voice brightened recalling the moment the vice president's wife, Lady Bird Johnson, and Mrs. Jean Smith, President Kennedy's sister, had walked into the room.

"When I opened the door to my room, they could see a long row of tiger skins [laid out on the floor]. The paws all lined up. The heads attached." It sounded pretty gruesome to me, but she breathed in deeply, as if recalling the smell of the orange blossoms at Tet instead of taxidermy specimens.

I understood a moment later, when she continued, "If I had the photographs, I would at least have something of my husband. He was such a skilled hunter. Magnificent. He killed the most beautiful beasts, and every one of his prizes, he turned over to me."

The irony of Madame Nhu's lost tiger skins didn't escape me. I knew that while the Americans had called her the Dragon Lady, those Vietnamese who had dared speak out against Madame Nhu referred to her instead as the Tiger Lady—out of cultural respect for the dragon.

I wonder now at all my continued enthusiasm for her. After all, she had stood me up—literally, at the church, and figuratively. She continued to dangle the promise of her memoirs in front of me, but I kept running into doubts that they existed outside her imagination. She had been referring to these so-called memoirs since 1963. She said she had written so many hundreds of pages that papers were collected all over her apartment, even under the couch. Why on earth should I believe that now, nearly fifty years later, she was finally ready to gather them together into a manuscript? When I tried to press her, she snapped at me. It was a quick flick of the sharp tongue I had heard so much about. "You should not speak about what you don't understand," she had chided, and it stung. But the truth was, I knew that if I didn't play along, I would never have anything to show. And her desire to have something of her husband again, I have to say, tugged at my heart strings, just as she had guessed it might.

Madame Nhu's challenge turned out to be fairly easy. After a couple of e-mails and telephone calls to the archivists at the Lyndon B. Johnson Presidential Library in Austin, Texas, I got what I was looking for.

When I opened the attachments on my computer, my breath caught in my throat. The sepia-toned photos brought a destroyed world back to life.

Four women stand in what is clearly a bedroom, a satiny upholstered creampuff of a place with endless curtains hanging over windows and around doorways. Elaborate moldings and parquet floors finalize the palace feel. And there they are: a row of gaping-mouthed tiger hides laid out end to end, running the length of the room right to the foot of the bed. What did it feel like to touch bare feet to them? Were their hides coarse and wiry? I puzzled over how Madame Nhu remembered to avoid tripping over ears, eyes, and teeth when she got out of bed in the morning.

I recognized three of the women in the photograph easily, and I assumed the fourth must be the ambassador's wife or the wife of another highly placed American official. The vice president's wife, Lady Bird Johnson, stands backed up against the edge of the bed, her white pumps planted squarely on the parquet, as if she has taken care to walk around the dead beasts instead of across them. Nicely dressed for a palace visit in a sleeveless sheath and heels, Lady Bird smiles gamely for the camera, but she looks just a little wilted by the heat. Her gloves are off, her hat is askew, and her curls droop in the humidity. She looks right into the camera, her eyebrows hitched in surprise.

Madame Nhu seems much more at ease. Wearing a long-sleeved *ao dai* with a scooped neckline instead of the mandarin collar, she welcomes her guests into the draped room with an open palm. In the next picture, she stands with her hips squared toward the camera, her shoulders thrown back. She seems to possess a ballet dancer's physical awareness. Madame Nhu looks like she might be ready to smile—at least her chin is lifted in the camera's direction. The strength of her presence distracted me from noticing her size compared to the Americans until much later. She was tiny. Without her heels and elaborate beehive, she might not have made it to Lady Bird's shoulder.

President Kennedy's sister, Jean Smith, has the same square jaw as her brother. She is wearing a full-skirted gingham dress and pearls, and she seems unable to tear her eyes from the tiger hides surrounding her feet—not even to look up for a photograph—as though afraid they might spring to life and attack. Her elbows tucked tightly to her body, one arm holds onto the other, like a security belt, her knees pressed together as though they might buckle otherwise.

Jean Smith was the youngest of the Kennedy siblings. Her husband, Stephen, was the president's political advisor and finance chairman, but Jean had pitched in her time and energy for Jack too. She worked tirelessly on the campaign, hosting tea parties and knocking on doors. After the election, President Kennedy would inscribe a photo to his youngest sister, thanking her for all her hard work. Jean had been thrilled, honored, she said, to have her hard work recognized—until she found out that all her sisters and her brothers' wives had gotten the same.[1]

Madame Nhu, the glamorous Asian dynamo, and Mrs. Jean Smith, the all-American woman, had more in common than could be supposed from a casual glance at the picture of them standing together. Both women were carried along by their families' strong ties to politics. Both had husbands who worked for family; both families were Catholic and anti-Communist and committed to doing the "right" thing. Both women were charming and savvy, and both professed a seriousness of purpose. It seemed like there should have been a natural affinity, not only between the women but between the newly inaugurated Kennedy administration in Washington and the Diem regime in Saigon.

President Kennedy himself had announced Johnson's trip to Southeast Asia, calling it a "fact-finding mission." There were conflicting reports about what was actually happening in South Vietnam. What was there to show for the millions of aid dollars the United States had poured into the tiny country since 1954? Were these Ngo brothers helping the fight against communism as they claimed, or were they hindering it? The last year had seen an uptick in violence and Communist activity, which may have been why Vice President Johnson didn't want to go. "Mr. President," Johnson had said, "I don't want to embarrass you by getting my head blown off in Saigon."[2]

Of course, no harm came to anyone in Johnson's entourage in South Vietnam. The Diem regime took good care of the Americans, hosting them in the guesthouse on the palace grounds. That first night in Saigon, the Johnsons, the Smiths, and Kennedy's new ambassador to South Vietnam, Frederick Nolting and his wife, enjoyed a fine French dinner in the rooftop restaurant of the Caravelle Hotel.[3] As they looked out over their wineglasses at the city's twinkling lights, the view convinced them that, indeed, this was a charming place worth saving from the Reds. Graceful women drifted under the acacias along wide tree-lined streets; the happy sounds of children frolicking in the square floated up to them on the cool evening breeze. But there was also a distinct tension in the air, an awareness of imminent danger, of Communists lurking in the shadows. Intelligence reports had confirmed that many of the people who had fought with the Viet Minh during the war against the French and had stayed in the South were now determined to unify the country under one leadership: Hanoi's. The Communists were having more success than anyone was comfortable admitting.

The Communists were said to control about one-third of the southern countryside. They had created bases in the delta and the highlands; the same Viet Minh weapons used against the French, wrapped in plastic and buried in the rice paddies for nearly fifteen years, were dug out and repurposed. Le Duan, South Vietnam's Communist chief, was in charge of organizing the old fighters into new squads. He had an impressive revolutionary pedigree, having spent seven years in French jails before meeting up with Ho Chi Minh in China in the 1940s. So although a southerner, Le Duan had the ear of his comrades in Hanoi. He was able to plead his fellow southerners' case: Our people are suffering under Diem and ready to fight. They must rise up. If we do not lead them, they will form their own resistance, and we will become irrelevant. The Politburo agreed with Le Duan and resolved to fight a military struggle in the south in addition to its political efforts. In 1959, a secret mission was authorized to travel down the Truong Son Route to bring arms and other supplies for waging war. The West would come to call the treacherous jungle path that snaked down the western edge of the country the Ho Chi Minh Trail.[4]

A year later, the Communist Party Congress in Hanoi committed itself to the military struggle even further. In December 1960, Hanoi formed the National Liberation Front (NLF), the proper name for the southern Communist effort to reunify the country, though the Americans would simply call them the Viet Cong. Regardless of their name, the downfall of the Diem regime was their number one goal. Hanoi had authorized them to overthrow the South Vietnamese president and his "colonial master," the United States, by whatever means necessary. By the time of the Johnsons' visit to Saigon, Communists were killing an average of five to eight hundred South Vietnamese army soldiers, government workers, and civilians a month. The figures were kept secret.

The grim numbers coming out of Vietnam were manipulated for two reasons, and both had to do with politics. On the American side, the US ambassador to Vietnam, Frederick Nolting, and the senior military commander, General Paul Harkins, were concerned that negative evaluations might undermine President Kennedy's resolve to keep American aid money and advisors flowing to Vietnam. When Secretary of Defense Robert McNamara went on a two-day fact-finding mission around the country, Nolting and Harkins prohibited their staffs from telling him anything that might give less than a favorable impression. Evasions were a slippery slope leading to the kind of outright manipulations that later took place, such as basing enemy casualty counts on intuition and peeling red stickers off a map that were supposed to indicate where the Communists had a foothold when it looked like there were "too many." American newsmen, while not censored outright, were made aware of US guidelines when it came to filing "undesirable dispatches." Specific numbers were to be avoided, as were indications of tactical strengths and weaknesses. Anyone who violated those ground rules would not be taken on missions anymore.[5]

The other reason to keep any bad numbers quiet was that President Diem, personally, would be mad. After the 1960 coup attempt, Diem had issued a verbal order to his army commanders not to conduct any operations that might incur serious casualties. The president had concluded that the dissatisfied army paratroopers behind the coup attempt had been angry with the regime for casualties suffered on offensive operations. Diem couldn't, or wouldn't, see that the regime's nepotism, Catholic bias, and repression of freedoms were the real triggers generating resentment. Diem didn't want another coup, so he did not want the army to suffer losses.

American advisors to the South Vietnamese army would eventually find out that orders from the very highest levels "not to fight" were completely undermining their advice to engage the Viet Cong, but that didn't stop them from passing fake body counts along to Washington. Communist losses were inflated, South Vietnamese casualties were downplayed, and no warnings on the iffy numbers were attached. Those numbers were translated into policy, and the policy was that the war was going well.[6]

The NLF goal—to smash the southern regime—was a top-down directive from Hanoi that was to be carried out from the ground up. The assault was to begin "in the villages . . . work its way up through the district and then provincial governmental levels until at last there would be an attack on the central government itself." The NLF Central Committee issued specific orders about what to target to maximize the impact of sporadic and random terrorist assaults: communication centers, warehouses, airports, and US offices were "particularly" singled out.

The early victims of the NLF terror campaign were from rural areas: Long An, Tay Ninh, An Xuyen, and An Giang provinces. Terror activities included a Buddhist temple sacked, a hamlet school burned and two teachers forced at gunpoint to watch the execution of local men, and a parish priest killed when a bullet smashed through his windshield; a farmer who ignored Viet Cong orders to turn his rice field over to another farmer was taken into a flooded paddy and shot. In December 1960, the violence moved closer to the city when the kitchen at the Saigon Golf Club was dynamited, killing one worker and injuring two cooks.[7]

The NLF terrorists were so successful because they were making ingenious use of common materials. For example, the standard bicycle bomb was deadly, effective, and nearly impossible to detect until it was too late. The entire bike frame was filled with explosives; thin wires attached to blasting caps inside the frame led out past the brake cables, which helped camouflage them, and connected to an electric headlamp fitted with a kind of stopwatch. It took only a small flashlight-battery-powered mechanism to blow the bicycle apart and unleash its terrible destructive power in the middle of a busy street. The Viet Cong called their two-wheeled variation on the Trojan horse the "iron horse." They recruited Vietnamese youth as terrorists—the optimum age was about eighteen, but boys as young as thirteen or fourteen were perfect "city saboteurs," or grenade throwers. Restaurants and hotels began to install steel grilles in front of the verandahs; people were afraid to sit on patios, go to movie theaters, or even visit the market.[8]

On March 22, 1961, only a little over a month before the Johnson trip to Saigon, a truck carrying twenty young girls was blasted off a desolate patch of road in the Rung Sat forest. The girls were on their way home to Phuoc Tuy province from Saigon, where they had just spent the afternoon watching the First Lady, Madame Nhu, make a rousing speech praising Vietnamese women on Hai Ba Trung Day. The celebration commemorated the Trung sisters, ancient Vietnamese heroines who had fought off the Chinese. Madame Nhu held the sisters up as role models for the brave women of modern South Vietnam. For these girls, however, the day ended in tragedy. In the moments after their truck hit the planted land mine, a volley of gunfire rained down.

The driver managed to get the lumbering truck in gear and made it to the nearest military outpost, but two girls were already dead.

The next week, Madame Nhu visited the hospital in Cholon where four of the young victims of the attack were recovering. One had lost an eye, another a leg, and one woman was crippled from a spinal injury. Madame Nhu also went to see the site of the explosion and talked to the girls who had survived the ambush uninjured. In the hamlet of Ti Giay, home of twenty-three-year-old Nguyen Thi Bang, Madame Nhu placed a wreath on the freshly dug grave and expressed her sorrow to the murdered girl's mother and sister. At the gravesite of Tang Thi Ut, Madame Nhu looked at the victim's fiancé and, her voice breaking with emotion, promised that this "inhuman and cowardly outrage perpetrated by the Viet Cong" would not go unavenged.[9]

The day after his arrival, Vice President Johnson met with President Diem in the palace office, where they talked about the specifics of US aid. While Johnson formally presented his gift—a set of American Heritage hardback books on US history—and his credentials, the wives took a tour of the palace with Madame Nhu to see the tiger skins. The picture of the meeting in the office downstairs shows Johnson bending deeply at the waist to meet Diem. After their meeting, the American vice president laid out an eight-point program that included more arms and more money. Later that afternoon, Johnson, ever the gregarious Texan, waded into the streets of Saigon to mingle with the South Vietnamese people. Reporter Stanley Karnow remarked that Johnson was shaking hands and smiling like he was "endorsing county sheriffs in a Texas election campaign," but in a sense, that was his job. Johnson had been assigned to reassure the South Vietnamese that the United States would continue to provide arms and money to improve social conditions and fight communism.[10]

Madame Nhu was seated in a place of honor next to the vice president, on his right, at the official luncheon. They had met only briefly on the day of his arrival. Madame Nhu had been at the airport, along with other officials' wives, to greet the delegation. Upon deplaning, the vice president strode toward her, crossing over the receiving line to shake her hand. His manners tickled Madame Nhu again at lunch.

She wasn't used to men waiting for her to sit before they took their own seat, any more than she was used to being addressed ahead of men like the president and her husband. But Madame Nhu liked Johnson's gallantry even if she didn't quite know what to make of it. Over lunch, he insisted that she agree to visit his ranch in Texas. She giggled nervously, covering her mouth with her napkin, but he insisted so much that she finally agreed to come—"when you become president," she promised. After that, Johnson took Madame Nhu's left hand in his huge paw and, in front of his wife and a table of diplomats, pulled her out to the balcony. "Show me the sights," he drawled. She'd have had to scramble to match his giant Texas steps, but the vice president didn't seem to mind. He had smiled at her for all present at the official reception to see.

In May 1961, Madame Nhu was surer of herself than she had ever been. Her ambitious project to reshape society was taking hold, with women as the agents of change. The work was more than gratifying, she had written hastily in her journal that January; she hadn't realized she was so smart! Madame Nhu had come up with the idea for a Women's Solidarity Movement the summer before. It would be a group of civil servants dedicated to helping the families of Vietnam's armed forces. They might bring food to someone in the hospital or deliver medicine to rural families; they also held blood drives and wrote encouraging letters to soldiers at the front. The idea was to give women a purpose outside the home, a way to participate in society more fully and realize how important they were to the building of this new country.

Madame Nhu also organized another, more militaristic group. Her own daughter Le Thuy joined this reserve unit of women organized as a paramilitary unit. They were trained in gun handling and first aid and marched in parades dressed in stylish military garb that nipped in at the waist. Madame Nhu called the members of her women's militia "my little darlings."

Madame Nhu's inspiration for her "darlings" came from the legend of the Trung sisters, two young ladies who had led their country to victory over China nearly 2,000 years before in 40 AD. The Communists used the legend too—they found a class issue in the narrative—but for her purposes, Madame Nhu emphasized the strength of women and mothers in battle. In the story, sister Trung Trac avenges the murder of her husband by a Chinese commander. Her younger sister and a posse of noble women ride by her side. One of these ladies is so pregnant that she gives birth during battle and continues to fight with the infant strapped to her back. Madame Nhu hoped that the story would inspire the women of her day to learn the skills to defend their homes. She even commissioned a bronze statue of the Trungs, which would welcome boats into the Saigon port. But when it was erected, the Trungs' faces and figures resembled Madame Nhu so much that rumors started to fly. Did Madame Nhu want the women of South Vietnam to honor the ancient heroines or their First Lady? The sculptor very possibly imposed the likeness himself in an attempt to flatter the First Lady, but the most popular interpretation was that she was using the women's movement to serve her own ends—again.

Most of the women who joined the Solidarity group were upper-class wives in Saigon. They joined to curry favor with Madame Nhu or to insure their husband's civil service jobs. Madame Nhu still had no idea how to connect to the majority of Vietnamese women. She took people's enthusiasm for her at face value. When Madame Nhu went into the countryside to check on the integration of her women's groups into the villages, she was given flowers and greeted warmly. She told Elbridge Durbrow, the former American ambassador to Vietnam, how on her arrival the women in these villages all thanked her for the Family Code abolishing polygamy and divorce. "She had not realized how well known and popular she was." Nor had she realized that the people might be anxious to tell the First Lady only what she wanted to hear.[11]

The Diem regime consisted entirely of family members or yes-men. You were either with them or against them. Government ministers and National Assembly men might go around shaking their heads and privately admitting their displeasure, but in formal matters of state, no one dared speak up. Books—whether nonfiction, novels, or, most ludicrously, poetry—were subjected to censors. Government permits that could be revoked at any time kept the local press under control, and members of the foreign press had to submit their copy to censors. The repressions were from the Communist playbook, but that was the problem: South Vietnam was supposed to be a free country. Resentment built up, silent and corrosive.

American intelligence sent from Saigon back to Washington catalogs a range of gossip linking Madame Nhu and her husband to corruption and influence peddling and accusing them of giving the president poor advice. As one diplomat remarked astutely, "It doesn't make any bit of difference if none of the wrongs attributed to her are true, the serious thing is that people believe it." The reports are skeptical of the influence Madame Nhu's women's organizations could really have on the country. They seem to consider them a vanity project.[12]

Madame Nhu shrugged off the few criticisms of her work that reached her as unserious. She was impatient with the pettiness of the people around her and wrote out her frustrations in her diary: "Intelligence breeds ambition, but isn't it terrible when one has to work with idiots to carry out great plans? God must have created those idiots to test me." Obviously, these people couldn't see the big picture, and Madame Nhu was moving too fast to stop and explain it to them.

Still riding high, Madame Nhu presented her colleagues at the National Assembly in 1961 with another set of grand ideas about how to protect women, the family, and the country. These she named the Morality Laws. Madame Nhu banned dancing and beauty contests as distracting to a nation at war. She also outlawed gambling, fortune-telling, cockfighting, and prostitution. She made contraception illegal—"We are underpopulated," she said—and also banned underwire bras. It was time, Madame Nhu preached, to practice austerity. Never mind that the outline of her own longline bra showed through the thin silk of her *ao dai*.

The Morality Laws didn't accomplish much besides angering the people—who kept dancing anyway. Chubby Checker and the Isley Brothers made the twist so popular that those defying the dancing ban would go to private nightclubs known as "twisteasies." The ban didn't just apply to imported rock and roll; sentimental Vietnamese tunes took the hit too. This was especially distressing for Vietnamese army soldiers, who sang constantly out in the field, for camaraderie or for a sense of comfort in an otherwise scary place where they could run into an ambush or a booby trap at any moment. "Rainy Night on the Frontier" was a particular favorite: "When the sky is turning rose . . . the young man is thinking of the one at home. . . . And his heart is full of love." Nonetheless, it was banned for not being anti-Communist enough.[13]

The laws were patronizing, implying that Madame Nhu knew better than her people what they should and should not be doing, wearing, and listening to. The resulting outcry over the fussy laws obscured Madame Nhu's general point—and it was a pretty good one. The dollars pouring into South Vietnam made Saigon seem like a party town instead of a city on a war footing. American aid to South Vietnam was supposed to create a middle class of businessmen and entrepreneurs who would support Diem. A comfortable lifestyle was the best defense against Communist instigation. But the commodities-import programs just subsidized an otherwise unaffordable lifestyle. The United States gave South Vietnam the goods to buy, helped the Vietnamese avert inflation, and paid for a high standard of living—plus most of the national expenditures. But it wasn't just the Vietnamese who benefited. The Pearl of the Orient was turning into a playground for 12,000 American servicemen in country. The number of bars on the rue Catinat had multiplied. Pizza shops opened, and cabbies doubled their rates for the American clientele. Businesses started with the purpose of finding Vietnamese girls as escorts for the lonely American servicemen. Advertisements promised beauty, charm, and class. It cost a GI $2.50 to look through photos of Miss Lee's girls and another $2.50 if he actually wanted to meet one in person at the agency. A real date could be arranged for under $8, plus the cost of actually taking the girl out. All of the Westernization provided more material for the Communist propaganda machine. If the South Vietnamese were trading their young girls for American weapons, it was easy to believe the country was also selling its soul.

Madame Nhu defended her strict laws. "You know, in order to keep the Communists down, you must have a line and stick to it." She was right. The popular conception of Americans "buying" South Vietnam would be a great recruiting tool for the Communists, and Madame Nhu was sharp enough to see the problem early. But she used a fire hose to douse a burning match. The people hated her for her imperious manner. Years of colonialism and war had already ground down her countrymen. Madame Nhu liked to talk about representing "her people," but she barely knew them. Instead, her laws and rules were a bloated extension of her own personal morals and ubiquitous reminders of her power. Her lifestyle in the palace reeked of extravagance and wastefulness when most Vietnamese still lived in the countryside and struggled to get by. She was in no position to deny them a little fun.

Madame Nhu's husband was no more popular than she was. His position in the Diem administration was loosely defined as chief councilor to the president, but he was largely believed to be the man running the show. To illustrate Nhu's immense power, correspondent David Halberstam tried to superimpose him onto an American context for the readers of the *New York Times:* "Imagine Diem as the President of the United States; in such a situation Nhu would have controlled all the country's newspapers, headed the CIA, the FBI and the Congress, served as the Attorney General and Secretary of State, and written all the reports the President saw. What Diem knew of the outside world was what Nhu wanted him to know; what he saw he saw through Nhu's eyes; the people he met he met only after Nhu had approved them."

Nhu created different organizations to carry out the political strategies he concocted. There was the Republican Youth, blue-uniform-wearing young men who were supposed to represent the political voice of South Vietnamese youth. Instead of expressing their own political opinions, they mostly parroted the sayings of their founder and leader, Ngo Dinh Nhu. The Republican Youth had 1,386,757 members at the end of 1962, nearly 300,000 down from two years before. The ranks had been purged of any potential Communist saboteurs; 21,061 of the young men had firearms, and they claimed to have killed 234 Communists. Out of their own ranks, they had lost nearly 500 to Communist assassinations and 2,413 more to kidnappings. Those statistics didn't seem to dampen their enthusiasm for their leader. At Nhu's reelection ceremony—he had just been voted national chief of the Republican Youth, again—the vice president of South Vietnam and members of the National Assembly stood by while Nhu received delegates of the youth corps. Although it rained throughout, Nhu stood, soaking wet, in his official uniform while one by one the youth swore on bended knee to carry out their leader's orders and uphold the Republican Youth constitution, seeking nothing short of mobilizing the entire population of South Vietnam to struggle against the Communists.[14]

Another of Nhu's pet projects was the Strategic Hamlets Program. The British had used something like it in Malaya to fight Communist insurgents there. Peasants moved to fortified areas protected by the army, defended by layers of barbed wire, ammunition, and guns. Nhu tried to replicate the British strategy; in theory, strategic hamlets would cut off the Communist access to supplies and manpower. Nhu liked this plan so much because, again, it brought the political revolution out of Saigon and into the rural areas. More than a military tactic to defeat the Communists, it was a logical outgrowth of his social and economic revolution, as well as an opportunity to build a new political base, for Diem, in the countryside. But because of Nhu's quick anger and favoritism, local officials falsely reported strategic hamlets where they didn't in fact exist. They were not exactly cozy settings. The villages were surrounded by booby-trapped bamboo thickets, and two watchtowers looked out into the jungle or rice paddies. Between two fences of barbed wire stood rows of spears, their tips coated with human excrement to infect the wound of any would-be trespasser. But installing barbed wire was time-consuming, and the steel itself was a valuable commodity. Instead of the fourteen tons of barbed wire specified for the construction of each hamlet, ten tons of barbed wire were stretched to build 163 not-very-secure ones. The locals were usually not compensated for loss of land, and people were uprooted at bayonet point without warning from their homes to be relocated because Nhu's strategy was to move into heavy Communist areas without advance notice, preparation, or consent. He made no allowances for the time needed to put other services in place that would have won people over, like security, medical help, and schools. Instead of a pattern of secure villages, Nhu had created what looked like a countryside dotted with small concentration camps.

Most terrifying of all was Nhu's Service for Political and Social Research of the Presidency (SEPES), which was basically an organization of informers supposed to function like a Vietnamese CIA. The Americans were generous with funding to help it get going. Soon, though, it earned a sinister reputation. SEPES was more than just an intelligence-gathering organization. It meted out justice through special police sections that employed harsh measures. Since it was hard to distinguish between hardcore revolutionaries and patriotically motivated collaborators, both groups were equally persecuted. The men SEPES rounded up could be beaten or given electric shocks to their genitals, but mostly they were just left to languish as political prisoners, making up two-thirds of the 30,000 inmates kept in the tiny nation's fifty jails.[15]

Nhu always made sure to defer to his brother, the president, in public, but the perception was increasingly that Nhu was in charge. That made him a target. On a hunting trip to Dalat, the Viet Cong attacked his convoy, and Nhu's head bodyguard was killed in the ambush. The government tried to keep it quiet, presenting the incident as a simple car accident on a dark country road. They never did explain why the car was riddled with bullets.

In an interview with reporter Marguerite Higgins, Nhu was candid about how much people disliked him, "I am hated, and so is my wife," but he was resigned to his role. "Every government has to have the tough guy, the man who does the dirty and unpleasant work. Even Eisenhower had to have a Sherman Adams [Higgins's footnote: Nhu took great pride in following closely the inner workings of the US government]. . . . In Vietnam, where violence and virulence are everywhere, I am the person who takes on the unpleasant jobs. It is I who am vilified, so that others may be spared."[16]

The popular discontent with Nhu and his lovely wife was well known to the Americans even before Johnson's visit. So why did the vice president make all those rosy promises of American commitment to the regime? As Johnson would explain in an official debrief on the trip, it wasn't that Diem and his family were especially deserving. Diem was complex, remote, and surrounded by people "less admirable and capable." But the fact remained that there was simply no one else for America to use to hold the line against communism in Southeast Asia. When he was in Saigon, Johnson had gotten a little carried away in the excitement of the moment and heartily proclaimed Ngo Dinh Diem the Winston Churchill of Asia.

"Did you really mean it?" asked journalist Stanley Karnow.

"Shit," Johnson drawled in response, "Diem's the only boy we got out there."

Karnow couldn't print that in the *Saturday Evening Post,* but *New York Times* reporter Homer Bigart had already coined a phrase for the American predicament in Vietnam: "Sink or Swim with Ngo Dinh Diem." It was the first line of a little song Bigart had made up to be sung among friends in the Saigon press corps to the tune of "I'm an Old Cowhand":

We must sink or swim
With Ngo Dinh Diem
We will hear no phoo
About Madame Nhu.
Yippee-i-aye, i-aye, etc.[17]

On the morning of February 11, 1962, two dissident pilots swooped low over the palace and dropped their bombs. Their target was the right wing of the palace, where the Nhu family resided. The Chinese nurse of the youngest child was crushed by a falling beam and killed. The Nhus' oldest daughter, Le Thuy, kept a clear head in the chaos. The sixteen-year-old scrambled to save the two youngest children, aged two and not quite ten, when the main stairway collapsed in a fiery crumble.

An entire section of the bedroom floor had given way just as Madame Nhu was running into the bathroom for a dressing gown to put on over her nightgown. She escaped a direct hit but fell two stories onto a pile of iron, wood, and gravel and came to in a heap of smoldering ashes. She would discover that she had three severe third-degree burns and deep lacerations on her arm, but strangely she felt no pain at all. She couldn't feel anything except that it was difficult to move, difficult to pick her way through the mess that had landed on her. But she knew she had to get out of there. A valley of light beckoned; a soft wind blew the smoke away from her. She had never seen so clearly. She saw beyond the ruins. Beyond the long broken shadows of the palace a brightness was rising. Goodness and Mercy. Staggering toward her was a figure in the flames. It was her husband looking for her, crying out with joy when he found her because he had thought she was dead. All their marriage troubles set aside, they were united—at least for the moment. Madame Nhu fainted into her husband's arms.

Madame Nhu lost nearly everything she possessed in the fire. A few dresses that had been at the dressmaker's survived, as did, I would later learn, a diary. Her trophies, the precious tiger skins, were a heap of burned fur. She had only memories left. But to her surprise, she was not despondent. Something new had opened in her, just as it had when she marched across the bridge in central Vietnam as a twenty-one-year-old woman with an infant in her arms. She would profess never to care about something as trivial as clothes or material possessions again.

The photographs of the women among the tiger skins in Madame Nhu's palace bedroom were made all the more poignant by the coming calamity that would transform the palace into a scene of wreckage.

I pasted each picture carefully into an album, one photograph per page and each page protected by a thin wisp of vellum. The album I had chosen was red, for luck of course. I sent it packed in Styrofoam peanuts by priority mail. In response, she gushed and fawned and praised me. My fulfillment of her challenge was surely a sign of something divine. But she wasn't quite ready yet, she said, to make good on her promise of handing over the memoir. I should be patient, she chided.

Of course, I should have known better.

CHAPTER 11

Young Turks and Old Hacks

"David Halberstam died yesterday," I mentioned carefully to Madame Nhu in April 2007. "It was a car crash." I wasn't sure how closely she kept watch on current events. I was even less sure how she might react to hearing the name of the *New York Times* reporter and prolific author, whom she had known in Saigon all those years ago.

His obituary had run in the morning paper:

> Tall, square-jawed and graced with an imposing voice so deep that it seemed to begin at his ankles, Mr. Halberstam came fully into his own as a journalist in the early 1960s covering the nascent American war in South Vietnam for the *New York Times.*
>
> His reporting, along with that of several colleagues, left little doubt that a corrupt South Vietnamese government supported by the United States was no match for Communist guerrillas and their North Vietnamese allies.[1]

"Mmmm, *The Best and the Brightest,*" she said, surprising me by immediately calling up the name of his 1972 book. "No, I did not know he had died. Too bad."

She didn't sound very sad, but that wasn't surprising. From what I knew of Halberstam's reporting, he hadn't liked Madame Nhu, and the feeling had been mutual. He had called her "proud and vain" and accused her of "delving into men's politics with sharp and ill-concealed arrogance." In his 1964 book *Making of a Quagmire,* Halberstam had said of Madame Nhu, "To me, she always resembled an Ian Fleming character come to life: the antigoddess, the beautiful but diabolic sex-dictatress who masterminds some secret apparatus that James Bond is out to destroy."[2] He had written so critically about Madame Nhu's thirst for political power that she was said to have told someone in 1963, "Halberstam should be barbecued, and I would be glad to supply the fluid and the match."

Maybe her feelings had mellowed over forty-four years, or maybe her memory had softened. But Madame Nhu's response to David Halberstam's untimely death forty-four years later shocked me with how fondly she recalled him. "He was intelligent, one of the rare ones who told the truth."

Indeed, he had, both in *The Best and the Brightest,* which Madame Nhu had mentioned, and in the astute, on-the-ground reporting that won him a 1964 Pulitzer Prize. Halberstam's truths had made the US government uncomfortable and the military brass mad. He had been one of the first to point out that the war in Vietnam was not going well. He showed how, time and time again, the United States was bungling its mission in Southeast Asia. The academic and intellectual "whiz kids" in the Kennedy administration had arrogantly imposed policies that defied common sense. To Madame Nhu, it must have been at least a little vindicating to see the men who brought her family down tarnished by Halberstam's reporting.

But Halberstam had also loudly, and repeatedly, blamed the Ngo family for the American failure in Vietnam. His reporting was read very carefully in Washington. President Kennedy himself asked the CIA to study every story the young journalist wrote, and each of those CIA reports generated pages upon single-spaced pages of analysis. The

CIA concluded that the young journalist was more accurately informed about the facts on the ground in South Vietnam than most of the military "advisors." He was right when he said that the Reds were making gains and right again in stating that the Communist guerrillas were well armed and "had the run of the delta."[3]

The CIA came to another important conclusion about Halberstam's reporting. His "invariably pessimistic" stories were contributing directly to a political crisis in South Vietnam. The CIA was holding David Halberstam responsible for the Ngo regime's crack-up. His reporting, they said, was contributing to its downfall. Had Madame Nhu ever known that little detail?[4]

Halberstam and the other young men of the press corps in Saigon believed in the American mission in South Vietnam. They supported the domino theory so wholeheartedly that when they saw their government's policies being dragged down by Madame Nhu and her family, the pressmen seemed to take it upon themselves as good Americans to alter the situation in South Vietnam, as well as report on it. Their goal was nothing less than regime change.

They blamed the Ngos for nearly everything that was going wrong with the American-supported effort in South Vietnam. Not until after Diem and Nhu were gone did Halberstam himself conclude that for all his reporting on the faults of the Ngo regime, he had simply failed to be pessimistic enough. The problem wasn't just the arrogance of the aristocratic Diem, the obtuse intellectualism of Nhu, or the self-serving machinations of Madame Nhu. American chances for success in Vietnam had bogged down in a much more layered quagmire. But by then, it was too late.[5]

Madame Nhu never seemed to have understood the role of the press in Vietnam. She thought reporters should stick to a common line and expected them to repeat what the palace told them. To look for outside sources was disrespectful. She, Nhu, and Diem didn't lie, at least not intentionally, to the press. They believed the absurdities they were peddling—like the great gains their army was making in the countryside or the devotion of the people to the regime. The reporters, they felt, were not interested enough in the right story lines. Why not talk about the health programs or social benefits? Instead they focused on the bad. Madame Nhu tried to scold them. "You all act as if you are all just spectators here, don't you realize you are with us and we need your support?"[6] The palace and the press talked past each other. The reporters caricatured her, and she just heaped more scorn on them.

For all that, on hearing of David Halberstam's death, Madame Nhu seemed to have blocked out the young reporter's intention to inspire the overthrow of her family's regime. She remembered instead how he had flattered her. "He compared my power to that of the president!" She said it as if he had merely complimented the cling of a black dress that she knew she looked good in but didn't want to admit it: Oh, this old thing! As if ascribing so much power to her was absurd, but flattering all the same.

David Halberstam had indeed identified Madame Nhu's greatest strengths: her consistency and determination. He commented on her complete faith in herself and her cause. But Halberstam also saw how that righteous certainty, in its execution, could be a fatal character flaw. Madame Nhu couldn't or wouldn't see that part. Instead she simply liked his description of her: "Madame Nhu had a real zest for the ceremonies of leadership. She was the only one of the family who walked the way a dictator should walk—with flair and obvious enjoyment, trailed by a line of attendants—turning slowly first to the right, then to the left in acknowledging the crowd. It was always a virtuoso performance."

The description could almost be read as a compliment if it weren't for its last line: "This was the way Mussolini must have done it."[7]

"I received him," Madame Nhu told me, as if she had bestowed an honor on the upstart journalist who had only been in the country a few months. It wasn't so easy to get in front of South Vietnam's First Lady. The potential interviewer had to go through an elaborate procedure. First he had to formally request a private audience and write a personal letter to her explaining what he wanted to ask. If the interview was approved, inevitably, the reporter would be kept waiting for the five feet and ninety-two pounds of Madame Nhu to make a dramatic entrance. She would make a show of arranging her *ao dai,* smoothing the silk pleats, and sitting down daintily so as not to rumple the fabric. The chair was so ornately carved that it resembled a throne—all the more so when she pushed a little buzzer in the arm. Somewhere a bell would ring. Halberstam writes of his own encounter with Madame Nhu's interview techniques in *The Making of a Quagmire* and describes being served tea and peppermint candies "by little male servants who bowed and scraped so low that the gesture resembled some form of medieval torture."[8]

Halberstam had arrived in Saigon just as another correspondent was leaving. Francois Sully, a Frenchman working for *Newsweek,* had gotten on the First Lady's bad side. He was being expelled after fifteen years in country. The reason? An article on August 20, 1962, was accompanied by a photograph of Madame Nhu's darlings—her paramilitary squad—with the caption "Female militia in Saigon: The enemy has more drive and enthusiasm." The US mission in Saigon was not sad to see Sully go. His reporting was gloomy when the official policy was still resolutely optimistic. But Halberstam took note of the opinions that mattered. Sully left Vietnam as something of a press hero. Two young girls stopped him in a store and asked for his autograph. As Sully prepared to pay the usual exit taxes on his departure, the local official smiled, shook his hand, and refused payment. He called Sully "a true friend" of Vietnam for telling the truth, however painful.

Associated Press reporter Malcolm Browne shared the 1964 Pulitzer with Halberstam for their coverage of Vietnam. They also shared a similar view of Madame Nhu. "She was a very vain sort of person," Browne confirmed later. "She was always very glad to talk to us correspondents, if she could be assured that what we wrote would be flattering," which was becoming less and less the case. Browne too gave Madame Nhu some grudging credit. "She was one of Diem and Nhu's strongest assets," not that he thought that a good thing for the US effort in Vietnam. "She would walk out into a crowd, at great risk to herself," he recalled. "She was infuriating, but courageous."

Browne had taken the June 1963 photograph of the burning monk. It was a horrific picture. The monk's face twisted in pain and horror. Thich Quang Duc had set himself on fire to protest the Ngo regime, and Madame Nhu could only say that she would "clap her hands for another monk's barbecue." That photograph, and her Marie Antoinette–like response, raised awareness of what was going on in South Vietnam as much as any stories written by foreign correspondents. Browne's picture was on President John F. Kennedy's desk when he sent a new ambassador to South Vietnam, Henry Cabot Lodge, who understood it to be his duty to do everything he could to neutralize Madame Nhu.[9]

John Mecklin, a former pressman turned government official, had covered the end of Indochina from 1953 to 1955 and came back in 1961 as the US Information Agency officer. He recognized the history-making impact the reporters were having and in his memoir, *Mission in Torment,* credits the reporting of men like Halberstam and Browne with bringing down the Diem regime. It occurred to me while reading his book that Madame Nhu had been right. The journalists had painted Madame Nhu as paranoid and crazy; she in turn thought the press was out to get her. Both sides were correct.

I drove out to Maryland to visit Stanley Karnow, who wrote the definitive, nearly eight-hundred-page *Vietnam: A History,* which I had taken with me on my first trip to Vietnam. He invited me onto his screened-in porch, where we drank instant coffee, black, and Karnow lit one cigarette after another as he recalled those days in Saigon.

Madame Nhu was, Karnow said, more feminine than feminist, "so coquette, always flaunting her sexiness." She was saucy, perky, cavorting, and a "loose cannon—no one could control her." Americans, Madame Nhu said, were using their aid money to "make lackeys of Vietnamese and to seduce Vietnamese women into decadent paths." She claimed that American reporters were working against her, that the *New York Times* had taken a $40,000 bribe to print an interview with a Viet Cong leader, and that the venerable American paper was part of an "international Communist conspiracy" to sink her country. Karnow remembered Diem privately flinching at the things his sister-in-law would say. She accused the American embassy of threats and blackmail, told the rest of the world it needed "electroshock to resume its senses," and denounced US Army Lt. Colonel John Paul Vann, advisor to the top South Vietnamese army general, as a "foreign militarist" who was "confusing the [South Vietnamese] officers." Karnow didn't think Madame Nhu's brashness was a strength. "Even if she was not stupid, she wasn't particularly perceptive. She didn't realize that she was fanning the flames" of public opinion against the regime.

Like Browne and Halberstam, Stanley Karnow wrote about the dangerous mistake the United States was making by backing the Ngo regime in Saigon. But unlike the others, Karnow ventured so far as to speculate that, as horribly as they might have abused the word "freedom," had Diem, Nhu, and Madame Nhu stayed in power, they "would never have let in US troops," or at least not in such great numbers. The war in all its horror might not have happened.

Madame Nhu's favorite English-language newspaper was the *Times of Vietnam,* published by her close friends in Saigon, Ann and Gene Gregory. The Gregorys had been in Saigon longer than most other Americans, arriving in 1952 as part of the US Information Service. After a brief return to the United States, they came back when Gene received a Ford Foundation Fellowship to conduct research on the developing social and economic structures of a country "just beginning to emerge from feudalism."[10] The Gregorys left government and academia behind when they bought what was then a weekly English-language paper. A 1963 profile of the Gregorys in *Newsweek* described the otherwise "fat and deceptively sleepy eyed" Gene as sharp enough to realize early the potential for his paper if he opened up its columns to the palace as a place to express its views. The *Times* became so successful that it soon turned into a daily paper. Describing it as a successful venture might be misleading. It had a circulation of only a few thousand copies, but who needed large numbers when you had the most important audience in the country?[11]

The other foreign correspondents did not mix well with the Gregorys in Saigon. The couple lived in a cream-colored mansion in an otherwise all-Vietnamese suburb. Ann was blonde and as full of pep as her husband was soft, and the pudgy Gene struck people as sorely out of whack with the other vigorous young newsmen swarming the city. His profession as a journalist was so out of character that for years people had assumed it was just a bad cover for his real work as an intelligence operative, a sort of "flabby James Bond character" who pretended to be so close to the Nhus because his mission was to keep tabs on them. But that theory fizzled. The Gregorys gave over too much of their paper to burning their fellow correspondents to be anything other than sincere regime sycophants. One of their front-page headlines blasted United Press International reporter Neil Sheehan by printing, "UPI LIES, LIES, LIES." When David Halberstam's editors asked him to write a piece about the newspaper, he wrote back that to write anything at all accurate about those people would be libelous and to write anything nonlibelous would be too charitable.[12] The Southeast Asia scholar Bernard Fall had known the Gregorys when he was finishing up his doctorate in political science at Cornell University. They had had a falling out, something about money he might have owed Ann, who had helped him type up his dissertation. When they met each other again, thousands of miles away in Saigon, the reunion was anything but pleasant. Fall wrote a note to his wife, Dorothy, about it: "I want you to know this so that you can take proper action with the U.S. authorities in case anything at all befalls me here," implying that Ann and Gene had been spreading highly critical rumors about him and that a bad word from them to the wrong people was highly dangerous.[13]

The *Times of Vietnam* was invaluable to the palace. It gave the regime a place where they could get their views across—in English. It was presumed that Gene Gregory afforded to be chauffeured around town in a black Peugeot because the Gregorys were in such good graces with the Nhus. Ann ran the paper on a day-to-day basis and helped Madame Nhu with the English translations of her proclamations about the latest Women's Solidarity Day or the anniversary of the Trung sisters. Madame Nhu's speeches were invariably long-winded and often incredibly boring, and they didn't always make sense.

In my own research on Madame Nhu, I had copied out enough of her speeches to recognize their rambling pattern. She used past, present, and future tenses, and she was painfully repetitive. Only a good friend, like Ann Gregory, would have found enough space in her paper to print them even in part. Yet, as often as not, the *Times* reproduced entire speeches. The paper soon became known as Madame Nhu's mouthpiece. She even claimed authorship of some of the articles herself, like one accusing American intelligence officers in Saigon of being "Nazi-like cynical young men" who were plotting to overthrow the government. Madame Nhu's style was too distinctive to pass off as anyone else's. Who else went around accusing people of being "intoxicated"? The *New York Times* reporter Halberstam was "intoxicated." President Kennedy was "intoxicated." The Buddhists and even her own parents—"intoxicated." The *Times of Vietnam* printed Madame Nhu's "campaign for disintoxication," in an article that began, bafflingly: "A campaign of disintoxication must be opened immediately to disintoxicate those who really want to be disintoxicated."

For all the trouble Madame Nhu caused with her talk of "Nazi-like" CIA spies, her accusation that the United States was plotting to overthrow the Diem regime proved to have been accurate a few weeks after the article ghostwritten by Madame Nhu appeared. The Ngos' downfall brought the Gregorys down too. The *Times*'s press was burned to the ground. Ann Gregory had to flee and take shelter in the US embassy. She would leave Saigon for Switzerland shortly afterward, where she and Madame Nhu continued to talk. When I asked Madame Nhu about her friendship with Ann, she giggled and said the two of them had had such fun together it was like being young again.

Madame Nhu had her defenders in the more mainstream press as well. Marguerite Higgins had worked for the *New York Herald Tribune* as a war correspondent for two decades before moving to *Newsday* and being assigned to Vietnam. She proved sympathetic to the Dragon Lady's plight.

Higgins arrived in Vietnam to interview Madame Nhu and take a look around the country in 1963. She had first experienced the country when she was six months old and sick with malaria. Her family had been living in Hong Kong, and the doctor there ordered the baby's parents to take her to the mountains of Dalat in French Indochina to breathe fresh, clean air. Dalat's man-made lakes made reinfection more likely than a cure, but baby Marguerite got lucky—more so than her maternal grandfather, an officer in the French colonial army, who had died of a tropical disease in Vietnam. Higgins got lucky again when she was assigned to cover the French defeat at Dien Bien Phu in 1954. She was walking next to the famous Magnum photographer Robert Capra when he stepped on a land mine and was killed. By then, Higgins was famous herself. *Life* magazine had lauded the sparkling-eyed young woman in her rolled-up khakis and tennis shoes as an audacious girl wonder in the boys' club of foreign correspondents. The caption under her photo read, "Higgins still manages to look attractive."[14]

Like Madame Nhu, Higgins had earned a reputation as openly ambitious. Both women could be ruthless and were fearless when it came to facing their enemies. At the end of World War II, while reporting on the liberation of Dachau, Higgins had commandeered a jeep and driven toward German territory. She herself disarmed and accepted the surrender of dozens of retreating Axis soldiers, quitting only when the jeep could carry no more weapons. She was in Seoul on June 25, 1950, when the North Koreans invaded. She swam to shore after her boat sank and then had to walk fourteen miles, but Higgins emerged famous. She was the first woman to win the Pulitzer Prize for international reporting, and the Associated Press named her Woman of the Year in 1951.[15]

Like the other correspondents in Saigon in 1963, Higgins believed wholeheartedly in the domino theory. But she was way more outspoken in her anticommunism than other American reporters. Higgins advocated the use of the atomic bomb against Communist China and called the fight against communism the "Third World War." She was willing to do what it took to defend America—and Higgins preferred that those battles take place "far from San Francisco and New York." She was more tolerant of the Saigon regime's obvious dictatorship, as long as it dictated under the guise of democracy. Higgins would later deny it, but *Time* magazine quoted her as having told another reporter over dinner in Saigon that American correspondents in South Vietnam "would like to see us lose the war to prove they're right." It was an inflammatory comment.[16]

When Higgins met Madame Nhu at the palace, the First Lady was smiling and "looking not a bit fierce." She described her admiringly: "Her beautifully coifed head was piled high with black hair, and wispy bangs covered her forehead. Her white silk *ao dai,* the traditional dress of Vietnam, hugged her well-proportioned figure closely in a way that suggested a womanly pride in it. She wore black pumps with high French heels. Her long mandarin-type nails were decorated with pink polish."[17]

Higgins openly admired Madame Nhu's personal courage, and she could sympathize with how any woman with a fiery and determined personality ran the risk of being defamed in public opinion. Higgins had been the subject of much speculation about her sexual adventures. She had been called "as innocent as a cobra" and derided as masculine simply because she was successful in a man's world. When someone told Homer Bigart of the *New York Times* that Higgins had given birth to her first child, he was said to have replied, "That's wonderful. Who's the mother?" The response was all the more cruel because the baby girl died five days after her premature birth.

Higgins's arrival in Saigon in the summer of 1963 coincided with Madame Nhu's description of the monk's suicide as a "barbecue." It really was a barbaric thing to say. But when Higgins asked her about the barbecue remark, she was satisfied with Madame Nhu's response: "I used those words because they have shock value. It is necessary to somehow shock the world out of this trance in which it looks at Vietnam." Within minutes of meeting her, Higgins saw the real problem Madame Nhu faced all too clearly. How could America, a country Higgins described as "a bland, aloof, uncaring, don't involve me society," understand "a fierce totally involved Oriental Valkyrie"?[18]

Higgins saw Madame Nhu as a more complete person than the Dragon Lady she had been prepared to meet. She had no problem with Madame Nhu using her good looks; sex appeal had been an integral weapon in Higgins's arsenal too. Madame Nhu was obviously a caring mother: when her four-year-old daughter ran into the room where the interview was taking place, Madame Nhu didn't raise her voice but patted the child playfully on the head and gave her a ribbon to occupy herself with during the rest of the conversation. Higgins saw Madame Nhu as an affectionate and respectful wife even if, as Madame Nhu admitted to Higgins during their interview, her love for her husband was "not the sweeping passionate kind." Higgins could relate to that too. Before marrying her own husband, she had sighed to a friend that only if a man was as interesting as war would she see the point in getting married. She saw no hint of Madame Nhu's rumored luxury or wealth, and she saw no problem with her desire for power. "Power is wonderful," Madame Nhu had told her. Higgins agreed.

For all those reasons and more, Higgins resolved that she would help Madame Nhu. She was acting as a friend, she said, and "as an American citizen not as a journalist." As such, Higgins gave her suggestions for how to phrase things, including entire passages to include in her future speeches on the topics of war, Buddhism, and press control. She also gave Madame Nhu some much-needed advice about what not to say in front of the press, clueing her in to words that make an unfavorable impression on the public she should be trying to win over. Madame Nhu thought she could just ignore her detractors and rise above the rumors of war profiteering, money laundering, and overseas bank accounts. She couldn't grasp that people's perceptions, even if inaccurate, created a reality she needed to confront. Higgins did. She would try to clear Madame Nhu's name from any association with corruption. Higgins wrote to Madame Nhu's mother,

> The Department of State and the Central Intelligence Agency say that there is no evidence of any corruption on the part of your daughter or any member of the Ngo Dinh Nhu family. There is no sign that they collected masses of money for their own personal use. Does that fit with your understanding of Madame Nhu's situation?
>
> Do forgive me for coming so straight to the point. If you feel disinclined to answer, I shall quite understand.
>
> Sincerely, Marguerite Higgins

Madame Nhu's mother responded with a one-sentence reply that, however curt, confirmed Higgins's opinion: "I do not believe President Ngo Dinh Diem and the Nhus to be corrupt."[19]

Madame Nhu earned herself the public support of another American friend in a very high place: Clare Booth Luce. Luce was a former war reporter herself and a convert to Catholicism. She too had experience with being in the public eye as a talented, beautiful, rich, and controversial woman. A successful playwright, she worked her way up from a position as secretary at *Vogue* and married the publisher of the *Time* and *Life* magazine empires, Henry Luce. Marrying well didn't quite satisfy her. Luce was elected to the House of Representatives from Fairfield County, Connecticut, and appointed as President Dwight Eisenhower's ambassador to Italy in 1952. She knew a thing or two about ambition.

Together, the Luces supported Republican, anti-Communist politics. They were members of the China Lobby that had supported Chiang Kai-shek before Mao took power. *Time* magazine had championed the Diem regime from the very beginning, hailing the president and his family as resilient, deeply religious nationalists. So it was no surprise that Clare Luce stood up for Madame Nhu. Luce said that what was happening in Vietnam was "remarkably like what happened to Generalissimo Chiang Kai-shek and Madame Chiang in China when the Department of State pulled the rug out from under them and Mao Tse-tung took over in China."

Luce took it upon herself to make things right this time around and wrote a cover article for the *National Review* defending Madame Nhu. She portrayed the South Vietnamese First Lady as a devoted mother and Catholic, a kind of cross between Jackie Kennedy and Eleanor Roosevelt. "For a moment, however brief, in history, some part of America's prestige if not security, seems to lie in the pale pink palm of her exquisite little hand." In a valiant but belated attempt to remake Madame Nhu's image in November 1963, Luce compared her to an American pioneer woman and called her a do-gooder and a feminist.[20]

The day before the article appeared in the press, Luce had a long telephone conversation with her friend "Dick," Richard Milhouse Nixon, who would go on to become the thirty-seventh president of the United States. At the time, Nixon was nursing deep political wounds, having first lost the 1960 presidential election to John Kennedy and then the race for governor of California in 1962. Luce and Nixon talked about the collapsing situation in Vietnam and the usefulness of the image of the beautiful, beleaguered Madame Nhu.

Luce was not defending Madame Nhu out of the goodness of her heart. As a staunch Republican, she wanted Kennedy gone. Luce believed JFK was losing Southeast Asia to the Communists, and she thought Madame Nhu's take on the situation in Vietnam was pretty accurate. The American presidential election was coming up, and Luce thought someone like her good friend Dick would better represent her conservative and anti-Communist values in the White House. Luce used all her charm to convince him that Madame Nhu was worth defending publicly, but she must have heard some doubt on Nixon's part because, before the end of their telephone conversation, Luce declared, "I wish *I* were running for President!"[21]

Why didn't more women feel the same pull to Madame Nhu as Marguerite Higgins and Clare Booth Luce? Why did the combination of glamour and seriousness fail so miserably in Madame Nhu when it worked so well for other women in politics—such as Kennedy women like Jean Smith, Robert's wife, Ethel, and especially Jacqueline Kennedy, the president's wife and the First Lady of the United States? Maybe it was because people considered their kind of feminism subversive. It wore a dress well. Madame Nhu had plenty of lovely *ao dais,* but she was either laughed off as a female out of her league or vilified as the "real man" in the Ngo family.

Madame Nhu was not the first woman the Americans called the Dragon Lady. The name seems to trace back to a fictional character from the 1930s comic strip *Terry and the Pirates*. That cartoon Dragon Lady was a sneaky seductress. She was made from fiercely sketched ink strokes that defined angular cheekbones and slanted eyes. She was interested only in money and power. From then on, any Asian woman who didn't conform to the submissive, meek, and otherwise obliging feminine fantasy about the Orient was labeled a "dragon lady." China's last empress, Xixi, was one, as were Soong May-ling, who would become Madame Chiang Kai-shek, and Madame Mao. Hollywood's first Asian American movie star, Anna May Wong, was cast either as a delicate flower in a demure supporting role or as a sly and deceitful dragon lady in movies like *The Thief of Bagdad* and *Old San Francisco.*

When Madame Nhu became First Lady of South Vietnam in 1954, America was a racist country. Jim Crow laws segregated people by skin color; anti-miscegenation laws meant that movie star Anna Wong couldn't play a romantic lead in a movie unless she had an Asian costar—it would have been illegal to show her kissing a white man on the screen in many states. The Japanese bombing of Pearl Harbor made the Asian evil genius the archetypal villain. Although the American victory in World War II put an end to the internment of Japanese Americans in camps, racist attitudes didn't change overnight. Asian scholar Sheridan Prasso argues that the American victory in the Pacific reinforced stereotypes of Asians as weak. By dropping the atomic bomb on Hiroshima and Nagasaki, the United States proved its masculine dominance. By the time of Korea and Vietnam, the nation was ready to stand up for other "compliant, feminized peoples who might otherwise succumb to the evil lure of Communism." Prasso unearths American descriptions of Asian leaders that dwell on these feminine qualities: Mao had a high-pitched voice, as well as long, sensitive woman's hands and a feminine mouth; Ho Chi Minh was small and frail, earnest and gentle; Diem was "as fragile as porcelain with delicate features and ivory skin."[22]

Vietnam was supposed to be an exotic, decadent place, the women obliging and demure. So Americans found Madame Nhu totally confounding. She didn't fit their expectations of an Oriental woman any more than she matched the American ideal: she was the exact opposite of the smiling blond woman on the cover of the December 1962 *Saturday Evening Post*. That issue presented a composite of the "American woman" and revealed her attitudes about family, sex, religion, and society. Mr. Gallup, king of the polls, had surveyed the nation, and the results were in. The American woman was a hardworking full-time housewife and mother. "Although the divorcee, the childless wife, [and] the working mother" existed, they were so atypical and therefore "extreme," that the authors excluded them from the survey. "Our study shows that few people are as happy as a housewife." A wife's responsibility: "You have to put your husband first." And unlike men who must search for meaning in life, the poll concluded, American women were born knowing their purpose precisely: to be a good wife and a good mother. As for wanting more, the authors concluded, women were easily satisfied with food, clothes, and a little help with housework. "The female doesn't really expect a lot from life."

A major change for American women was in the wings. With her publication of *The Feminine Mystique* in early 1963, Betty Friedan would give voice to the "problem that has no name," women's second-class status in society, and the book would launch the modern feminist movement in the United States.

The Madame Nhu whom American women read about in newspapers didn't hesitate to ask for credit where she thought it was due—and to request it loudly. She was unapologetic about liking power and wanting more. A majority of American women "disapproved" of the idea of having a woman as president, and 20 percent of all women said female involvement in politics was a generally bad thing. Women were simply too emotional. The American public in 1963 had certain ideas about just what was appropriate in a First Lady. Madame Nhu was not it.

Jacqueline Kennedy played the part much better. She looked like a movie star, was well educated, and spoke French. But Jacqueline Kennedy was also trapped by the conventions and stereotypes of the era.

While Madame Nhu was open in her admiration for Jacqueline Kennedy, using the words "elegant" and "refined" to describe her, the feeling was not mutual. Madame Nhu, Jacqueline Kennedy said, "was everything Jack found unattractive." The First Lady of the United States was very specific in a recorded interview from 1964. Politically powerful women were pretty awful in general. Indira Gandhi, the future prime minister of India, was "a real prune, bitter, kind of pushy, horrible woman." But in judging others, it was Jackie who sounded ugly—and like a relic from a bygone era.[23]

Her defenders might say that Jackie Kennedy recognized the constraints of her era, validating them to gently subvert them, turning them inside out. Perhaps. In 1964, she was all too clearly a product of her time and place. She bragged in her familiar breathy voice about her "Asiatic" marriage to Jack, equating subordination with femininity. As for Madame Nhu, a real woman who happened to be from Asia, who refused to bow and scrape and act demure, Jacqueline thought she was just awful. Madame Nhu acted as if she resented getting power from men, instead of being grateful, and that resentment made her unsexy and masculine. "I wouldn't be surprised if they were lesbians," Jackie whispered about Madame Nhu and Clare Booth Luce. Those kinds of women—ambitious women who wanted something to claim for themselves and weren't ashamed of it—were not welcome in the Kennedys' America of 1963.

CHAPTER 12

Burning Monks

MADAME NHU HAD BEEN pleased with my success in finding the tiger-skin pictures for her—so pleased, she said, that she had decided it was finally time to send me a single-paragraph summary of her memoirs.

> *Summary of my book: The Holy Church must be defended.* Having received the Mission to spread the word around the world, so that others could know the Truth of what was happening in Viêt-Nam, I began my travels on September 11, 1963, at the Interparliamentary Union in Belgrade. In my absence, Vietnam was crucified as the "Christ of Nations." . . . Everything comes back on the Holy Church, as the Secret of Fatima, to save the world from the Apocalypse . . . Madame Ngô-Dình-Nhu.

What was this? The secret of Fatima? Christ of Nations? Instead of a precise summary of a once powerful woman's life, the paragraph sounded like an extract from a religious diatribe. When I asked Madame Nhu where her personal memories were—the smells, the tastes, the sounds—she replied obliquely.

"Coming," she promised. "I just need to know that I can count on you."

I should have known better.

My next challenge—the final one, Madame Nhu promised—was to find the text of a particular speech delivered in August 2009 by an American, a Catholic bishop named William Skylstad, during a trip to Vietnam from Spokane, Washington. Someone had told Madame Nhu about the bishop's visit to an area close to the city of Hue, a place close to her heart. The bishop stopped at the Shrine to Our Lady of La Vang. To Madame Nhu the symbolism of an American bishop visiting La Vang—what's more, a bishop who was the president of the US Conference of Catholic Bishops—could represent only one thing: an apology for what had happened to her family. I had never heard of the bishop or the place, but I promised Madame Nhu that I would look into it.

Believers say that sometime at the end of the eighteenth century, a vision of Mary appeared in what is today the Hai Lang District of the Quang Tri Province of central Vietnam. At that time, Catholics in the country endured terrible persecution; their religion marked them as colonial sympathizers, and Vietnamese emperors were still trying to fight the French incursion. The Nguyen dynasty issued edicts to destroy churches, and Emperors Ming Mang and Tu Duc encouraged the repression of Catholicism by any means, even violent ones. Nhu's own Catholic ancestors had almost been wiped out. More than one hundred members of the Ngo clan had been herded into a church and burned to death in the early 1800s.

Mary was said to have appeared to a group of Catholics hiding from a massacring mob in the woods. She materialized wearing a Vietnamese *ao dai* and holding a child. Surrounded by lights, she told the people to keep praying and reassured them that their prayers would be granted.

The story was told and retold for a hundred years. By then, the French colonial influence in Vietnam had freed Catholics to worship openly, and the spot became a pilgrimage destination for hundreds of thousands of Vietnamese Catholics. On August 22, 1928, priests of the Catholic Church consecrated the site in front of 200,000 pilgrims. Madame Nhu was just a little girl, living with her Buddhist family way down in the delta. But she discovered La Vang in 1943 as a new convert to the faith when she had moved to Hue to be with her husband's family. Maybe she was drawn to the place because the consecration happened on her birthday. Maybe she liked the image of Mary. Or maybe she just liked getting out from under her in-laws and having a good excuse to leave the city. In 1959, thc Diem government declared the area a national shrine. The church of La Vang was then promoted to a basilica minor in 1961, reflecting its timely anti-Communist recognition by the Vatican.

Ultimately, when it came to the speech, I came up empty handed. The bishop's office was as kind as could be. The bishop himself asked his secretary to send me his notes on the trip. I was able to tell Madame Nhu that the seventy-five-year-old had worn his black cassock and red sash despite the heat—the temperature had been about 104. There were 1,500 people at the shrine for Mass, but as for the speech itself, whatever the bishop had said had vanished into the humid air.

Madame Nhu's disappointment at my lack of results was audible. She wanted Bishop Skylstad to have said that Mary had appeared in Vietnam but never in the United States. She wanted him to link Mary's not appearing to Americans and what had happened to her family. She wanted to hear that the Catholic bishop acknowledged the terrible act Americans had committed and that they were paying the price. But I couldn't get that for her.

"C'est dommage," that's too bad, she sighed. "You were like an angel."

"Madame, I am sorry." But was I really? I wasn't sure anymore. Her calls had become increasingly erratic, coming late at night or much too early in the morning. Lately, she seemed frustrated when I couldn't talk—because of the baby or her timing. I had even started to avoid the phone when the caller ID read "Unavailable." When we had gone out of town for a week over the summer, there had been thirty-seven hang-ups on the voice mail, sixteen of them consecutive. I was certain who the persistent caller was.

I began to doubt that Madame Nhu would ever give me her memoirs or, after reading the summary she was so proud of, that they would be readable. I was getting tired of the cat-and-mouse game. So I challenged her.

"I am not sure what good the speech would have done for your memoir anyway," I said. "People want to know what actually happened. To you. Not your religious interpretation of things."

There was a sharp intake of breath. The hiss of contempt in her voice filled my ear.

"The Vietnamese *know* the truth. Anyone who is worth it knows the truth. Too bad for the others. Who cares about the rest of you."

I had triggered the same defense mechanism that had once walled her off from the world in Saigon. When Madame Nhu was First Lady, it was always "the diplomats" or "the Communists" working to discredit her. Her husband said that "foreign powers" were against them, "maybe . . . because we are Catholic." I wasn't working against Madame Nhu in any way or for any reason. My intention was to help her. I wanted to get the memoirs that would help people understand and sympathize with her. But I had dared to contradict her, and for my sin, she would punish me with a long and stony silence.

Madame Nhu hung up on me. It would be almost a year before I heard from her again.

That same stubborn insistence on always being right got Madame Nhu and her family into more trouble in 1963 than they could get themselves out of. The trouble with the Buddhists had started in Hue, with the oldest of the five living Ngo brothers, Ngo Dinh Thuc.

Thuc was dressed in his customary clerical robes when his car approached the outskirts of Hue one morning early in May. His heavy features and drooped jowls were far removed from the lean good looks of his brother Nhu, but Thuc's manner was distinguished and confident.[1]

Thuc, the archbishop of Hue, was being chauffeured back into the city after a visit to La Vang's cathedral on the morning of May 7,

1963. Six months before, the pope himself had elevated the church of La Vang from minor basilica to a full basilica. Practically, not much had changed besides the installation of a *conopaeum,* an umbrella-like structure with silk panels of red and yellow that would be used to shelter his Holiness if he came to Vietnam for a visit. But the designation for La Vang was special to Thuc, because he had helped turn the worn red patch of earth into what it was now: a pilgrimage site, a center for the cult of the Virgin Mary, and a financial "cause." Thuc had overseen the construction of the marble Holy Rosary Square, the dredging of Tinh Tam Lake, and the erection of three concrete banyan trees to represent the Trinity. Government officials, from the vice president down, gave money even if they weren't Catholics, as it helped to be in the good graces of Diem and Nhu's big brother.

As the archbishop of Hue and the Ngos' older brother, Thuc was the head of the family. He stayed in the presidential palace when in Saigon, living for months at a time with Diem and the Nhus. It was a good vantage point from which to promote Catholicism. To pad his donations, Thuc also transferred what should have been public funds for the state of South Vietnam to the church. He blurred the line between church and state when Thuc was granted "concessions" from the government, transferring land, farms, businesses, and real estate to the church, making the Catholic Church the largest landowner in the country.[2] It would have been hard for Diem to say no to his older brother, especially as Thuc could claim to have the strong arm of God on his side. Thuc's corruption didn't benefit him directly—the land and the money went to the church. Those in the closest ranks of Diem's Catholic circle knew where the money and lands were going, and they didn't complain.

But most Vietnamese were not Catholic. They were Buddhist, at least in combination. The most popular Vietnamese religion is still a mix of Buddhism, Confucianism, and Taoism with some ancestor worship thrown in. Most homes have an altar in the front of the house, as do many Vietnamese shop fronts. Madame Nhu had grown up in a household that identified with Buddhism and Confucianism. The smell of the joss sticks reminded her of the family altar in her Hanoi home, when on the new moon day the incense mingled with the essence of orange and peach blossoms that her mother arranged before guiding the children to kowtow at the altar, overflowing with gifts. Madame Nhu should have known that Buddhism could conjure up powerful feelings of home and family for the Vietnamese, but the Catholic family she had married into didn't see things that way—especially not Archbishop Thuc, who interpreted the loose form of Buddhism practiced by most Vietnamese as religious ambivalence. He saw that ambivalence as a challenge and opportunity. His dream of converting Vietnam into a Christian nation seemed tantalizingly close. And Thuc did not do much to hide his own personal ambition: to be a cardinal in the Catholic Church, or even more.

On the drive back from La Vang, Thuc noticed flags flying all around Hue, colorful squares of garish blue, yellow, red, white, and orange in honor of Buddha's upcoming 2,527th birthday. The city of Hue was as close as Vietnam had to a religious center for Buddhism. It was the historic home of the Vietnamese emperor, who had served with the mandate of heaven.

But the flags were technically illegal. An obscure flag-flying law declared that only national flags could be flown in public places, and no religious flags were allowed anywhere unless they were the banners of a religious "institution." Buddhism was no such institution. A leftover French colonial regulation labeling it an "association" had simply been rolled into the new country's laws in 1954. There had been so many other pressing problems. Unlike an institution, such as the Roman Catholic Church, an "association" like Buddhism was subject to government controls and restrictions. Had no one thought about changing the law? Or, as the frustrated Buddhist leadership accused, had no one been willing to change it?

Thuc ordered the flags taken down. Hearing about it later in Saigon, Nhu was enraged by his older brother's thoughtlessness. "Why did my brother insist on sending such a stupid order about the flags? Who cares what flags they hang out?"

The Buddhist leaders cared very much. They had been waiting for a chance like this and quickly made the most of it. The Buddha's birthday celebration quickly turned into a protest. Thousands of people streamed over the bridges into the center of town. They waved banners for religious equality, but many were likely only too glad for an excuse to join a protest against the government. It was pretty clear that the Buddhist protests could not be characterized as a purely religious expression. The fact that the marchers had written their banners in English showed that they aimed to capture Western photographers' attention. The Buddhists knew that if they wanted regime change, then they needed the sympathy of the foreign press.

Government troops and city law enforcement officials were waiting in the city center to make sure nothing got out of hand. And then, all of a sudden, it did. Two explosions erupted. No one knew where they had come from or which side had detonated them. The crowd was ordered to disperse, and when it didn't, fire hoses were turned on them; civil guardsmen fired shots into the air. Chaos descended. Grenades were tossed into the crowd. A wave of human screaming followed the crack of explosions closely. When the smoke cleared, nine people had been killed, including two children, and fourteen were injured.[3]

As a knee-jerk reaction, the government in Saigon blamed the episode on the Viet Cong. Diem and Nhu claimed Communists were responsible for the mess in Hue. Communists had exploited the situation, they said.

Perhaps if the brothers had only made a sincere effort to apologize, the crisis might have stopped there. But instead, Diem and the Nhus applied the lessons they had learned throughout the years, from standing up to the Binh Xuyen in 1955 to facing down the paratroopers in 1960: Show no weakness. Do not negotiate. In the face of instability, apply more pressure.

The Ngos felt wrongly accused. Wasn't it enough that freedom of religion was spelled out in the constitution of South Vietnam? Why did the Buddhists have to insist on new and separate treatment for their religion over everyone else's? Would the other religions and religious sects—the Hoa Hao and Cao Dai and the few Protestants and Muslims—demand the same? Their demands were divisive, and South Vietnam needed unity to fight the Communists. The Ngos just didn't see religious persecution as a legitimate complaint and viewed the Buddhists as political opportunists. Security forces, layered with secret militias and spy networks, together with general repression under

Madame Nhu's morality laws, made the situation ripe for an explosion, but the Ngo regime treated the Buddhists as they had the gangsters and the coup plotters. It was a colossal misjudgment.

The Buddhists kept gathering. In cities all over South Vietnam, they took up the fight against the Diem regime. They protested for their right to public assembly and called for the right to fly the Buddhist flag in public. They also called the Ngo regime out for its Catholic bias. Bald monks gathered in their saffron robes and addressed crowds of curious onlookers with battery-powered bullhorns. The police would show up and disperse the crowds, but they were careful. Beating and arresting monks would be terrible public relations for a regime already under close watch.

Killing and violence are anathema to the Buddhist philosophy of peace, with one great exception: self-immolation. The sacrifice of one's mortal flesh for the collective cause of others is permitted. As one Buddhist spokesperson put it, "A Buddhist monk has certain responsibilities that he must take care of in this life on his way to the next life."

One month after the May protests, an elderly monk named Thich Quang Duc emerged from a white car at the busy intersection of Phan Dinh Phung and Le Van Duyet in the center of Saigon. Two young monks walked alongside him and helped the old man lower himself onto a square, tufted pillow. He folded his legs into the lotus position, his knees a few inches from the ground. Then, working hastily, his young assistants closed in again, dousing the old man's orange robes with pink fluid, even sloshing his face and the back of his bald head. When they had stepped a safe distance back, Thich Quang Duc struck a match and let it fall into his folded robes. The fireball engulfed him. The bonze sat unmoving, like a pillar, as the smoky yellow flames consumed him.

The monks had tipped off some members of the international media that "something very important" was going to happen, but Malcolm Browne was the only journalist in Saigon to show up. The Buddhists had left the specifics deliberately vague—they did not want the police alerted—and they had guessed correctly that their spectator would not intervene, although he certainly had time. Unlike a regular gasoline fire, which burns furiously bright for just a moment, this blaze was intense and sustained. Browne looked on in horror at the blackening figure surrounded by licking flames, but if he felt compelled to act, he was also keenly aware of his duty as the only camera-toting journalist present to document the travesty in Saigon. "I could see that although his eyes were closed his features were contorted with agony. But throughout his ordeal he never uttered a sound or changed his position, even as the smell of burning flesh filled the air." Behind the burning body, two monks unfurled a banner in English: "A Buddhist Priest Burns for Buddhist Demands." Another bonze spoke into a microphone in both English and Vietnamese: "A Buddhist priest becomes a martyr." Browne guessed that the ordeal lasted ten minutes before the flames subsided. Thich Quang Duc pitched over, twitched, and was still. He was the first and most famous, but he wouldn't be the last. By the end of that terrible summer, six more Buddhists, including monks, a nun, and a young student, had lit themselves on fire.[4]

As the Buddhist situation flared in Saigon, the United States, on whose support South Vietnam depended completely, was threatening to dissociate itself from the regime. The Americans wanted Diem to open up his government, to talk with his political opponents and bring them into the fold—in other words, they wanted him to behave more like a democrat than a dictator. Diem was taking "considerable action" on some matters, but on others, the Americans felt he was stalling or making matters worse. And he was refusing to cooperate with the foreign press—to "retrograde effect." The regime's "attitude towards the US press reflects [its] attitude in general towards the US government and people," and if the Nhus were "openly contemptuous," Diem was simply "indifferent." As American ambassador Henry Cabot Lodge reflected in his 1967 *Vietnam Memoir,* "The United States can get along with corrupt dictators who manage to stay out of the newspapers," but Diem and the Nhus couldn't follow those rules.

Diem was frankly tired of steeling himself against demands from Washington. He wasn't a puppet and resented being treated like one.

Born under French colonialism, he wasn't going to be a victim of American "colonial imperialism," so Diem was very sensitive to any encroachments on his sovereignty. As Edward Lansdale pointed out in a secret memorandum to Secretary of Defense Robert McNamara in 1961, "If the next American official to talk to President Diem would have the good sense to see him as a human being who has been through a lot of hell for years—and not as an opponent to be beaten to his knees—we would start regaining our influence with him." Americans already criticized the way he ran his army, they disparaged his family and closest advisors, Nhu and Madame Nhu, as "evil influences," and now they were pressing Diem to quiet the mess with the Buddhists. Diem couldn't help but frame any concession to the Buddhists as a concession to the Americans: "If we make a concession now, the United States will ask for more," he rationalized. "How many concessions do we have to make to satisfy them? . . . I wish to increase the army; the United States refuses to supply weapons and other means. The United States only wants to send troops to Vietnam."[5]

Madame Nhu's Women's Solidarity Movement issued a declaration that the *Times of Vietnam* printed in full the very next day: a robe does not make a bonze. It admonished Vietnamese and Americans to take a hard look at the real motives behind the monks' demonstrations. Madame Nhu charged the Buddhists with using their religion as a cover for communism. The Buddhists were "exploited and controlled by Communism and oriented to sowing disorder and neutralism."[6] To accuse someone of communism in the Cold War chill of Saigon in 1963 was an incredible insult. But it didn't end there. Included in the pronouncement was a passing swipe at "those inclined to take Vietnam for a satellite of a foreign power," by which Madame Nhu clearly meant the United States. Officials in the US embassy were stunned that such a diplomatic gaffe could go unpunished. "If that statement is policy, it's a disaster," they warned.[7]

But Madame Nhu's most offensive pronouncement was yet to come. And this time it was not buried in any women's group declaration; she came out and said it herself. The Buddhist suicides were "barbecues," she declared. With that one sentence, Madame Nhu sealed her fate. The varied grievances against the government suddenly all became believable after Madame Nhu gave such a cruel voice to the regime.

President Diem tried to control the damage by going on the radio to say how profoundly troubled he was by the death of Thich Quang Duc. Then he reiterated that as the constitution protected Buddhism, he was personally its guardian. Negotiations with the Buddhists continued, and a document that would come to be known as the Joint Communiqué of June 16 resolved the Buddhist flag-flying issue—at least in theory. On religious holidays, the Buddhist flag could be flown outside pagoda walls as long as it was accompanied by a larger national flag. The Buddhist flag could be flown alone only inside the pagoda. On national holidays, no religious flags were to fly at all. Most tellingly, in a revealing moment of weakness, Diem made a point to tell reporters that Madame Nhu did not speak for the government. To most people the Diem presidency really comprised three people: Diem, Nhu, and Madame Nhu. This attempt to silence the most visible member reduced his power, especially when, as quickly became apparent, Madame Nhu showed her complete unwillingness to be silenced.

Madame Nhu couldn't let it go. It seemed too unfair: the Buddhists got concessions when the regime had done, in her mind, nothing wrong. She refused to apologize and dug herself in deeper. "I would beat them [the Buddhist activists] ten times more," she said to David Halberstam. If there was another suicide, even if there were another thirty, Madame Nhu said she would clap her hands in delight.

Privately, the Ngo brothers continued to depend on Madame Nhu, who had advised the brothers well in the past. Keeping with that tradition, Nhu came to his wife in the middle of the night on June 15, the night before the communiqué was signed to resolve the flag-flying issue, and asked, "What should we do?" Madame Nhu had already told Diem what she thought of the document—and him. "You are a coward," she had spat at the president. Diem just shook his head and told her she didn't understand. This time, the problem had international implications. It was too big for her.[8]

That night she was too tired to argue more. She told her husband that they were in an impossible situation. To fight the Buddhists would cause more trouble, but to sign the document revising the flag order would admit guilt and open them up to further risk if the Buddhists wanted them to make amends or demanded retribution. "Get Diem to sign it," she sighed about the joint communiqué. But it was very important to her that one thing not be overlooked. When Diem signed the document, he should write in that none of what he was agreeing to had ever been illegal in the first place—reiterating the fact that the constitution protected religious freedom. Presumably Nhu passed the advice on to Diem because the president did just that, in his neat tight script: "The points put down in the Joint Communiqué were approved in principle by me at the very beginning." Madame Nhu's solution appeased the Buddhists on the flag flying without ever admitting that the government had behaved badly, and Madame Nhu thought the brothers ought to be grateful to her for getting them out of a tight spot, again.[9]

With the communiqué signed, the Buddhist mess should have been settled. But the flag flying was never the real problem. It was simply the spark that had ignited the underlying issues, and those continued to smolder. The palace was infuriated that the foreign press, the Americans especially, couldn't let the issue go. Reporters were giving voice to people dissatisfied with the regime, and the more voice they received, the more they protested. There were mass demonstrations in Saigon, Dalat, Nha Trang, Qui Nhon, and Hue. Monks continued to stage public suicides. Their banners no longer asked the Ngos for religious tolerance; now they called for an overthrow of the government. People seemed to respond with enthusiasm. How was the government supposed to react? Its authority was being flouted daily. Nhu confided to his wife his fear that negotiating with the Buddhists had looked like weakness. At the hint of impotence, the brothers would lose political allies; people once too scared to defy them would be no longer so afraid. The palace was vulnerable to attack. The Vietnamese people needed to be reminded who was in charge, and so did the Americans.

On August 20, President Diem enacted martial law. Troops would occupy strategic points in Saigon, but the pagodas, Diem said, were to be handled with special care. Diem didn't want any of the monks hurt.

He said he didn't want any more trouble, and his generals seemed to believe him. But Nhu had a different plan.

The very next day, Nhu's combat police and special forces, the "shock troops," were called in. He had ordered the men to dress in regular army fatigues. The plan was to make it look like the Army of the Republic of Vietnam (ARVN) was defying Diem's presidential order to take it easy on the pagodas. It was a crazy act of duplicity, but he was desperate to keep the unhappy Americans at a distance from the ARVN generals, whose ambitions to take over the country were growing as the Ngos' iron-fisted control on opposition appeared to be slipping. Nhu was well aware that the Americans would not tolerate a brutal campaign against the Buddhists. Thinking the ARVN had embarked on a rogue assault on the pagodas would be sure to drive a wedge between them. But by faking army involvement in the pagoda raids, Nhu played right into the hands of those who most wanted him gone.

The screams of Buddhists, the war cries of their attackers, shattering glass, pistol shots, and, over it all, a pagoda gong being struck again and again filled the night of August 21, 1963. Xa Loi pagoda was Buddhist headquarters in Saigon. It was usually a restful place that gently echoed the steady drone of monotone chanting and reverberations of brass gongs. That night it became the scene of a two-hour orgy of violence and a blatant show of power and might. David Halberstam looked on in shock, seeing in the horrific scene unfolding around him "the crumbling of an American foreign policy." Madame Nhu also watched the assault from a tank parked not far away from Halberstam, but she viewed the situation far more optimistically. Justice was being served.[10]

Her good mood carried into the next day, when a press correspondent described the First Lady as in a "state of euphoria, chattering like a schoolgirl after a prom." Madame Nhu compared the late-night crushing of the "Communist Buddhists" with the 1955 rout of the Binh Xuyen gangsters, except she didn't seem to realize that only one side was doing the shooting this time. She didn't dwell on the fact that the victims were weaponless, bald monks. It was the "happiest day of my life," she said, and another victory for the Ngo family.[11]

It was also Madame Nhu's thirty-ninth birthday. That day a cablegram had arrived at the palace from her parents in America. Maybe she expected a routine, if formal, note, the kind of restrained birthday greetings that parents of a certain pedigree sent to their adult child. But she should have known better. It was the second cable from them in five days.

The first had been a ciphered cable. In strong, almost threatening words, her mother and father urged her to leave Vietnam with her four children. "Get out of the limelight," they told her.[12] Madame Chuong had also personally delivered this message to Henry Cabot Lodge as he was about to leave Washington for Saigon: the Ngo regime was so hated that "unless they leave the country there is no power on earth that can prevent the assassination of Prime Minister Diem, of his brother Nhu, and of my daughter, Madame Nhu."[13] Madame Nhu had not known about the meddling of her mother meeting the incoming ambassador behind her back, but she been infuriated enough by the letter. She was no longer a child, and they couldn't tell her what to do. In their second cable, her parents seemed to agree. It was not a birthday message at all but a letter of resignation. The Chuongs quit their prominent ambassadorial posts, her father to the South Vietnamese embassy in Washington, her mother as special observer to the United Nations in New York. Chuong wrote, "I cannot go on representing a government which ignores my advice and of which I disapprove." The regime publicly denied that Chuong had resigned in criticism of the government. They said he had already been fired.[14]

What had been just talk before, of barbecuing Buddhists and beating them harder, had become a chilling reality. The raids on the Buddhist pagodas were a manifestation of what Madame Nhu had been saying for months. Diem never publicly broke with his brother over the pagoda-raiding scheme, but he did send a private letter to Madame Nhu, a directive from the president of South Vietnam to a member of the National Assembly: she was to make no public statements about the raids and to give no more statements to the press.

For once, it seems, Diem acquiesced to American demands to silence his First Lady. But he cushioned the blow. A meeting of the fifty-nine members of the Interparliamentary Union was coming up at the end of September in Belgrade. It wouldn't look so much like banishment if Madame Nhu was the South Vietnamese representative. How much more trouble could she possibly get into?

Madame Nhu was happy to go. She could take people up on other offers she had received and extend her trip. She had been invited to speak at the Overseas Press Club in New York City, and why not, she thought. If they wanted her, she was sure she could make a convincing case for herself and her country.

A grainy, unpublished photo captures the family on the palace stairs on the brink of Madame Nhu's departure. The oldest child, daughter Le Thuy, was going along on Madame Nhu's travels abroad, and Nhu and the three other children had gathered to bid them good-bye. They smile into the camera and Madame Nhu lays a reassuring hand on her youngest daughter's shoulder. Only the four-year-old looks at all uncertain about the future as the rest of them make their way to the airport.

An impressive crowd gathered around Madame Nhu as she prepared to make what would be her farewell address at Saigon's Tan Son Nhut Airport. A dozen men, wearing skinny ties and dark suits despite the heat, leaned in toward the deceptively diminutive beauty smiling in their midst. To a casual observer, it might have looked like the reporters were naturally drawn to her, like moths to a flame, incapable of resisting the Diem regime's most flamboyant character. The brooch on her left shoulder dazzled, and her eyes were bright with excitement about her upcoming trip. She wore a well-tailored brown *ao dai* over flowing white pants and high-heeled pumps. Over her arm, she carried a travel bag for the long flight and a fur stole. Her hair was held impeccably in place, high off her head, in a stylish beehive. If it weren't for the microphones and bulky recording devices of the era, she might have looked like a woman classically surrounded by admirers on bended knee.

Instead, the men surrounding Madame Nhu at the airport that day were some of her fiercest critics. To them and their American readers, she had become a "female monster," complete with a "serpent's tongue" and red-painted "talons." In their stories about South Vietnam, they had likened her to Lucrezia Borgia and then to Marie Antoinette.

Malcolm Browne would remember seeing the Nhus say their goodbyes at the airport. They pulled together for a brief moment for one last worried kiss, looking like any normal couple. As her plane took off, Nhu's eyes followed its ascent into the sky, his hands covering his ears to block the roar of the engines. Could anyone have known it would be the last time he would see his wife? By the time Madame Nhu's plane was in the air that day, the wheels of the regime's bloody denouement were already in motion.

With hindsight, the image of reporters circling Madame Nhu with their microphones takes on a distinctly more ominous cast. Instead of moths to a brightly burning flame, it recalls a more sinister image of sharks circling. Perhaps instinctually they smelled blood in the water.

CHAPTER 13

Too Beautiful to Ignore

MADAME NHU LANDED IN New York hours behind schedule. Her Pan American flight from Paris had encountered turbulence somewhere over the Atlantic; strong headwinds had pushed against the plane. It wasn't the only force resisting her. Hurricane Flora was lingering off the American coast, although much farther south. It had already killed 4,000 in Haiti, and it was anyone's guess where she would go next or what damage she would do when she made landfall in the States. Madame Nhu's plane touched down at Idlewild Airport in the calm before the storm.

That the airport would be renamed JFK, and that the president whose memory it honored would be assassinated in a matter of weeks, would have been unthinkable in the soft evening light of October 7, 1963. It would have seemed impossible that what the American public still considered the little war in Vietnam, a far-off land in the exotic Orient, would spiral into destruction for the next decade. The Gulf of Tonkin incident was still a year away; the only American servicemen in Vietnam were 15,000 military advisors—a far cry from the 200,000 who would be in country by the end of 1965. In 1963, there were still no troops on the ground.

But Vietnam had come to the United States—at least in the petite figure of Madame Nhu about to launch a cross-country press tour. She should have been scared. Everything was at stake—her family, her country, even her safety. She seemed to acknowledge the danger. She felt, she confessed, like she had been "caught by the skin of the neck like a kitten and thrown into an arena with lions."[1] So she should have been walking on eggshells. She should have stayed quiet. She shouldn't have come to America at all. But that would have made Madame Nhu predictable, and she was anything but.

She deplaned boldly enough, wearing freshly applied pink lipstick and a blazing smile. Transatlantic travel still meant luxury—lavish meals, served on china, and endless drinks. People dressed up to fly. Madame Nhu wore a dark mink stole over her slimly tailored brown sheath; sharp-heeled pumps peeked out from under the hem of her white pants. She made her way down the gangway without having fixed her hair, which had slipped during the long flight, but just a little. One insubordinate lock bounced behind her left ear as she headed toward the terminal.

A few of the lower-ranking attachés from the South Vietnamese embassy in Washington, DC, were at the airport to greet Madame Nhu. She raised a gloved hand to wave at them in the imperial way, with a stiff wrist. There were also members of the South Vietnam United Nations delegation, and beyond them, a sea of white faces and bright lights.

How long did it take Madame Nhu to note the other conspicuous absences? There were no official representatives from the United States. No one at the federal, state, or even local level had come to meet the First Lady of the Republic of South Vietnam, the United States' formal ally in the Cold War battle against communism. There were only a police lieutenant, his sergeant, and the four New York City patrolmen assigned for her security. Also missing were her parents, the former ambassador Chuong and his wife. Although they were in fact visiting New York that day, it was not with the purpose of greeting their daughter. Instead, the Chuongs were sounding the alarm all across the city about the damage the power-hungry Nhus were doing to South Vietnam. They warned that the government there could not be reformed. Madame Nhu's own parents were calling for her ouster.

Madame Nhu carried on, making her way down the tarmac to the Pan American terminal—a huge and hovering circle that looked like an alien spacecraft. One hundred reporters and photographers jostled each other to get a better view of her first steps on American soil. The newsmen must have marveled at how this tiny woman could be at the epicenter of so much trouble. Microphones and cameras were ready to document any sign of self-doubt, a chink in the silken armor. But Madame Nhu was used to collecting herself in front of a crowd. Her smile looked genuine enough.

Madame Nhu went to a podium set up for her arrival. To reach the microphone she stood on a little stool. Her voice rang firm and clear as a bell as she delivered some prepared remarks—she was looking forward to the trip ahead, she said. Her half veil would have cast a shadow over anything else that might have shown in her eyes.

A reporter from the back of the room asked Madame Nhu about the obvious gaps in the crowd. Madame Nhu turned to her eighteen-year-old eldest daughter, who had accompanied her on the trip, for translation help, and Le Thuy moved closer to her mother. Le Thuy wore her hair in a bell-shaped bob. An oversized bow was fastened so low on one side that it looked like it might fall out at any moment. It was a fashionable look at the time. Twenty-three-year-old Mary Tyler Moore wore her hair the same way on the *Dick Van Dyke Show* episode set to air later that week. Looking like an obedient schoolgirl, Le Thuy murmured into her mother's ear a combination of Vietnamese and French.

Madame Nhu closed her eyes and nodded briefly.

"I've become, in spite of myself, a controversial person. I don't want to embarrass anyone." Now that she was here in America, Madame

Nhu said she would do her best to "try and understand why we can't get along better."

When Madame Nhu spoke English, she lilted, and some of her words purred together. Her tone was almost flirtatious. But the sad little shrug of her shoulders before she ducked into her waiting Cadillac limousine showed the room full of mostly men exactly what they were waiting for: a carefully measured glimpse of something fragile and human inside the woman they had dubbed the Dragon Lady.

Madame Nhu's coast-to-coast itinerary would take her to twelve American cities in twenty-two days. She was booked for seventeen radio and television broadcasts, plus seventeen speaking engagements, eleven of them at universities and colleges. She had also been invited as the guest of honor to fifteen more formal luncheons and dinners. But the American enthusiasm had a dark edge.

The invitations to speak with the press and at private events, press clubs, and academic institutions had been issued despite the wishes of the US government. Such freedom of the press—and blatant disregard for government wishes—would have been unthinkable in South Vietnam. Decades later, Madame Nhu still didn't understand. She would cite it as an example of her disillusionment with Americans. How, she wondered, could the American media and the country's most distinguished schools invite her, only for the government then to try to say, "Don't come."

The American people wanted a spectacle. The American government was trying to prevent one. So it had done what it could, diplomatically, to prevent her from visiting the country. Harlan Cleveland from the State Department pulled aside South Vietnam's new ambassador to the United States in Washington to ask if the regime had taken any steps to "tone down" Madame Nhu. The new ambassador from Saigon had already made clear in highly classified conversations with US officials that he personally thought she should be "eliminated," but he remained oblique about how that could be accomplished. Out of concern for his job and maybe his neck, he had to be subtler. He sent five cables to Saigon before Madame Nhu's arrival. He was merely told that the First Lady had been privately instructed to "quiet down." Everyone knew that couldn't be trusted to work.

The American reporters were good at their jobs. They could goad Madame Nhu into making a scene. It helped that the lady was "unfortunately too beautiful to ignore." So the American government tried to shame the media instead. An unnamed official high in the Kennedy administration went off the record to reproach the biggest players in the media: CBS, NBC, *Time, Newsweek,* and the *New York Post.* They were paying this Dragon Lady too much attention. Didn't they realize the possible harm of giving Madame Nhu a platform to bring her case to the American people? The American stake in South Vietnam was high, and this little lady threatened everything.[2]

Since Madame Nhu was sending shivers down the spine of the Kennedy administration, she became a convenient friend in an election year to his opponents, such as the Doughertys, who had made their fortune in Texas and had an oil well in their front yard, and the formidable Clare Booth Luce, Republican senator and wife of Henry Luce, founder of the Time-Life empire. They were among many conservatives and Republicans to extend the South Vietnamese First Lady a warm welcome to America. Marguerite Higgins proved a constant friend as well. She had written down what to say and what to avoid saying. Those don'ts included some of Madame Nhu's favorite phrases: she was to stay away from using expressions like "systematic conspiracy" and "intoxicated monks." Higgins also warned Madame Nhu not to criticize President Kennedy so blatantly.

As it was not recognizing her as an "official" visitor to the United States, the State Department bluntly told Madame Nhu that it could not guarantee her safety. She was on her own. The lack of diplomatic protocol around her arrival in New York sent the message loud and clear. The only official recognition of Madame Nhu's visit was made in protest. Senator Stephen Young, a Democrat from Ohio, said that Madame Nhu had gotten "too big for her britches" and should be sent back to South Vietnam. Representative Wayne L. Hays, chairman of the House Foreign Affairs Committee on Capitol Hill, went on the congressional record to lodge a formal complaint against that "evil woman" having entered the country on a diplomatic visa. And although Madame Nhu didn't know it, she had even received a warning from the president of the United States himself.

In August and September, Madame Nhu had sent letters from Saigon and then Paris to Vice President Lyndon Johnson, asking about whether she would be welcome in the United States. She felt a certain comfort asking Johnson—she had gotten to know him during his official visit, and their teenage daughters had become friends. So Madame Nhu thought she would appeal to the gentlemanly side of the giant Texan. She had been able to charm him not so long before and now she teased him in a letter not to let himself be "frightened by a lady."

But President Kennedy was personally vexed about her potential visit. In his view, Madame Nhu emasculated the men around her. The State Department had warned in August that she undercut authority by appearing to lead men around "by her apron strings." Kennedy had no intention of letting that kind of usurpation of power happen on US soil. A draft of a reply to Madame Nhu's letter went from Johnson's office to the White House; Johnson wanted Kennedy to approve it himself.

"This is not the kind of letter that you write a charming lady," chided Kennedy with a mocking smile. He was reading it in his steam bath, a kind of alternate office for the president, who suffered from excruciating back pain. It was said that he did some of his best thinking in the bath. In fact, Kennedy's advisors often gathered around the president, who received them naked from the waist up and covered with a towel below—at least that's how he was usually described. Meanwhile, the aides wore their suits and ties and even sat on the toilet or crouched on the humid floor tiles.

Kennedy took a moment to muse about how to craft the letter back to Madame Nhu. "It's got to be more gentle and more . . . " The thought trailed off as he went to work on crafting a reply. Kennedy expounded on her beauty and charm. He also gave her what can only be read as a warning about "certain political facts of life." The letter asked her to consider, "in as coldly objective fashion as possible, the question whether your coming here will help or hinder." Vice President Johnson read the redraft and found it "pretty good." He dutifully signed the letter and sent it off to Madame Nhu as his own.[3]

Madame Nhu may not have known who the author really was, but she read the message between the lines. I can only imagine the square set of her chin as she scratched out an indignant reply with a fountain pen. Her decision not to stand by silently was one of conscience, she said. She would go the United States. And summing up the intensity of her intent with characteristic drama, she wrote, "I refuse to play the role of an accomplice in an awful murder."

Presumably, the "murder" she mentions in her letter was a rhetorical flourish. The White House secretary who filed the correspondence must have thought so when she scrawled "no reply needed" across the top. But weeks later, when Madame Nhu's husband and brother-in-law were, in fact, awfully murdered, the phrase in Madame Nhu's letter reads as an eerie presentiment. By the time Madame Nhu had written those words, the coup that would topple and kill the Ngo brothers already had US support. The plot should have been very clandestine, with coded wires, eyes-only memos, and back-alley Saigon meetings. Yet Madame Nhu seemed to know about it. And she was set on coming to the United States for an extended visit in the country she was all but accusing of premeditated murder.

Madame Nhu had been "strongly dissuaded" from coming, she explained to a CBS correspondent on the transatlantic flight from Paris. She was referring to the letter from Kennedy and the State Department's refusal to guarantee her safety, as well as to other messages she had received from anxious Vietnamese diplomats.[4] But Madame Nhu persisted anyway, in what she called her "feminine spirit of contradiction—maybe if they had invited, had insisted that I come, I would not!" And then, according to the reporter, Madame Nhu had giggled and fluttered a little like a butterfly in trouble. Was her visit a coquettish whim, as she had tried to convince the journalist on the flight, or was she a "power-hungry propagandist," as her father, the ex-ambassador, claimed?

The truth was that Madame Nhu was more powerful than the tottering government she had left behind in South Vietnam. The Ngo regime was failing, and she knew it. It was weak and defensive while she was vibrant and declamatory. She believed in herself more than she believed in her husband and his brother. She would not stay at home and be a quiet housewife while the mob gathered around her. She, after all, had faced gunfire before; she had gathered her skirts and her infant and crossed the bridge unharmed. She had faced down the Binh Xuyen gangsters and the grandiose General Hinh. Madame Nhu was sure of herself, and her self-belief had never betrayed her.

Madame Nhu's bold self-confidence was backed by innate political skill. Even those, like former ambassador to South Vietnam Lawton Collins, who thought her a "vixen of the first order," couldn't help but find her politicking—and her fearlessness—remarkable. The foreign journalists who had witnessed her displays of courage in Saigon admitted to a grudging respect for her audacity—and Madame Nhu must have sensed that. She didn't mind their tagging her the Dragon Lady; she could understand the fascination. "I looked fearless and that was true." So what if the Americans had invited her and then said, "Don't come"? Since she wasn't allowed to stay in her country, she might as well enter into the place she had likened to the biblical lion's den and see what she could do about fixing the fraying relationship between South Vietnam and America, wielding at least the illusion of power from the inside.

She knew that she had nothing to lose.

Columbia, Harvard, and Princeton clamored to have Madame Nhu visit their campuses. *Time* magazine, the *New York Times,* and television networks competed for face time with the First Lady. Some of America's most powerful political families feted her. The American government's efforts to shush her only reinforced that she was indeed a powerful personality to be reckoned with. All the attention, even the negative kind, paid to her visit padded her confidence.

Madame Nhu's stay in New York centered on the seventh floor of the Hotel Barclay. The luxury hotel was used to protecting the privacy of its guests, including celebrities like Marlon Brando and Bette Davis. On the ground floor was the flagship Caswell-Massey pharmacy. Greta Garbo and Katherine Hepburn were clients. Sarah Bernhardt once ran out of the company's famed cucumber night cream and had the store express ship thirty jars for her European tour. The lobby of the hotel itself had plush carpets and wood paneling. A giant gilt birdcage dominated the entry.

Madame Nhu did not leave her hotel at all the first day. She stayed cocooned in Room 708, a suite with heavily draped windows that gave her only a sliver of a view into midtown Manhattan. From there, Forty-Eighth Street passed in front of the hotel to meet the avenues, Lexington and Park, at perfect right angles. That symmetry was unremarkable in itself, but the city went on and on like that, a neat grid paved with shiny black Cadillac sedans, soft-topped Buicks, city buses, and of course yellow taxicabs. The world must have looked so orderly and affluent from up there. Pedestrians observed the boundaries of sidewalks. Streetlights regulated traffic. Dark-suited businessmen went about their daily affairs inside the buildings that stood shoulder to shoulder with her hotel like brothers competing for who was taller. It all confirmed what Madame Nhu believed—that Americans might be a genuine people, but they were arrogant. And no wonder; looking around New York City in 1963 confirmed that can-do confidence was built into the American infrastructure. There was nothing self-effacing or humble in sight.[5]

Belgrade, Rome, and of course the last stop on her journey west, Paris, had been beautiful in that old-world way—the twisting streets and crumbling plaster, the historic associations and faded glory. It was a sensibility Madame Nhu could appreciate and the foundation of the only world she had ever known. European aesthetics and standards of beauty had shaped colonial policy in Indochina. But the sound of all these Western cities was so foreign. They were a dissonance of honking and bleating and sirens. In contrast, the carts and bicycles that swarmed the roads of Saigon were a muted whirr that even a good rain could drown out.

Just beyond the Hotel Barclay's awning there were protesters. They had been on the street since the night before, chanting, "Phoo on

Nhu! Phoo on Nhu!" These were not like the quiet monks who had been lighting themselves on fire in Madame Nhu's country. Nor did they resemble the American hippies or wild-haired peace activists who would take up the antiwar cause in just a few more years. The young men wore suits and ties; the women wore sensible shoes and stockings. They marched in orderly lockstep circles and carried placards on their shoulders, bearing the messages "End Diem" and "End the War in Vietnam" stenciled in clean block letters. Looking back at video clips of the protest, it seems quaint and quite harmless, a controlled expression of free speech. The painful societal schisms associated with the Vietnam War would come later—at the Democratic convention in Chicago in 1968, where police beat back protesters who were burning draft cards, and of course at Kent State. But the group outside Madame Nhu's hotel in 1963 was a radical one for its time. Most Americans still believed wholeheartedly in the domino effect and generally trusted their government. When President Kennedy said that the United States had a responsibility in South Vietnam to stop communism, the policy went largely unchallenged.

A boy in a crew cut and glasses stepped out of the oval formation to be interviewed by Ben Horman, a CBS news reporter. The earnest youth wore a sweater vest under his blazer and carried pens in his front pocket. Horman asked him, almost condescendingly, "So do you think we should pull our forces out? And just let the commies take over?" The young man's Adam's apple and nerves threatened to choke him, but he squared his jaw and spoke into the CBS microphone: "It's for the Vietnamese people to decide." Then he repeated the statement for good measure. "It's for the Vietnamese people to decide."[6]

Madame Nhu disagreed entirely. The Vietnamese people could not be trusted with the decision, any more than the Americans could. The notion that South Vietnam might not be worth fighting was anathema for her.

She emerged refreshed from her hotel the next day. Fifty newsmen and television cameramen were waiting for her in the lobby. She rewarded them with a quick smile, showing a row of pearly teeth. The men shouted for her attention, but she only gathered her fur tighter around her and slid past.

From then on, Madame Nhu seemed to be everywhere all at once. Helping that impression was the fact that boutiques around the city put mannequins with almond eyes and puffy hairpieces in their shop windows. One fashion designer ruefully commented that he doubted Madame Nhu would be a lasting fashion influence in New York because American women were not small enough, or flat chested enough, to pull off her look effectively.

Everywhere she went Madame Nhu stopped traffic, literally. Two hundred protesters showed up to picket the first event, but those numbers were dwarfed by the one thousand attendees at Madame Nhu's lunch at the Waldorf Astoria hosted by the Overseas Press Club. *Time* magazine reported that women in minks heavily outnumbered the working newsmen. "Is she 40?" asked one matron in the audience. Madame Nhu had just turned thirty-nine. "You don't have nails like that and do much around the house," another woman in the audience muttered. Some of her audience had forgotten—perhaps they never knew—why Madame Nhu was in New York. She was trying to save her family. She was trying to enlist support for the fight against communism. She was not there to prove herself a capable housewife.

The next day three hundred people crowded around simply to watch her emerge from her limousine and dash into Radio City Music Hall. Madame Nhu had to travel around New York under heavy police escort, snarling traffic up and down the avenues as she made her way from midtown to Times Square, from Columbia to Sarah Lawrence to Fordham.[7]

On her fourth day in the city, she nearly collapsed. Madame Nhu had taped a television show the day before and had just come from a lunch with the publishers of *Time* magazine. When she took the stage at Sarah Lawrence College in the late afternoon, her voice was shaky. A woman who had been in the audience said Madame Nhu was "obviously not well" and that she had to stop several times to sip from her glass and swallow some sort of pills. She wavered on her feet under the bright stage lights and excused herself from the stage before she fainted. It was a far cry from her usual spirit. But in this case, it seemed to work in her favor.

A group of women standing around in twin sets and knee-length pencil skirts gathered after the talk outside the auditorium to chew gum, smoke cigarettes, and compare notes on their impressions. "I couldn't hate her!" one young woman exclaimed, and her friends nodded in agreement. Then they chimed in like birds pecking the same seed: "I was disarmed." "She was pretty." "I'm sorry she didn't feel better." But another woman announced her disappointment. The Dragon Lady she had been expecting had not showed up. The term "just didn't seem to fit that sweet woman."[8]

It might have helped that the Ngo family had hired a New Yorker as program director for Madame Nhu's trip. She and two assistants worked in adjoining rooms at the Hotel Barclay during Madame Nhu's stay. They coordinated the details of the cross-country visit but protested to the media that they were not public relations consultants—and certainly "not advising anybody on what to say."[9]

A public relations firm had already fired Madame Nhu and the rest of the Ngo family as clients. The Oram Group was a well-known and well-respected consultant for social and political causes. Their clients included Planned Parenthood and the NAACP, as well as environmental, religious, and civil rights groups. The American Friends of Vietnam had hired the Oram Group sometime during the Eisenhower administration. For $3,000 a month, the firm was charged with promoting President Diem and making sure that the US government and taxpaying public would stand firm behind the embattled president of South Vietnam. Harold Oram himself had helped orchestrate Diem's triumphal visit to the United States in 1957, when President Eisenhower had personally greeted him at the airport in Washington, and 50,000 people had turned out to watch his motorcade pass through the city. When Diem made his way to Manhattan, the city held a ticker-tape parade. But the staff of consultants at Oram and the directors of the firm had later split among themselves on the question of Diem: was he a strong leader or a repressive dictator? By 1962, they had made up their minds. Oram ended all commitments to represent and promote South Vietnam as a good cause. The firm wasn't going to do anything to help Madame Nhu on this trip.[10]

Like any good tourist to the Big Apple, Madame Nhu took in the sights, including a show at Times Square and dinner at a nightclub where she listened to jazz. She seemed game for it all. Madame Nhu was making a real effort to show the Americans that she appreciated their culture. The decision to play the good sport on American soil was a smart tactic. She knew she needed to soften her image. By visiting all the sights, taking in all the tastes and sounds that New York City had to offer, she was trying to say that American style and entertainment were great—in America. She wanted to show that she wasn't a militant moralist all the time. But Madame Nhu did not apologize—at least not sincerely. A few weeks before, in Rome, Madame Nhu had commented to the press that the American military in Vietnam acted "like little soldiers of fortune." It was a terrible thing to say, even if she didn't really understand what she was implying. The new ambassador in Saigon, Henry Cabot Lodge, had strongly condemned her for it, and the newspapers had run with the story, calling her flagrantly anti-American and accusing her of desecrating the sacrifice of the 112 American soldiers who had died in South Vietnam. All of this helped build the tension and frenzy surrounding her visit to the United States.[11]

Madame Nhu refused, or maybe she was unable, to tone down the defensive bristling in her voice. Even though she had apologized for causing offense, she couldn't drop the issue. Instead, she decided to hammer home what she meant to say. The "Americans bring their houses on their backs [to Vietnam]. . . . They live at great expense."

She had a point. South Vietnam was a country at war. Moderation would have been more appropriate. As with any couple in a troubled marriage, fights over money just exacerbated the tensions between the US and South Vietnamese governments. By 1963, the United States was pouring $1.5 million into South Vietnam every day, nearly $550 million annually. Americans thought the South Vietnamese should be doing more with the massive inflows of cash, but the South

Vietnamese argued that too much of the money earmarked for South Vietnam went to "operational expenses" for American servicemen and advisors—bringing cold Cokes, hamburgers, and color televisions to comfort the advisors stationed in the jungles. The Ngo brothers wanted a cutback in the number of American advisors; instead, the Kennedy administration signaled that it would put more men in South Vietnam but cut the overall aid package. At the same time, the Communists needed only point to the Americanization of South Vietnam—from the economy to the fashion to the shelves of the grocery stores—to make their nationalist point.

So much had been made of the phrase "the monks' barbecue" and now the "soldiers of fortune" comment that, Madame Nhu complained, her deeper meaning had been lost. "I could not make myself heard in my country." She was heard just fine by the 4,000 to 5,000 students who packed the auditorium to hear her at Fordham University on day five of her visit. The all-male audience had given Madame Nhu a roaring welcome when she walked on stage. She wore another silk *ao dai,* this one with a boatneck, her hair tidily twisted up. She showed no signs of the shaky exhaustion of the day before. This was a different crowd altogether. Row after row of men gazed up at the little figure on the stage. They were dressed in severe suits and dark ties and rippled with appreciative laughter when Madame Nhu told them, "I'm ready to answer questions—but I don't want to deprive you of your lunch." They were charmed and seemed more than willing to go along with Madame Nhu when she beseeched them with a final request, "Whatever you hear, please don't condemn me." She was given a standing ovation.

In front of the men at Fordham, Madame Nhu seemed to have overcome whatever shyness or lingering doubts might have plagued her. That success was followed by cheers from a capacity audience at Columbia University. Even though detractors had repeatedly pelted her limousine with eggs and chalk as she traveled through the city, Madame Nhu seemed to realize by the end of her first week in the United States that she would be just fine, no thanks to the government that refused to acknowledge her.

On Sunday morning, Madame Nhu and her daughter went to Mass at the Church of Saint Agnes on Forty-Third Street near Grand Central Station. Madame Nhu wore a salmon-pink *ao dai,* and Le Thuy wore turquoise; with their matching smiles the mother and daughter looked like they could have posed for a Howard Johnson ad. Madame Nhu had every reason to smile—her interview on NBC's popular show *Meet the Press* would air that evening, and she had just received a huge bouquet of flowers from the students at Columbia in apology for the protests she had encountered on campus the day before. It was a nice touch, but even nicer was a visit from New York City's public events commissioner. It would be Madame Nhu's first formal face-to-face greeting from a government official at any level. All the fuss around Madame Nhu had made her "his concern" as a New York City representative.[12] She must have been tickled that even he had trouble making his way through the Barclay lobby. Madame Nhu had been in the country nearly a full week, and the excitement surrounding her still hadn't died down. Curiosity seekers, media, protesters, and fans still swarmed her hotel. After his meeting with Madame Nhu, the official conceded to the press that she was "a dynamo." She simply couldn't and wouldn't be ignored.

CHAPTER 14

Closed Doors

IN 1943, SOONG MAY-LING, the wife of Generalissimo Chiang Kai-shek, travelled across America, from East Coast to West, New York to California. Her itinerary was very much like Madame Nhu's twenty years later. They had called Madame Chiang the Dragon Lady too—for being determined, daring, and deliberately alluring. And like Madame Nhu, Madame Chiang was on a crusade against the evil threat posed to her country by communism.

But the context was different. Madame Chiang's 1943 visit took place less than two years after the attack on Pearl Harbor. The willowy Chinese woman who took the floor at the US Senate cut a dashing figure; she was an inspirational hero for the Americans—they had fought a common enemy during World War II, the Japanese. If Madame Chiang said the Communists were another threat to China's security, America was ready to believe her. The American public was enchanted with what she wore, how she spoke, and even her daily toilette. The papers chronicled every detail of her trip.

For as exotic as Madame Chiang appeared, with her crescent-shaped eyes, glossy black hair, and fine-boned physique, she was also just familiar enough. She had gone to school at Wellesley. She knew how to talk to Americans. This wasn't her first trip to the States, and she was used to the culture.

Madame Chiang had been aware of an American paradox that made her innately skeptical of how she was treated. In her experience, Americans could profess to be charmed with the romance of the Orient but still hold racist and condescending attitudes. Madame Chiang bristled at any implied racism or condescension because she was Chinese, and she insisted on top ceremonial protocol during her visit to the United States. Like Madame Nhu, Madame Chiang was not technically the wife of a titular head of state: Chiang Kai-shek was a man of many titles, but president of China was not one of them. Regardless, President and Mrs. Roosevelt greeted Madame Chiang personally when her train pulled into the station in Washington, DC. She rode with them in their car to the White House. Once there, the Roosevelts put her up in the Rose Room and had the bed made up with silk sheets for her sensitive skin. For the entirety of her stay, nearly every night for a month, the Roosevelts invited Madame Chiang to dine with them in the evening.[1]

In stark contrast, Madame Nhu was still getting the silent treatment from the Kennedy administration and the entire US government.

Madame Nhu arrived in Washington, DC, on October 15, 1963. She had been speaking to Princeton University students in New Jersey earlier in the day, and the day before that she had been in Cambridge, Massachusetts, at Harvard Law School and Radcliffe College. She was going to spend one more week on the East Coast, in and around the nation's capital, before flying to Chicago. It was a grueling schedule. Increased security had been procured; maybe the protests were predicted to be worse in Washington than they had been in New York. So Madame Nhu had a whole entourage trailing her through the District of Columbia and its environs. She rode with her daughter in the lead car, a long black limousine. Streets were cleared; traffic was held up;

even the motorcade of the president of the United States had to wait for her to pass. Hearing the self-congratulatory way Madame Nhu remembered it fifty years later, you would think she had been Moses parting the Red Sea.

Madame Nhu turned up on her parents' doorstep on Wednesday evening, the day after arriving in Washington. The Chuongs' new house was modest. After leaving the diplomatic pomp of the South Vietnamese embassy behind in August, the former ambassador and his wife had moved onto a tree-lined street in a residential corner of northwestern Washington. The solidly built brick house had two floors and only five rooms. It was a comfortable enough home, but for a couple with imperial bloodlines used to living life among servants and impeccable luxury, a middle-class American home must have seemed a huge step down.

It was not family nostalgia that brought Madame Nhu to their front door, although she knew that her father, during his otherwise dignified resignation speech, had choked up at the mention of his daughter. She was suspicious of her father's emotion. Chuong referred to her in public only as Madame Nhu. He told reporters that he simply "did not wish to know her." Indeed, he and his wife felt a call of duty to tell their point of view in order to "cover the stench" that their daughter was making. Former president Harry Truman, whose daughter was the exact same age as Madame Nhu, was said to have reached out to compliment Chuong on how superbly he was handling his tempestuous daughter.[2]

Chuong tried to belittle his daughter in her role as First Lady. She "has not the power she is supposed to have," he sniffed when asked about the inner workings of the Saigon government. In a CBS interview that aired on network television, he elaborated. His boss of nine years, President Ngo Dinh Diem, was just the front man. The real power in Vietnam belonged to his younger brother and Chuong's son-in-law, Nhu. Madame Nhu might have been infected with the same "power madness" as her husband, but she was "only a shadow."[3] Chuong was trying to make his daughter seem smaller, but he failed.

Instead he reconfirmed what the Americans had come to suspect and fear: that together the Nhus had enormous power over Diem. That made Madame Nhu more, not less, influential.

The insults still struck a nerve. When an Italian journalist asked Nhu about his father-in-law, Nhu spoke for himself and his wife. For once he let the mask slip, and his words expressed a retributive violence that seemed utterly alien to the discreet librarian he had once presented himself as. If Chuong tried to return to Saigon, Nhu said calmly, as if remarking on the weather, "I will have his head cut off. I will hang him in the center of a square and let him dangle there. My wife will make the knot on the rope because she is proud of being a Vietnamese and she is a good patriot."[4]

The house was dark when the limousine pulled up to the curb. Le Thuy rang her grandparents' doorbell while her mother waited slightly behind her. Madame Nhu stood with hands on hips, out of the immediate line of sight of anyone looking through the peephole. One fluttering pant leg could be seen through the side slit in her *ao dai,* her heeled foot tapping—with impatience and perhaps nerves. Madame Nhu played the role of the petulant daughter perfectly. Only two days before she had even sounded like one when she whined to the NBC reporters on *Meet the Press* about how her father had been against her since her childhood.

Exasperated with the waiting, Madame Nhu swept Le Thuy to the side and rapped her knuckles on the door herself. There was still no answer. Madame Nhu was keenly aware that the twenty reporters or more who had trailed her to the scene were watching her every move. Lightbulbs flashed against the white trim of the house, catching the humbled First Lady as she stood there. Now Madame Nhu was indignant at being ignored—and at being ignored in front of a crowd. She pushed her shoulders back and marched into the backyard. Poking holes in the lawn with the spikes of her heels, she made her way to the back entrance, where she darted up a few patio steps and peered in through the windows.

The rooms were dark and the walls inside still mostly bare. She might have noticed the borrowed chairs her parents were using or the uncarpeted living room. A photograph of the couple stood propped up on the mantle, and the only art was a delicate painting of Madame Chuong's hands on silk. Perhaps there were still boxes to unpack. When the Chuongs had left the embassy behind, they had surely taken more than this with them—like their collection of books and vases and Asian art. The family picture once on a prominent display in the embassy, the one that showed Madame Nhu as a small child clasping her parents' hands, was nowhere in sight. There was a small phonograph that Chuong had kept next to his desk at the embassy. He had used it frequently to play recordings of Shakespeare's plays. They were "full of wisdom," he said; Chuong liked to listen to centuries-old tales and absorb their insights into human behavior. The tragicomedy playing itself out in real time on his front lawn had all the urgency—and potential for destruction—of the final act of a Shakespearean drama.[5]

It was all the Washington newsmen could do to keep up with the First Lady as she stalked off her parents' property. Madame Nhu was upset. "I don't understand. I called and talked to someone here just moments ago." But the moment had passed, and now the Chuongs were not at home, or they had done an excellent job of pretending not to be. Madame Nhu and Le Thuy folded themselves into the back seat of the limousine, and the car took off. It sped through the quiet streets of the capital until it pulled up short in front of the Vietnamese embassy. When Madame Nhu made her way to the door and knocked, a figure dressed in white opened it almost immediately. "Chau!" Madame Nhu cried out. And then, according to the reporters who arrived just in time to witness the scene, Madame Nhu threw herself into the arms of the small man. Someone would later explain to the press that Chau had been the family cook for many years. He ushered Madame Nhu and Le Thuy inside the embassy, away from the prying press. The new South Vietnamese ambassador had told the Americans confidentially that he didn't care much for the First Lady, but he was smart enough to have laid on a pleasant dinner—his job, if not his life, would have been at risk otherwise. And since the newly arrived diplomat had kept Chau on staff after the Chuongs had left, the kitchen probably still had plenty of ingredients on hand to re-create some of the dishes Madame Nhu had loved as a girl—maybe the northern soup flavored with ox tail and anise or grilled pork meatballs wrapped in large lettuce leaves with mint and cilantro. Madame Nhu's last taste of home came not from her parents, who left her standing in the cold, but from the cook they had once employed. It was a bitter if familiar reminder, like her childhood all over again, when her parents had left her on her grandfather's estate and handed her care over to nurses.

When Madame Nhu was still in Europe before coming to America, her mother had summoned a close Kennedy aide to her new home for a "vital" meeting. When he arrived, she told him pointedly: get Kennedy to get rid of the Ngos. Diem was incompetent; her son-in-law, Nhu, was *un barbare.* As for her daughter, Madame Chuong said that she had advised people in the Vietnamese community in New York and Washington to run Madame Nhu "over with a car" when she arrived. If they couldn't do that, they should throw tomatoes and eggs. Looking over the edge of her teacup, she vowed to the Kennedy aide that if the White House wasn't going to do anything about silencing Madame Nhu, she, Madame Chuong, was quite capable of organizing "something against this monster."

That conversation was written up and classified "secret." An official with a sense of irony had scrawled along the side of the document "mother's love."[6]

Over Madame Nhu's next few days in Washington, she would go against the advice she had received from Marguerite Higgins, the reporter at the *New York Herald Tribune.* The First Lady went back to criticizing the American government, an attack calculated to disrupt and wound the Democratic administration, which she accused of being soft on communism. Certain unnamed liberals surrounding Kennedy, she said, were "not red yet, but pink."

Still, the crowds seemed sympathetic to Madame Nhu. Five hundred people packed into the National Press Club to see her on Friday, October 18. The audience interrupted her speech more than twenty times with applause—on average once every three minutes that Madame Nhu was on stage. In response, she purred and smiled graciously. She was overwhelmed, she said, by the goodwill of the American people. However, she continued a little sadly, she was also dismayed. The Kennedy administration had continued to give her the silent treatment. She understood, she said, that this was not a state visit. "But there are ways in which these things can be done." Madame Nhu adopted a "more in sorrow than in anger" tone and suggested the Kennedy administration could have handled the whole business, indeed its whole policy with respect to South Vietnam, a little better. She implied that the administration didn't really know what it was doing or with whom it was dealing. Her insinuations must have infuriated Kennedy. But, as so often, Madame Nhu wasn't wrong.

CHAPTER 15

Coup d'État

ALMOST A YEAR HAD PASSED SINCE Madame Nhu and I had given up on each other. When she started calling again in the summer of 2010, it was as if nothing had happened. I played right along, as she wholly expected, but my willingness came as a surprise to me. I found it funny how I had missed her and yet dreaded getting dragged back in.

Madame Nhu's voice was gravelly. For the first time, she sounded like the eighty-six-year-old woman she was. She had been sick, she said; she had undergone surgery on her feet and moved out of Paris. I had guessed that something had happened to her. When I called her about three months after she hung up on me, ready to apologize for upsetting her, I had gotten the standard international tone for a number no longer in service. First I worried that something terrible had happened. I scanned the obituaries daily, holding my breath and exhaling when I didn't see her name in boldface. I couldn't imagine that she would change her phone number only because of our disagreement. But I also couldn't imagine that she would have gone so long without calling me. So much for being her angel, and so much for those memoirs—or so I thought.

"My children," she said by way of explaining her silence, "they wanted me closer to them. I live in Rome now." She prattled off the news of the last few months, described her health troubles, and added, almost as an afterthought, that by the way the memoirs were done. She was ready to send them to me.

There were a few technical difficulties between that conversation and my receiving the memoirs in my e-mail inbox, something to do with her children and their full-time jobs and, I inferred, their depleting reserves of patience for their mother's memoir project. I couldn't rationally explain my own obsession with getting Madame Nhu's story, but by 2010, perhaps it was that I had spent so much time, nearly five years, hoping and waiting for them that it was a hard habit to break. I expected the memoirs to fulfill my curiosity about Madame Nhu. I would understand her, I would be able to put her in context, and I could put a neat check next to her name on my list of quirky fascinations, and maybe move on.

Instead, the two volumes that landed in my inbox baffled me. The title didn't help at all: *Le Caillou Blanc*, or *The White Pebble*. Later my mother made a bit more sense of it for me. In France, they say of a momentous event that its date is marked with a white pebble. But at first, scrolling through the pages was like reading something written in code. There were letters and numbers in parentheses, biblical references in bold headings, and italicized subheaders organized chronologically. It appeared Madame Nhu had made a grand catalog of her life, but it was a maze to be deciphered—yet another obstacle to obtaining Madame Nhu's grand narrative. It was much too foreign for me to make out, at least at first glance.

Thankfully, she sent pictures. I pored over them, wishing I could hear the characters speak. There was one of herself at eighteen, taken on the eve of her wedding, in the moment before everything changed. Studying a glossy portrait of her husband, I noticed for the first time that Nhu, the so-called Rasputin of Vietnam, had a slightly upturned button nose. Instead of looking cold and frightening, he was, well, cute.

The parts of Madame Nhu's writing that resembled a conventional memoir were thinly seeded throughout some two hundred pages, but the biographical nuggets were rewarding. This definitely wasn't the memoir she was said to have sold to the *Saturday Evening Post* in the days after the 1963 coup; nor was it the memoir that Madame Nhu was writing when she was too busy to give press interviews in the 1960s and 1970s for less than $1,000 a pop. I doubt these pages had ever existed anywhere as physical copy. If she had been writing them, she was writing them in her head. The two volumes e-mailed to me seemed to have been drafted recently, maybe even in the months since we had last spoken. I hadn't known many things.

Madame Nhu described herself at her desk writing. She wrote of falling and hitting her head. It was heartbreaking to read about her being so vulnerable and old. She talked of land disputes in Italy between her son Trac and their neighbors, who were trying to encroach on their property. But when she dipped back into the rich loam of her memory, she came up with sparkling details, like the rain in Dalat that was so heavy, it filled Le Thuy's backpack on her walk to school. Or her elegant *pousse,* with wheels so big that I easily imagined myself in her place, bouncing along the canals in Hue, feeling a bit like Cinderella on her way to the ball. Her writing style was not linear; at times it was barely coherent. But if you could hang on through the rapids, it was fascinating. I suggested to her that if she hoped for a wide readership, the manuscript would need a good bit of editing, but it would be a valuable addition to the historical record.

"No." Her voice was raspy and her breathing labored, but she came across the line taut as a steel cable and sliced cleanly through the patter of our otherwise pleasant morning chat. "I trust you completely with the memoirs. You are fully responsible. But there will be no editing. No changes are to be made. They are to be published as they are written. Volume number one, followed by number two. And," she added, "I am anxious to get this in print as soon as possible. I don't have long."

I was flummoxed. I had access to the inner thoughts of one of the world's most famous recluses. I was tantalizingly close but still trying to fit together the pieces of the puzzle. I felt like a character in an ancient Vietnamese fable who finds an enchanted treasure. Each time I got within reach of understanding Madame Nhu, she slipped away again, her elusiveness making her ever more the object of my attention.

The last time we talked, Madame Nhu sounded worse, her voice sandpaper in her throat. "There are days when I want to close my eyes and go in peace. But what wakes me up is only the feeling that there is something that I have to do, and something I have left to say." Madame Nhu's dying wish was to express herself. She was asking me to help her, but I no longer knew how.

Madame Nhu talked to her husband for the last time on October 27, 1963. They had spoken every few days while she was away, first in Europe and then in the United States. It had been a long trip. Madame Nhu and Le Thuy had left Saigon six weeks before, and now it was almost time to go home. They planned to fly from California to Vietnam with a stopover in Japan. Nhu was going to meet them in Tokyo to accompany them the rest of the way, and Madame Nhu was trying to finalize the itinerary over a tinny long-distance telephone call connecting her from San Francisco to Saigon.

There was a small cyst on her eyelid, she explained to Nhu. She wanted to get it taken care of, but she supposed it could wait a few more days until she got to Tokyo. "Would that be alright?" she asked him. If she did it in Japan, she reasoned, "it will be cheaper!" Madame Nhu was trying to lighten the mood. It could be hard to read a person over thousands of miles of transpacific cable, but Nhu's voice sounded small and strange to her.

"I'm not coming to Japan anymore. I am staying in Saigon."

Madame Nhu chose not to insist. She didn't want to get into a disagreement over the phone, so she bit her tongue. "Fine." She would get the surgery done before flying home. In Los Angeles, why not? Doctors there were used to working on beautiful, famous faces. She would stay ten more days.

After Washington, DC, Madame Nhu's stops had included cities and colleges in North Carolina, Illinois, and Texas. She had taken part in US Day on October 23 at Dallas Memorial Auditorium, where she had been called onto the stage and handed a bouquet of flowers.

US Day was a protest rally specifically organized to take place one day before the UN Day celebration of the US membership in the United Nations at the same location. Banners reading "Get the US out of the UN" and "Get the UN out of the US" were unfurled. The anti–United Nations gathering brought together ultraconservatives who opposed the Kennedy administration in Washington—members of the John Birch Society, the Minutemen, and the National Indignation Convention. A man named Lee Harvey Oswald was there. Madame Nhu's proximity to Oswald in Dallas on US Day, combined with the chain of tragic events about to unfold in Saigon, make Madame Nhu a main character in some of the wilder Kennedy assassination conspiracy theories.[1]

The accusations are baseless—death was far from Madame Nhu's mind in Texas. She was too busy enjoying her time as the VIP guest of billionaire oilman Dudley Dougherty at his sprawling ranch, San Domingo, just outside Beeville in southern Texas. He encouraged Madame Nhu to speak her mind freely to the press and gave her and her daughter a taste of Texas hospitality. Le Thuy especially seemed to enjoy it; on the ranch she changed out of the *ao dai* she had worn on the speaking tour into pants, kitten-heel boots, and a sweater, topping the Western outfit off with a cowboy hat. Le Thuy held a shotgun for the first time on the skeet range, downing clay pigeons with the twelve-gauge at an impressive rate of six out of ten. It wasn't beginner's luck—Le Thuy had plenty of machine-gun training from drilling with her mother's paramilitary organization in South Vietnam—but she still impressed her hosts and landed her first "real" boyfriend, Dougherty's twenty-four-year-old nephew, Bruce B. Baxter III, from Corpus Christi.

Young Baxter followed Le Thuy and her mother from Texas to California. His ardor was undeterred by California's governor Pat Brown, who made what *Time* magazine declared the "understatement of the month." Governor Brown said on the eve of their arrival, "Madame Nhu is a controversial figure. She is not the first to visit California, nor will she be the last. I urge all Californians to act like civilized Americans and let the lady have her say." Baxter, for one, acted like a gentleman. He invited the mother and daughter to dine out with him at a

Chinese restaurant in San Francisco, and when Baxter left, presumably to return to Texas for a few days, he couldn't stay away for long. He met up with Le Thuy again at her hotel in Los Angeles. The couple lounged around the Beverly Wilshire pool area before heading out on the town, spending two hours at Hollywood nightspots, but always in the company of their chaperones, two middle-aged men.[2]

Eight thousand miles away in Saigon, Ngo Dinh Nhu had bigger things to worry about than his daughter's first romance or the price of his wife's eye-cyst surgery. For all Madame Nhu's press attention and powerful new friends, things in Saigon had continued to worsen. Nhu had sounded so strange on the telephone with Madame Nhu because he knew by then that things were all but hopeless.

Nhu's attack on the pagodas in August had poisoned whatever goodwill remained in his relationship with the Americans. Before then, the general thinking in Washington was that the United States had simply been "insufficiently firm" in its dealings with Diem and Nhu in Saigon, but after the August raids and Nhu's flagrant disregard for the American directive to resolve tensions with the Buddhists, Washington's policy changed radically. The brothers were incorrigible, and they would have to be replaced.

On August 24, a top-secret cable sent to US Ambassador Henry Cabot Lodge in Saigon instructed him to confront Diem with uncomfortable and immediate demands: give the Buddhists what they want, and get rid of Nhu. If Diem didn't agree or act quickly, "we must face the possibility that Diem himself cannot be preserved." Lodge was given the green light to pursue alternative leaders. Although American leaders in Washington would not manage the tricky details of a regime change, the cable assured Lodge that "we will back you to the hilt on actions you take to achieve our objectives."[3]

Of course, a US ambassador couldn't exactly solicit regime change. That was Fred Flott's job. An American Foreign Service officer from the Midwest, Flott understood it was his task to do the dirty work the ambassador himself could not—to make contacts with opponents of the Diem regime and funnel American support to topple the government of a friendly nation.

The Ngo brothers might not have known the full extent of what was going on in the American embassy in Saigon, but they had a pretty good idea. Someone loyal to the Ngos had installed small eavesdropping devices in the embassy offices that went undetected until the Ngo affair was well over.[4] But even without the spying technology, the shift would have been obvious to Diem and Nhu. On September 2, 1963, President Kennedy said in a *CBS National News* interview with Walter Cronkite that the Ngo brothers' "government has gotten out of touch with the people" of South Vietnam. Kennedy continued, "Now all we can do is to make it very clear that we don't think this is the way to win," and he called for "changes in policy and personnel," a statement widely interpreted as a threat to Diem to get rid of Nhu.

Ambassador Lodge took a hard line with the brothers in the Saigon palace right from the start. Instead of courting Diem's favor and smoothing ruffled diplomatic feathers, the ambassador kept his distance. The American embassy staff displayed "unabated hostility" toward Diem and Nhu, and Lodge's manner was prickly and imperious. When a reporter asked Lodge why he had not visited the palace in weeks, he replied, "They have not done anything I asked. They know what I want. Why should I keep asking?"[5]

Instead of taking face-to-face meetings with Diem, Lodge leaked information to the American press that he would hold American aid dollars hostage if Diem didn't do what he was told, and Lodge became publicly critical of anyone in the American government who was too nice to the Ngo brothers. One of his targets was CIA Saigon station chief John Richardson. It had been Richardson's job to work with Nhu and get close to him in the hopes of influencing him. Because he failed to demonstrate any influence, however, Lodge regarded Richardson as a failure. In a private letter to Secretary of Defense Robert McNamara, Lodge deftly waged a passive-aggressive campaign to get Richardson fired, implying that without ever "meaning to be disloyal," he was too complicit with "those we are trying to replace." Richardson was a symbol of American support. His withdrawal in October 1963 was yet another signal to Diem and Nhu that their time was nearly up.[6]

The brothers couldn't vent their frustration with the Americans outright, so they seemed to take it out on the South Vietnamese people.

Martial law had been lifted, but every day Nhu's police arrested dozens of "dissidents." People caught distributing antigovernment pamphlets or writing anti-Ngo graffiti were taken into custody; even schoolchildren were detained in holding cells.

The brothers in Saigon couldn't know that enthusiasm for the coup in Washington was waxing and waning. The White House itself was in disarray over all the conflicting advice it was receiving. CIA director John A. McCone consistently voiced criticisms of a coup. To a meeting of a Special Group on Vietnam, McCone said that replacing Diem and Nhu with unknowns was "exceedingly dangerous" and would likely spell "absolute disaster" for the United States. He said privately to President Kennedy too that this coup "would be the first of others that would follow."[7] But the Departments of State and Defense, on the other hand, were adamantly behind a coup. The United States was divided but had already passed the point of no return. Ambassador Lodge was firm in his belief: "We are on a course from which there is no turning back."

President Kennedy himself still wasn't sure what to think about a coup against the brothers in Saigon. He dispatched a nine-day fact-finding mission headed by his secretary of defense, Robert McNamara, and the chairman of the Joint Chiefs of Staff, General Maxwell Taylor, in October 1963. The cover for the trip was to check on the progress of the war against the Viet Cong, and the men kept with protocol by meeting with President Diem at the palace for more than two hours. Not appearing on the official schedule, however, was a game of tennis with Major General Duong Van Minh.

General Minh was known as Big Minh for two reasons: to distinguish him from another general of the same name and also because of his unusual size—he was close to six feet tall and two hundred pounds. Minh towered over his Vietnamese colleagues and literally looked down on the Ngo brothers, his bosses. A graduate of the École Militaire in Paris and a veteran of the First Indochina War who had fought alongside the French against the Viet Minh, he had backed Diem and fought against the sects and gangsters who threatened the early years of the Diem presidency. Now Minh was plotting against Diem and Nhu. In reporter Stanley Karnow's opinion, he was not the main conspirator, "but as the senior general, he was the man who crystalized the various factions who were all plotting against Diem."

Despite Minh's enormous frame, he played elegant tennis. The American officials, McNamara and Taylor, barely kept up in the crushing Saigon heat, but they managed to sweat out a good game of doubles on the grass courts of the Cercle Sportif. Then the group retired to a mahogany-paneled room in the club for a casual chat "about the game." On hearing about the match and private conversation, Nhu and Diem could only infer that the men had talked intrigue too. In fact, they hadn't. Minh was too scared of leaks that day. But Diem and Nhu were well aware of his links to plotters and the American embassy and the CIA.[8]

In Nhu's desperation he had tried other tactics, like leaking reports that he was in talks with the Communist government of North Vietnam. In late August 1963, Nhu met with Polish diplomat Mieczyslaw Maneli. A secret meeting with a Communist representative provoked the United States to try to understand: if Nhu really was ready to cut a deal with the north and come to a negotiated peace, would that justify taking urgent action to install a new regime, or would it force the United States to ease up on Diem and Nhu? Records show that in the meeting, Nhu talked about "paving the way for trade exchanges with the North," and he discussed his anger at the Americans but said he did not want to cut ties entirely with the United States. There is no record that the talks initiated with North Vietnam were more than preliminary. There simply wasn't time.[9]

By the last day of October, Diem and Nhu were down to their last tactic to try to keep the regime afloat. It was trademark Nhu, a smoke-and-mirrors scheme: he and Diem would fake their own coup. It was risky, but it was their only hope. A false coup was supposed to scare the Americans into renewing support for the Diem regime. Carefully selected phony coup leaders would pretend to be "neutralists," in the vein of the surprise 1960 neutralist coup in Laos that had severely damaged US interests in Southeast Asia. Losing South Vietnam to neutralists would be another domino down—a devastating blow to the American Cold War strategy.

To a casual observer, October 31, 1963, seemed like just another day in Saigon. That morning, President Diem chatted easily in his office with US Ambassador Henry Cabot Lodge and Commander in Chief, US Pacific Command Admiral Harry Felt. Felt was passing through Saigon on what looked like a routine inspection of American military assistance to South Vietnam, but in fact the South Vietnamese army generals plotting against Diem had orchestrated his presence, specifically timing Felt's visit to keep Diem in the palace all morning.[10] The South Vietnamese president warned his visitors that they might hear rumors of a coup and should pay no attention to them. At noon, shutters were lowered over storefronts. Motorbikes, pedicabs, and Renault taxis ferried people home, out of the midday heat for two hours of lunch and rest. The city was calm.

The palace was quiet too. The Nhus' younger children had left for Dalat. They were on school vacation, and the boys had begged their father to let them go hunting. He must have been glad that his sons were following his own passion for the sport. He let them go but made sure that fifteen members of the presidential guard accompanied them. His youngest child, four-year-old daughter Le Quyen, couldn't hunt, but she would go to the mountains with her brothers and her nurse. She could run more freely around the grounds there than she was ever allowed to do in the garden of the palace. Nhu couldn't have known it, but he had saved their lives by allowing them to leave Saigon.

At a little after 4 p.m. a crash of artillery fire broke out. The gunfire sounded like it was near the presidential guard barracks. Shooting so close to the palace had definitely not been part of the plan. Until that moment, the brothers had appraised the slow buildup of troops and tanks inside Saigon's city limits calmly. They had taken note of the developments in the city from the remove of their offices. Instead of raising warning flags, the movement of troops and armor had reassured Diem and Nhu. They believed their plan, code-named Bravo Two, was off to a good start. Just before the police headquarters fell into the generals' hands, a frightened police official had telephoned Nhu to tell him that they were under attack.

"It's alright," Nhu said. "I know all about it."[11]

Nhu was unruffled because he still thought that, according to plan, his forces would quash the "insurrection," leaving him and Diem hailed as heroes. In the ensuing confusion, Nhu also intended to conduct a very personalized bloodbath. Special forces and Nhu's hired gangsters would murder disloyal ARVN generals and senior officers. Troublesome Americans had been marked as well; reporter Stanley Karnow would learn that Ambassador Lodge and veteran CIA agent Lucien Conein were on the list of targets.

This wasn't the first fake coup scheme that Nhu had planned. The first, code-named Bravo One, had been shelved in October after Nhu's special forces caught wind of a brewing insurrection among the military ranks. Bravo Two, the countercoup supposedly now under way, involved almost cartoonish levels of deception: it was to be a coup inside a coup.[17]

But it soon became clear to the brothers that something had gone wrong. They gathered around the transmitter in the president's office. It remained quiet. They called the surrounding provincial chiefs, all military men. They called corps commanders and division commanders too. No one stirred. By the time Nhu realized what was really happening, it was too late. There was no way out of the city and no one to trust. The traitors had encircled the palace, forming a tightening noose. Nhu grabbed the mouthpiece. "Take up your arms." He barked the order out to the brothers' last remaining hope, the boys of the Republican Youth and his wife's paramilitary Women's Corps.

Their silence was a death sentence.

Diem and Nhu's plans had been hijacked. The man they had entrusted to carry out the phony coup, General Ton That Dinh, had turned on them. The youngest general in the South Vietnamese army, Dinh was described by those who knew him as a loud, whiskey-drinking paratrooper. Dinh made up for any lack of intelligence with sheer ambition, and he didn't travel anywhere without a personal photographer. His attempts to ingratiate himself with the Ngo regime had included converting to Catholicism and joining Nhu's obscure political party. Dinh's tactics worked, to a point. President Diem treated him like an adopted son. But Dinh's vanity made him easy prey for Diem's opponents. The conspirators convinced General Dinh that he belonged in the president's cabinet. When Diem refused him the position, Dinh's damaged pride made him ripe for the picking.[13]

Los Angeles was fifteen hours behind Saigon, and the First Lady was recovering in her suite at the Beverly Wilshire. She'd had the cyst removed from her eye hours earlier, and her dark glasses and gauze bandage were awkward. Thankfully, Le Thuy was there to help her, read to her, and keep her company.

Madame Nhu and Le Thuy were awakened in the night by a frantic telephone call from the attaché at the Vietnamese embassy. In a panic, he described the unfolding crisis in Saigon. He said roadblocks were being thrown across avenues leading from the city to the airport. Insurgent marine troops wearing red kerchiefs were arriving by the truckload in the heart of the city. Events were unfolding with great precision. This was it. The radio station, the post office, and the central police headquarters were all occupied, as were the Ministries of Interior and Defense.

Madame Nhu listened helplessly to the details of the unfolding crisis thousands of miles away. She writes, "If only I had been there," again and again in her memoir. She tells herself that she would have prevented the regime from falling, like she had in 1955, 1960, and again in 1962. She believed her absence this time had fatally weakened the Ngo regime. Of course, a rational person would say that there was no way she would have survived, and there is little reason to think that if Madame Nhu had been in Saigon, she could have done anything to prevent what happened. But rationally, she should never have survived crossing that bridge back in 1946.

The worst part was that she could not get hold of the children. Trac was fifteen, Quynh eleven, and little Le Quyen only four. The story they would later tell their mother was harrowing. When the coup started, they were still in Dalat. Up there, surrounded by army men, they no longer knew whom to trust. The children fled into the woods behind the house and spent the night in the cold rain. They walked all the next day to a mountain village where they were able to beg a bit of rice and ground meat. Then they waited.

The Ngo brothers fled to Cholon, the Chinese part of Saigon. Some said they used a tunnel in the basement of the palace to make their daring escape. Others say a black Citroen pulled up in front of the palace gates, and the two brothers, both wearing dark grey suits, simply walked out and climbed in. Either way, they were fugitives. It would be hours before the coup forces realized they were fighting for an empty palace. By then the brothers were hiding in the house of a merchant named Ma Tuyen.

Before dawn on November 1, 1963, the final siege on the palace began. Marching formations of South Vietnamese army rangers filed in behind a column of tanks. They pointed their barrels at the palace walls and began to fire. It didn't take long before the assault at point-blank range carved a jagged hole. American journalists Ray Herndon and David Halberstam claimed to have been the third and fourth people to enter the palace, right behind the first two Vietnamese lieutenants who scrambled through the hole in the wall. A white flag finally went up from the first floor window on the southwest corner of the palace, signaling to the other soldiers and cowering civilians that it was over. It was time to loot the palace.

A rush of people charged across the grounds and up the stairs. The silk drapes hung in tatters, and the palace's ornate mirrors and lamps, fixtures dating from the French colonial era, lay shattered on the floor. The rangers, army boys, and journalists poked through the rubble. They found Nhu's whiskey and, lying on his desk, the aptly titled book he had not gotten a chance to finish: *Shoot to Kill,* by Richard Miers, a memoir about his success fighting the Communists in Malaya. And while it turned out that Diem's reading tastes ran to adventure tales about the American West, the first eager boys pawing at Madame Nhu's silk negligees overlooked the brown-covered book in her drawers. Her diary was eventually found, discreetly slipped into a waistband, and kept for decades as an heirloom and souvenir.

At the palace that day, Fred Flott, the Foreign Service officer from the embassy, saw firsthand the fruits of his labors to overthrow the government: "the body of the first man I ever saw who was shot in the head with the M-16 rifle . . . it looked just like a tomato that somebody had stepped on. He was being hauled downstairs at the time. And there were soldiers doing a bit of looting, but there was also some semblance of discipline." Flott himself pocketed a few ashtrays from the palace as souvenirs and nodded a greeting to David Halberstam when they passed each other on the stairs. The embassy worker would remember that the journalist's hands had been filled with a ten-foot elephant tusk. Halberstam would admit instead to having taken a Laotian sword, probably from Nhu's collection.

The decorative sword wouldn't have done Nhu any good at that point. The brothers knew they were finished, so they didn't try to hide much longer. They moved from Ma Tuyen's house to another location in Cholon, the yellow and white stucco St. Francis Xavier Church. Diem called the army headquarters and asked to be put in touch with the generals to arrange his surrender. Troops began pulling up shortly after. The officers walked up to the front of the church and saluted the man who had been their president for nine years. Then they led him and his brother out and shoved them into the back of a small, tarpaulin-sided truck. Later, no one can say when, the brothers were transferred to an armored car. They would not come out of it alive.[14]

Saigon was in chaos. Camouflage-wearing rebels fired their rifles into the air in celebration. Mobs tore through anything associated with the Ngo regime. The offices of the *Times of Vietnam* were burned; the Catholic bookstore of Archbishop Thuc was smashed. And a determined crowd marched down to the waterfront. A forceful crowd pulled the statue of the Trung sisters, the one cast to look so much like Madame Nhu, from its pedestal using a few dozen meters of rope. One of the heads was broken off and rolled through the streets—like that of an ogress fallen victim to the guillotine.

Madame Nhu was stuck in the quiet luxury of the Beverly Wilshire, with its carpeted rooms and thick draperies and California sunshine, but she was desperate to get her children out of South Vietnam. She called Marguerite Higgins, the reporter she had met in Saigon and who had become a friend. A sobbing Madame Nhu asked, "Do you really believe they [Diem and Nhu] are dead? Are they going to kill my children too?" Higgins offered to help by calling on her connections at the State Department in Washington.

"Hurry," Madame Nhu had implored. "Please hurry."

Higgins called Roger Hilsman, Kennedy's close advisor and the assistant secretary of state for Far Eastern affairs, at 2 o'clock in the morning.

"Congratulations, Roger," she greeted him. "How does it feel to have blood on your hands?"

"Oh, come on now, Maggie," Hilsman replied. "Revolutions are rough. People get hurt." But Higgins's voice on the phone in the middle of the night asking about the Ngo children must have been a startling reminder of the power of the press. Hilsman's initial reaction quickly turned when he realized that the United States couldn't stand by and let something bad happen to children, no matter who their parents were. The proper and chivalrous thing to do would be to get the kids out of the country as quickly as possible. Hilsman assured her that President Kennedy would do anything he could to safeguard the children and promised to get them to a safe place.[15] Within three days, the children were out of harm's way in Rome.

The Americans were happy to help. They recognized that the deaths of the Ngo children in the coup would reflect horribly on the new regime the Americans would now have to work with. Things were off to a bad start as it was. The official story, that the Ngo brothers had committed suicide, was blown when two leaked photographs showed Diem shot through the head and Nhu's body filleted with a bayonet more than twenty times. One picture showed both bodies lying in a pool of blood on the floor of an armored car, their hands tied behind their backs. The other picture showed Diem's bloody corpse on a stretcher with a smiling soldier looking into the camera. The officer said to be responsible for the deaths of the Ngo brothers, Captain Nguyen Van Nhung, was found strangled at general staff headquarters three months later. His murder was never solved.

The Pentagon Papers, the US government's history of its political and military involvement in Vietnam, concluded about the 1963 coup, "As the nine-year rule of Diem came to a bloody end, our complicity in his overthrow heightened our responsibilities and our commitment in an essentially leaderless Vietnam." The generals behind the coup began to make arrangements for a civilian government. General Big Minh became president, and after delaying for what was deemed an appropriate period, the US government recognized the new government of South Vietnam on November 8.[16]

The South Vietnamese and American satisfaction in having found an alternative to Diem and Nhu was short-lived. Another general overthrew Minh's government only two months later in January 1964. In quick succession, seven more governments in South Vietnam would rise and fall. Exacerbating the political mess, the Viet Cong had organized into an efficient army, and the military balance began to tilt into their favor—although it would be a long time before the United States officially recognized it.

Fred Flott, the ashtray-stealing Foreign Service officer and unofficial liaison between the American embassy and the South Vietnamese coup plotters, was chosen as the official US government representative to accompany the Ngo children. Trac, Quynh, and Le Quyen had been cleaned up after their ordeal hiding in the jungle of Dalat. Their mother's friend, Nguyen Khanh, the swaggering, goateed general she had so distrusted during the coup attempt in 1960, brought the three children to Saigon on his private plane. He had nothing to fear from the new military junta, which knew he was safely on their side, so he could afford to do the children a favor.[17] The Americans took over from there, putting the children on a private US military C-54 aircraft to Thailand. Then Flott accompanied his three charges to Italy. They sat in first class on a flight Pan Am called the "milk run," stopping in Rangoon, Calcutta, Delhi, and Karachi, before finally landing in Rome. Flott sat next to fifteen-year-old Trac for the long trip.

> I really had a lot of respect for [him], because he rose to the occasion very well. He wasn't crying, sort of an Asian outward passivity or composure on the thing [the coup]. . . . And the kid read the account of the condition in which his father and his uncle had been found in the back of this armored personnel carrier, with their heads squashed by rifle butts, and all kinds of bayonet wounds in them and everything else, all

> cut up, and their heads squashed. And he was reading this with complete calm. He read English quite well, although we talked in French. But he didn't understand the word "squashed," so he said to me in French, "What's the word for squashed?" I said, "Ecrabouille." I said, "It means squashed, but you don't want to pay too much attention to the details, because the reporters probably didn't even see it, and it's the way they write their things." And he took it very calmly, went on and talked and eventually I got them to Rome.

Their uncle, Archbishop Thuc, was waiting for the children in Rome. Madame Nhu was still in Los Angeles. Flott recalled the handoff of the Ngo children to Thuc with bitterness:

> Archbishop Thuc met us there, at planeside. He was very hostile, because he knew I was sent by [Ambassador] Cabot Lodge to accompany the children. There were about 150 Italian newsmen there and other press people. I went up to the Archbishop to pay my respects, pay my condolences, and tell him I'd been asked by Ambassador Lodge to deliver the children to him, so they could rejoin their mother, so their mother could rejoin them. He wouldn't speak to me, wouldn't shake hands, nothing. Total distance, total ice treatment. Packed them into the car, not a word of thanks, nothing. . . . We had protected these kids from all possible trauma; there had been no scene, nobody came up and talked to them during the whole trip. But not a word of thanks to Lodge, to me, to Pan Am, or anybody. Archbishop Thuc packed them into a big limousine he had and tore off.[18]

It's hard to believe Flott felt entitled to any thanks from the Ngo family. After all, he had helped orchestrate their overthrow. Entire books have explored the extent to which the United States was directly responsible for the 1963 coup in South Vietnam and, by extension, the murder of the Ngo brothers. Few people have put it more succinctly than President Lyndon Johnson, when he grumbled during a February 1, 1966, telephone conversation with Senator Eugene McCarthy, "We killed him [Diem]. We all got together and got a goddamn bunch of thugs and we went in and assassinated him. Now, we've really had no political stability since then." Did the fall of the Ngo regime really make the war much worse than it ever would have been if Diem had stayed in power? Former CIA director William Colby thought so. He said, "The overthrow of Diem was the worst mistake we made." If the United States had sustained support for Diem, and if he had not been killed, Colby believed, the Americans "could have avoided most of the rest of the war, which is a hell of a note."[19]

Clearly, the Americans were involved in the Saigon coup. Some in the government were more for it, some more against, but everyone can agree that there was, at minimum, an implication that the United States, from President Kennedy on down, would support a coup against Diem. Because of that, America has had to bear the responsibility for it.

By all accounts, President Kennedy was profoundly disturbed by the Ngo brothers' deaths. In the cabinet room of the White House, General Maxwell Taylor recalled that "Kennedy leaped to his feet and rushed from the room with a look of shock and dismay on his face which I had never seen before." CIA man Colby confirmed the reaction, saying the president had "blanched and walked out of the room to compose himself."[20] But others wondered how the president could possibly be surprised. Had he really failed to comprehend that a coup would have enormous implications?

As Kennedy's friend Red Fay would recall, the president didn't just blame himself for the deaths of Diem and Nhu. He blamed Madame Nhu. "That goddamn bitch. She's responsible for the death of that kind man [Diem]. You know, it's so totally unnecessary to have that kind man die because that bitch stuck her nose in and boiled up the whole situation down there."[21]

On the day after the coup, President Kennedy dictated a memo for his records. He called Diem's and Nhu's deaths "particularly abhorrent" and accepted responsibility for having "encouraged Lodge along a course to which he was in any case inclined." His presidential thoughts on the Saigon assassinations were then interrupted by three-year-old John Jr. and six-year-old Caroline, who came squealing into the office for a moment with their daddy. Behind the crinkling of the tapes, you can hear little voices saying, "Hello," into Kennedy's Dictaphone. Just a moment later their father asked the children all about the changing of the seasons: "Why are leaves green? How is snow on the ground?" The exchange is all the more touching when you remember that these children would never see the change of seasons with their father again. Kennedy would be assassinated just three weeks later.[22]

CHAPTER 16

In Exile

MADAME NHU AND HER DAUGHTER lingered in California through the terrible, early days after the coup. The three other children had already arrived in Rome, but Madame Nhu just couldn't bring herself to follow them yet. She couldn't accept the news coming out of South Vietnam: that Diem and Nhu were dead and that the military had taken control of the government. Madame Nhu kept hoping for some sign that her husband and his brother had survived. A faked death could have been a page in another of her husband's ingenious schemes. The photos of the slumped, dead bodies left Madame Nhu unconvinced. The corpses were too badly mangled to identify. She would take three more years to fully accept their deaths and to accept that she would never be the First Lady of South Vietnam again. In the days after the coup, Madame Nhu relied on anger and indignation to keep her going.

On November 5, four days after the coup, she held a press conference in a room off the lobby of the Beverly Wilshire Hotel. Madame Nhu wore dark sunglasses, a simple pearl necklace, and a shimmering *ao dai,* captured in a poem by Laurence Goldstein as "the color of moonlight."

Her voice caught as Madame Nhu tried to read from her prepared statement. "Whoever has the Americans as allies does not need any enemies." She accused the United States of bearing responsibility for the coup and, clenching a tissue, composed herself enough to issue an eerie prediction. "I can predict to you all that the story in Vietnam is only at its beginning."

Her father, Tran Van Chuong, who had refused to see her at any other point on her monthlong tour of the United States, climbed a back staircase to Madame Nhu's hotel suite on the eighth floor. Father and daughter were reunited in private, and afterwards Chuong told the press that there was "no need for a reconciliation"; they had set aside their differences in light of the tragedy. Madame Nhu told Clare Booth Luce a quite different, and far more believable, version. Her father had come to visit her, she said, because he wanted to go back to Vietnam and join the new government, but obviously he could not do so without his daughter's blessing. Not even Chuong could talk his way out of that kind of political scandal. He couldn't just join forces with the people who had killed his son-in-law without some kind of explanation or Madame Nhu's help. He came to her hotel room at the Beverly Wilshire to ask if he could he tell the public that his widowed daughter had forgiven him.

But Madame Nhu would do no such thing. She wouldn't forgive him for quitting on the regime in August, and she wouldn't forgive him for not receiving her and Le Thuy on his doorstep. She would never, ever forgive him or her mother for having made her childhood as the invisible middle daughter so miserable.

Presumably, Madame Nhu knew that Chuong and his wife had been undermining the Diem government for years, but she might not have known all the details. Wesley Fishel, head of the Michigan State University Vietnam Advisory Group and contracted to consult for the Diem regime, became a close friend of Diem's during the early years of his presidency. His group advised on everything from public administration and personnel to economics and trade decisions, and many of its proposals shaped how the Diem administration ran. But

Diem didn't seem to have registered much of a response to Fishel's frank letter in 1960, a warning about Chuong's obvious "ambitions for higher office." Fishel told Diem that Chuong had "virtually succeeded in destroying the organization of your friends in America" from the moment he arrived in Washington as ambassador.[1] No one can answer why Diem kept Chuong in place, but at least after the coup Madame Nhu could take some small solace in the fact that her parents would not benefit from their betrayal. The coup her parents had helped lay the groundwork for would condemn them to a life in exile.

Madame Nhu couldn't have known that their lives would end in murder just twenty-three years later. She couldn't have known that the prized son they had cast her aside for would be their killer. The Shakespearean plays that Chuong had enjoyed listening to so much during his life, tales of madness, betrayal, family tragedy, and revenge, were in retrospect tales that foreshadowed his fate.

Quite suddenly, Madame Nhu found herself with practical concerns—like money. Her room at the hotel was $98 a night. A source close to Madame Nhu revealed to the *New York Times* that she had arrived in the United States with $5,000 in cash for what was supposed to be a three-week tour. The source also whispered that her wealth in South Vietnam had been greatly overestimated—all the funds had gone into the coffers of her husband's political party. There were no savings and few overseas holdings. "Money is definitely a worry," the associate confided to the *New York Times*. While sorting out what to do after the coup, Madame Nhu continued to rack up debts—and she no longer had a government to send the bill to. Allen Chase, a financier with a home at the end of a long, winding private drive in the Los Angeles Bel Air neighborhood, invited her to check out of the hotel and become his houseguest. Chase and his wife let Madame Nhu move into their bedroom while they themselves moved into a guest room.

James McFadden, publisher of the conservative magazine *National Review,* had been one of the few visitors to Madame Nhu, and the newspapers reported that she had been in negotiations with book publishers and, it being Los Angeles, movie people about selling her story.

But Madame Nhu's highest value might be realized if she stayed in the United States long enough to exert an influence on the upcoming election year. In a telephone conversation, Clare Booth Luce and Richard Nixon shared the sentiment that Madame Nhu had real potential to damage President Kennedy. Luce told Nixon that she was convinced "Jack Kennedy wants a negotiated peace!" and once Americans found out about his real intentions, a neutral South Vietnam, he would be unelectable. Madame Nhu, the grieving widow, was "still a figure in the puzzle."

But Madame Nhu had no real choice in the end. She had no money, and her Republican friends couldn't support her forever. She left half of her $1,000 bill at the Beverly Wilshire unpaid, and left the United States for Rome to be reunited with her three other children. Before leaving, Madame Nhu read a long farewell statement at the airport. "Judas has sold the Christ for 30 pieces of silver. The Ngo brothers have been sold for a few dollars."

While Madame Nhu blamed the United States for the coup in Saigon, others were blaming her. President John F. Kennedy wasn't the only one who faulted Madame Nhu for the coup in Saigon. United States Information Agency officer Everett Bumgardner called Madame Nhu the "friction point" between the Americans and the regime. She instituted "almost everything that I think went wrong with the Diem government that eventually led to his downfall."[2] Vietnam historian Joseph Buttinger is no kinder in his two-volume history on the Vietnam War: he describes Madame Nhu as the rock around the neck of a drowning man.[3]

But in the end, Madame Nhu was right about a lot of things that she never got credit for. She was right that the millions of dollars pouring into South Vietnam were hurting as much as helping in the war against communism. The "Americanization" of South Vietnam turned many nationalists toward the Communists, who warned that capitalism merely disguised American colonial intent. Madame Nhu had said that the Americans were conspiring against the regime, and indeed, from the ambassador in Saigon to the president in the White House, they were. As for the Communists "intoxicating" the Buddhists, they did have some influence in the Pagodas. Communist sources after the war revealed that their agents had indeed infiltrated the Buddhists and they could well have had a part in inspiring the uprising in the summer of 1963. By getting rid of Diem, the Americans, it seemed, had played right into the Communists' hands.

Madame Nhu also accused the press of being "intoxicated" by communism. There was the case of Pham Xuan An, who worked for *Time Magazine* and did circulate widely among prominent journalists who regarded him as a knowledgeable analyst. After the war, An was named a Hero of the People's Armed Forces by the Hanoi government, awarded four military-exploit medals and elevated to the rank of brigadier general in the North Vietnamese army. But whatever access An had to the reporters over the years, their expert views undoubtedly reflected what, they, themselves saw there. Nonetheless, it was a shock to learn that for all those years of contacts with American journalists, An had been a North Vietnamese agent.

Madame Nhu's parting words at the press conference at the Beverly Wilshire—"I can predict to you all that the story in Vietnam is only at its beginning"—also came true. US President John F. Kennedy wanted to get out of Vietnam. A trail of documents shows that he intended to reverse the American military commitment to South Vietnam. Scholars think that Kennedy might have promoted the coup against Diem and Nhu in a miscalculated effort to advance that withdrawal, but of course they can only speculate as Kennedy was assassinated three weeks after the Ngo brothers. Because of his early death, Kennedy escaped ultimate responsibility for Vietnam.

On November 24, 1963, Madame Nhu sent a condolence letter from Rome to Jacqueline Kennedy, writing of her "profound sympathy for you and your little ones." But she couldn't help but inject in a barbed reminder of the grief she was suffering herself. "The wounds inflicted on President Kennedy were identical to those of President Ngo Dinh Diem, and of my husband, and [came] only 20 days after the Vietnamese tragedy." Madame Nhu suggested that she was somehow stronger or better equipped to deal with tragedy than Mrs. Kennedy when she wrote, "I sympathize the more for I understand that that ordeal might seem to you even more unbearable because of your habitually well-sheltered life." In other words, now you see how it feels.

Soon after taking the oath of office aboard Air Force One in November 1963, the new American president, Lyndon Johnson, oversaw the escalation of the war in Vietnam. He would not, he said, "be the president who saw Southeast Asia go the way China went"; nor would he let the United States lose to North Vietnam, "some raggedy-ass, fourth-rate country." In the year that followed, Johnson authorized support for raids against North Vietnam, increased the troop levels from 12,000 Americans to 75,000, and used the reported attacks on an American vessel in the Gulf of Tonkin as justification for presidential war making. Things only got worse from there. US combat units were deployed in 1965, and the war in Vietnam turned into a proxy war between the United States and the Reds; China and the Soviet Union had also begun sending troops to help North Vietnam. By 1969, more than 500,000 US military personnel were stationed in Vietnam, but they still couldn't save the country from communism. The United States withdrew its forces in 1973, and on April 30, 1975, the Communist tanks rolled into Saigon. Vietnam was finally unified, but at devastating human cost. As many as 2 million Vietnamese civilians died, as did 1.1 million North Vietnamese and Communist South Vietnamese fighters and close to 250,000 South Vietnamese soldiers; in 1982 the Vietnam Veterans Memorial in Washington, DC, was inscribed with the names of more than 58,200 members of the American Armed Forces who died or are listed as missing as a result of the war. The sobering lessons of Vietnam still haunt American policy in Iraq and Afghanistan.

As the war in Vietnam exploded and the world focused on Tonkin, then Tet and My Lai and the Christmas Bombings, Madame Nhu faded into the background. Her life got stranger and sadder still. She had been given, anonymously after the coup, an apartment in Paris. Madame Nhu hadn't questioned the gift; after all, she figured the Americans owed her more than an apartment, and she was too busy fighting off extradition attempts. The new government in South Vietnam was petitioning the French government to abide by a 1954 judiciary convention agreement that provides for the extradition of alleged criminals, and the junta leaders had already issued a warrant for her arrest. They wanted Madame Nhu to stand trial in Saigon for "damaging the national economy" and "violating foreign exchange regulations." If the French sent her back to South Vietnam, she could all too easily guess what would happen next. Her brother-in-law, Ngo Dinh Can, had remained in Vietnam after the coup. Can had turned himself in to the American consul in Hue, where he had hoped to receive some protection. But the Americans turned Can over to the military junta, which convicted him of running the Diem regime's Hue operations. Can was imprisoned at Chi Hoa Prison in Saigon for months before being dragged into a courtyard and placed in front of a firing squad. Can was so ill from untreated diabetes that he had to be propped up to be shot.

Renting out the brand-new four-room apartment, light filled and facing the Eiffel Tower, was Madame Nhu's only potential income—and it would get her out of France before the new government made up its mind about whether to extradite her or not. The Americans were advising the French to go along with the new government in South Vietnam. Desperate to leave, Madame Nhu accepted the first offer she got, well below the 3,000 francs a month she was hoping for but enough to cover basic expenses. She moved to a patch of arid land on the outskirts of Rome, a property that her husband had bought in the hope of one day building a kind of Catholic retreat for government workers in the Diem government.

The oldest Ngo brother, Archbishop Thuc, helped Madame Nhu secure tenancy on the Roman land before moving on to his next church assignment: a parish in the South of France. In 1981, Thuc went rogue. He splintered from the mainstream Catholics and began consecrating bishops without the approval of the Holy See. Thuc was involved in a plot to appoint bishops to a council in Mexico, where they would appoint a new pope to overthrow the one in the Vatican. Needless to say, that didn't go over well with the church. Thuc died, penniless and in obscurity, at eighty-seven years old in 1984 at a monastery in Carthage, Missouri.

Things hadn't gone well for Madame Nhu either. On April 12, 1967, her beloved daughter, Le Thuy, died in a car crash outside of Longjumeau, France. She was only twenty-two years old. Madame Nhu always believed that her daughter was murdered. Le Thuy had been working toward her law degree. Imbued with passion and a sense of vengeance, Le Thuy had written in her diary that she would kill those who had hurt her country and killed her father. When Madame Nhu talked to me about her suspicions surrounding Le Thuy's death, I found her logic hard to follow, but she mentioned that four trucks had converged on Le Thuy's car on a twisty country road, an event so improbable that, in Madame Nhu's mind, it had to have been planned. The most damning evidence of Le Thuy's murder, and a conspiracy to cover it up, was that Madame Nhu's own lawyer afterward asked for her forgiveness; if he had done his best, Madame Nhu reasoned, he wouldn't have needed it. Her conclusions about Le Thuy's death were outrageous—and yet understandable. Of course Madame Nhu thought of her daughter's death as one more episode in the cloak-and-dagger drama that had ruined her life.

Luckily, to Madame Nhu's mind, her three remaining children had no interest in reliving history. Trac, Quynh, and Le Quyen were trying to make their lives over as European citizens. They attended prestigious schools, and two of them got jobs with international organizations: Quynh worked for a major American manufacturing corporation in Brussels, and Le Quyen worked for the Italian aid organization Caritas on refugee and migration issues. It seemed that after the Saigon coup and the assassinations of their father and uncle in 1963, the death of their sister in 1967, and the murder of their grandparents by their uncle in 1986, the three remaining Ngo children might be able to move beyond their terrible legacy. But on April 16, 2012, Madame Nhu's youngest daughter, Le Quyen, was killed on a Roman highway when her scooter collided with a bus. The Italian news channel Roma Uno uploaded a video to YouTube of the accident scene, rivulets of blood still seeping from under a white sheet on the road. It was viewed over 50,000 times in the weeks and months after her death. I can't help but draw parallels to the infamous Kennedy Curse: the Kennedys are the only other high-profile family I can think of whose members seem to suffer disproportionately tragic fates.

Madame Nhu was spared the anguish of burying another child. She had died nearly a year before, on Easter Sunday, April 24, 2011. She was eighty-six years old and passed away peacefully, her son assured me, taking comfort in the fact that she was going to be reunited with her husband and daughter in heaven.

For perhaps the last time in her own right, Madame Nhu made headlines around the world. Pictures of her from half a century earlier ran alongside her obituary; from there, they were uploaded to blogs and assembled into grainy video montages. The death of the so-called Dragon Lady of South Vietnam made the front page of the *New York Times*. She was "liked" on Facebook, tweeted, and "tumblred." Svelte and sinister and scheming—all the old clichés came roaring back. The media lingered on Madame Nhu's almost cartoonish Dragon Lady character for about a week—a pretty grand finale for someone who had been living in obscurity for the last forty-eight years. But Madame Nhu's resurgence couldn't last. The spectacular capture and death of Osama bin Laden turned attention away from what had happened in Vietnam in 1963 and back to America's contemporary wars.

It felt very lonely being back in the corner of my apartment that I called my office. I thought of Madame Nhu every time the landline rang. I had to remind myself not to scramble for the pad and pencil—it wouldn't be her. Tacked to the wall were dozens of pictures of Madame Nhu. I just couldn't bring myself to put them away; I couldn't even face the papers still strewn about the floor. Newspaper clippings and State Department memoranda and personal letters remained fanned out chronologically, and I kept averting my eyes from where Madame Nhu's memoir weighted down the west end of my desk. Before she died, I had begun a laborious process of cataloging the whos, whats, and whens, affixing a rainbow of Post-its along the way. Without her, the stack of white pages looked insurmountable.

And yet, as horrible and disrespectful as it felt to say it out loud, Madame Nhu's death was somehow liberating. I was not going to hurt her feelings, and she would no longer sit in judgment of my efforts. In hindsight, it seemed obvious. Madame Nhu kept refusing to meet me because she had known that to do so would have broken part of the mystery—and the mystery kept me coming back for her. Once she showed herself fully, she would have lost control. And she would never do that—at least not on purpose. Until the very end she kept herself just out of reach.

I struggled with what to do. Madame Nhu had trusted me with her memoirs and photographs, and after her death, I felt that responsibility keenly. I couldn't just let her last words collect dust in my possession; after all, she had told me over and over that she wanted one last chance to be heard. And yet, in her memoir, she was simply perpetuating her own version of the Dragon Lady myth. She wrote as if she were already far removed from reality. For example, in her memoirs, Madame Nhu comes off as self-centered and self-aggrandizing when she writes, "It is therefore for myself that, out of personal curiosity to uncover my long life, I try to remember, bit by bit, my passage as the Predestined little one of the Lord. . . . I think I will be better understood, and can help others on their journey, by recalling mine." She also credits herself with wholly redefining what it meant to be a modern Vietnamese woman: "I never stopped innovating, given the rules of modernity, what was known as the life of a woman."

Madame Nhu idealized herself and her family's history in her memoir's pages, never once questioning the dark shadow of the family's good intentions. The only fault she ever came close to admitting to me she almost whispered into the phone: "Perhaps I should have been a little more humble about our family's greatness."

But in the context of our relationship, which I would call a friendship, I saw Madame Nhu as a more complicated and more sensitive woman than she was willing to express in the pages she had sent me. I had found ways to respect her for her tenacity without excusing her bad behavior, and now I felt like I had been handed the chance to breathe some life into the remote, exotic place in history to which she had been assigned.

I had a dream about Madame Nhu not long after she died. I was at a villa in Rome, standing in front of a tiled atrium that looked like something out of my eighth-grade Latin book. From there I was led to a velvet couch by a graceful young woman I took to be Madame Nhu's long dead daughter, Le Thuy. She was most unfriendly to me, and I was suddenly scared of the tongue-lashing I would surely receive from Madame Nhu. I was kept waiting and waiting, until finally a shrunken and grey old woman appeared on the threshold of the hallway. I had the bizarre impulse to go and throw my arms around her, but she waved me back to my seat. She never came into the room, but I could hear her voice as clearly as if she were speaking into my ear: "I am far too busy here to receive you." Then the old woman linked arms with the young one, and they walked away from me. They had almost disappeared into the dark recess of the hall when the little old lady turned back to me with a genuine smile. She was happy where she was. Of course I am fully aware of all the tricks the subconscious can play, but I woke up with the strangest certainty that Madame Nhu was at peace. She no longer cared what I said or did.

After Madame Nhu's death, when her diary turned up in the Bronx, I found in its pages confirmation of the fascinating, contradictory character I had come to know over the phone. I have no doubt that she would not have wanted the diary to surface. Why, she'd have chided, would anyone care about the petty fights of a bad marriage? Who would want to hear about these small cruelties when they should be so dwarfed by the larger looming politics of the Cold War and fighting communism. She could not have seen that her intensely personal tale of marital woe was a window into the psychology of a woman with ambition to forge an identity and all the complications that she generated.

In the very first entry of her diary, on January 28, 1959, the thirty-four-year-old Madame Nhu, still youthful and not yet trapped in the despair of a doomed regime, nonetheless asks herself, isn't the best time to die right after one has been baptized? The depth of her depression was at absolute odds with the self-confident image she had always presented so carefully to the world. A few days later, she writes that she has come to a hard resolution. She has decided to accept that she will never be something more than she is. Her description of the resolution is vague, "renouncing pink and blue dreams," an end maybe to childish hopes and dreams, but the cryptic entry has a definite finality. "I can no longer be more, I will no longer be more."

In the diary, Madame Nhu comes across as a woman desperately preoccupied with her marriage. She writes that Nhu is hunting again. Nhu is in a bad mood because he's trying to quit smoking. Nhu has missed his flight to come home to her—deliberately, she implies. Only on one occasion does she recall him surprising her by doing something nice—buying her a crystal chandelier for their wedding anniversary. For all that Nhu might still gaze at her or lay a palm on her cool skin, Madame Nhu pities herself: "He is not young enough to do more." When he does rise to the occasion, he doesn't do it when or how she wants. Madame Nhu is bitter at the thought that Nhu got to spend his youth as he wanted, on whom he wanted, and at thirty-four, she is stuck with the little that is left. It is not hard to guess at what she wants. Madame Nhu writes that she has to find other ways to "cool the fire of her desires."

For all her evasiveness, the diary makes clear that Madame Nhu's emotional needs went unfulfilled until she found a place in politics. I can't help but feel for the woman revealed in these private pages. She was frustrated by her time, her place, and the traditions that surrounded her. She was slowly stifled in a passionless marriage and surrounded by others who lacked her spirit and desire. The future must have seemed terribly lonely.

"I love him less and less," she wrote to herself miserably. Yet, as she had before in moments of despair, Madame Nhu would rally. She would make a place for herself alongside her husband the only way she could, by insisting that she be recognized. Because of her leonine tenacity Madame Nhu was traveling independently in the United States during the coup. She did not fall when the Ngo brothers fell; she never gave up when those around her fled, and she survived them all: the perfidious generals, the duplicitous American officials, and even the false-faced plotters lurking in the shadows.

She even seems to have tasted love briefly in the form of a few affairs. In the diary she wrote about three men by their initials only: L, K, and H. The language is vague enough that I have to wonder if she ever actually acted on her impulse: "Happily have not met anyone yet who has it all," "it" being a desired combination of sincerity, admiration, and adoration—the qualities to match her own. But H seems to have come close, with what she describes as his dynamism and extraordinary way of courting her, though she doesn't provide any details other than to say he was a real Don Juan character. She coyly asks H, "Are you always like this with women?" and his reply pleases her to no end: "Do you really think women are like you? I had to cross oceans to find you."

The anonymous H understood Madame Nhu. I rather sympathize with him, even though I have no idea, beyond the initial, who he was. He loved Le Xuan, Madame Nhu, because of who she was: staggeringly beautiful, proud, willful, a woman who would not be consigned to the place that the men around her had fenced off for her. She would battle with empires, bandits, and the forces of history before she was done. She would be at the heart of the story, the center of the epic into which she had been cast, and no one would ever forget her. She was indeed worth crossing an ocean for, and I am glad that I did.

Acknowledgments

MY DEEPEST GRATITUDE GOES, of course, to Madame Nhu, for having lived a life as extraordinary as she did and for sharing her story with me. But this book would not have been possible without the help of many others.

Madame Nhu would have remained ever so much more mysterious were it not for the hospitality of John Pham and the generous spirit of Captain James Van Thach (US Army, Ret.), to whom I extend a sincere thank-you.

I have studied with many great professors and teachers through the years. Professor Jack Harris led my first visit to Vietnam with Hobart and William Smith Colleges, and Professor Hue Tam Ho Tai at Harvard University stands out for her brilliant scholarship on Vietnamese history. Ngo Nhu Binh, my Vietnamese-language instructor at Harvard, was the most dedicated teacher I have ever had the pleasure to study with. Although he wasn't a professor of mine, thanks to Professor Edward Miller at Dartmouth for his academic insight and advice.

I benefited enormously from the honesty and generosity of the people I interviewed. Many of them lived through a war I could only write about, and I was humbled by their knowledge. Thank you to Ambassador Jim Rosenthal, Mrs. Mauterstock, Pham Ngoc Lan, Lan Dai Do, Madame Bourdillion, Laurence Goldstein, and Dominique Matthieu. My eternal thanks go to the many writers and reporters who covered the Vietnam War—and to those who passed away while I was writing this book, including Stanley Karnow and Malcolm Browne. As a rookie, I feel lucky to have been included in the membership of self-described "Old Hacks." Thank you for letting me into your conversations.

I am indebted to the many librarians, archivists, and staff who made my research more fruitful at the following institutions: the John F. Kennedy and Dwight D. Eisenhower presidential libraries, the Hoover Institute, the University of Virginia, Syracuse University, Michigan State University, the Library of Congress, and the National Archives at College Park in Maryland. Special thanks go to Steve Denney at the University of California, Berkeley, for making and sending so many photocopies, to Margaret Harman at the LBJ Presidential Library for locating Madame Nhu's tiger-skin pictures, and to Bishop Skylstad for his reflections on Vietnam. Merci to the French archivists in the Centre d'Archives d'Outre-Mer in Aix and the SHAT Archives in Vincennes.

My special appreciation goes to Malgorzata Labno and Jessica Martino for digging up research and articles and to my talented friend Jessica Tampas for taking my author photograph. To Abby Lewis and Laura Pham Lewis, thank you for making the world seem like a smaller place. Tremendous thanks go to Suzanne Santos, Marjorie Elliott, and Sue Kelly for their careful reading of the manuscript draft and to Ted Moore for just the right phrase.

Thank you to Katherine Sanford and her parents, Peter and Susan Osnos, who encouraged my earliest efforts. I was incredibly lucky to land agent Lindsay Edgcombe at Levine Greenberg Literary Associates. She guided me to the great team at PublicAffairs, and I sincerely thank everyone there who worked on this book, especially Rachel King and Jen Kelland. My editor and the publisher of PublicAffairs, Clive Priddle, deserves my deepest thanks for shepherding this book through the process and for making every page better.

I would never have made it through the years of research and writing without the support of my friends and family. Thank you especially to my parents: my mother, Marie Catherine, and her husband, Richard; my father, Gary, and his wife, Suzann; and my in-laws, Carol and Tom. I am indebted to each of them, along with my sisters, Tally and Tama, and their families, for the patience and love they have shown me through this project. I owe a special line of thanks specifically for my mother's eagle eyes. Above all, I am thankful for the love and creativity of my children, Tommy and CC, and for my amazing husband, Tom; thank you for always believing in me.

A Condensed History

1802: Emperor Gia Long unifies a loosely associated group of territories into the country now known as Vietnam and makes Hue the imperial capital.

1859–1880s: The French colonize Vietnam, Cambodia, and Laos—the countries that become known as Indochina.

1910: Ngo Dinh Nhu is born outside Hue.

1924: Tran Le Xuan is born in Hanoi.

1940: The Vichy government orders the colonial administration in Indochina to collaborate with the Japanese.

1943: Tran Le Xuan marries Ngo Dinh Nhu and becomes Madame Nhu.

1945: The Japanese surrender, and World War II ends. Ho Chi Minh declares Vietnam an independent country but immediately meets with resistance from the French, who intend to retake their colony.

1946–1954: The First Indochina War, a war of independence between the French and the Viet Minh, takes on strategic importance during the Korean War and divides international support along Cold War lines; China and the Soviet Union support the Viet Minh, and the United States supports France.

1954: The French are militarily defeated at Dien Bien Phu. The Geneva Accords divide Vietnam into two countries along the seventeenth parallel. The capital of the Communist north is Hanoi; the capital of the south, the Republic of Vietnam, is Saigon.

1954–1963: Ngo Dinh Diem heads the government of the newly formed Republic of South Vietnam. His sister-in-law, Madame Nhu, is granted the status and power of First Lady of South Vietnam.

1960: The Communist government in Hanoi forms the National Liberation Front, an anti-Diem, anti-American guerrilla military force in South Vietnam, which the Americans come to call the Viet Cong.

1963: South Vietnamese president Ngo Dinh Diem and his brother Ngo Dinh Nhu are killed in a military coup supported by the United States. Madame Nhu begins a life of exile.

1964: The Gulf of Tonkin incident occurs. The US Congress gives American president Lyndon Johnson war powers, and official US military involvement in Vietnam begins.

1973: The United States withdraws its troops.

1975: Saigon falls to the Communists, and the country of Vietnam is reunified.

1995: Diplomatic relations between the United States and Vietnam are normalized, and the American embargo against Vietnam is lifted.

2011: Madame Nhu passes away in a hospital in Rome, Italy.

Notes

Chapter 2: Forgotten Graves

1. "Notes on People" section, *New York Times,* October 16, 1971, 37.

2. On Khiem's telling Warner about the hit list, see "Memorandum from the Director of the Bureau of Intelligence and Research (Hughes) to the Secretary of State," September 6, 1963, *Foreign Relations of the United States* (*FRUS*), *1961–1963,* Vol. 4, *Vietnam: August–December 1963* (Washington, DC: GPO, 1991), 122–123; and Marguerite Higgins, *Our Vietnam Nightmare* (New York: Harper and Row, 1965), 227. The author obtained information about the Ngo brothers not liking Khiem and secret meetings with his sister during a 2005 interview with John Pham.

3. Madame Chuong's telephone call to Hilsman is detailed in Department of State Telegram to Saigon no. 764 (November 8, 1963); for Lodge's response, see Embassy Telegram from Saigon no. 984, November 9, 1963.

4. Tran Van Khiem letter to Australian journalist Denis Warner, May 1, 1964.

5. Joe Holley, "Tussle over St. Elizabeth's: Preservationists Set Their Sights on What Could Become Department of Homeland Security Headquarters," *Washington Post,* June 17, 2007, C1.

6. On Khiem's being deported to France, see Santiago O'Donnell, "Man Charged with Killing Parents Deported to France," *Washington Post,* October 29, 1993, D6; and the records of the US Supreme Court, *Khiem, Tran Van, Petitioner v. United States,* 92–6587507 U.S. 924; 113 S. Ct. 1293; 122 L. Ed. 2d 684; 1993 U.S. LEXIS 1323; 61 U.S.L.W. 3582, February 22, 1993.

7. Le Chi is quoted in Saundra Saperstein and Elsa Walsh, "A Journey from Glory to Grave; Vietnamese Clan's Saga Began in Palace, May End in Court," *Washington Post,* October 19, 1987, A1.

Chapter 3: A Distinguished Family

1. CAOM, Tran Van Chuong Dossier, HCRT non-cote, notice de renseignements concernant Madame Tran Van Chuong, April 1951.

2. CAOM, Tran Van Chuong Dossier, HCRT non-cote, and CIA National Intelligence Survey, "South Vietnam Key Personalities," 1958 (Chuong is not accorded an entry, but his younger brother, Tran Van Don, former foreign minister of Diem's government, is listed with biographical notes.

3. The description of her birth is from Madame Nhu's unpublished memoir, *Le Caillou Blanc,* 2:39.

4. Neil Jamieson, *Understanding Vietnam* (Berkeley: University of California Press, 1993), 18.

5. CAOM, Tran Van Chuong Dossier, HCRT non-cote.

6. CAOM, Tran Van Chuong Dossier, HCRT non-cote.

7. Hue-Tam Ho Tai, *Radicalism and the Origins of the Vietnamese Revolution* (Cambridge, MA: Harvard University Press, 1992), 32.

8. CAOM, Tran Van Chuong Dossier, HCRT non-cote.

9. Madame Nhu, *Caillou Blanc,* 2:13.

10. Kieu information is from Tai, *Radicalism,* 109–111. In 1924, controversy exploded over Kieu. Was the poem about the survival of the Vietnamese through language and culture? Or, as seen through the prism of contemporary colonial society, was Kieu merely a symbol of elite collaboration and treason?

11. Madame Nhu, *Caillou Blanc,* 2:49.

12. Jamieson, *Understanding Vietnam,* 27.

13. Madame Nhu, *Caillou Blanc,* 2:13.

14. Despite debate about how deeply the practice of Confucianism was engrained in Vietnamese traditional life, scholars generally agree that most educated Vietnamese in the first half of the twentieth century saw their traditional heritage as strongly Confucian. See Jamieson, *Understanding Vietnam,* 10, 11; Alexander Woodside, *Vietnam and the Chinese Model: A Comparative Study of Vietnamese and Chinese Civil Government in the First Half of the Nineteenth Century* (Cambridge, MA: Harvard University Asia Center, 1988), 60–96. At the height of the Buddhist crisis in 1963, Chuong continued to publicly assert that his "religion" was Confucian.

15. Tai, *Radicalism,* 93.

16. Madame Nhu told her story to Associated Press reporter Malcolm Browne in 1961 interview.

17. Madame Nhu, *Caillou Blanc,* 2:14–15.

Chapter 4: Portrait of a Young Lady

1. CAOM, Tran Van Chuong Dossier, HCRT non-cote.

2. Crosbie Garstin in Mark Sidel, *Old Hanoi* (Oxford: Oxford University Press, 1998), 22.

3. Nicola Cooper, *France in Indochina: Colonial Encounters* (Oxford, UK: Berg Publishers, 2001), 43.

4. Tu Binh Tran, *The Red Earth: A Vietnamese Memoir of Life on a Colonial Rubber Plantation* (Athens: Ohio University Press, 1985), 30.

5. Cooper, *France in Indochina,* 150. There was a differentiation between the high status of the Indochinese over the African blacks in racial hierarchies. However, there was also a blurring between colonial territories. Medical experts on the effects of racial integration drew comparisons between the Indochinese and African populations, indicating a lack of distinction between nonwhite populations. "Imperial France blurred all native populations into one indistinguishable morass of disease and filth" (Cooper, *France in Indochina,* 152).

6. Cooper, *France in Indochina,* 93–94.

7. Tai, *Radicalism,* 30.

8. Nguyen Ky, "The French Model," in *Hanoi,* ed. Georges Boudarel and Nguyen Ky (Lanham, MD: Rowman & Littlefield, 2002), 62.

9. CAOM, Haut Commissariat Indo, carton 375, Surveillance of Nippo-Indochinese Relations by the Sûreté, CAOM Indo Rstnf. 6965.

10. SHAT Archives 10H 80, Note du Général Aymé sur les événements dont il a été témoin en Indochine du 10 mars au 1 octobre 1945.

11. Edward Miller, *Misalliance: Ngo Dinh Diem, the United States, and the Fate of South Vietnam* (Cambridge, MA: Harvard University Press, 2013), 42.

12. "Queen Bee," *Time,* August 9, 1963.

Chapter 6: The Crossing

1. After World War II, the Potsdam Agreement had imposed Chinese peacekeepers on Vietnam. Not allowing the French to retake Indochina was a way of conceding to the American worldview and showed Chinese impatience with colonialism. The Chinese took over at the sixteenth parallel but didn't last long in Vietnam; they had their own war to fight. So they struck a deal with the French that allowed the French back into their former colony in exchange for giving up French concessions in China.

Chapter 7: A Mountain Retreat

1. For details on the Chuongs' escape from the Viet Minh and shelter at Phat Diem with Nhu, see CAOM, Tran Van Chuong Dossier, HCRT Non-Cotes, Bulletin de Renseignements, May 29, 1947; the bulletin of July 10, 1947, describes the Chuong family's whereabouts since 1945. For Chuong's fruitless donations to the Viet Minh, see Bulletin de Renseignements, March 3, 1946.

2. Madame Nhu, *Caillou Blanc,* 90.

3. Eric T. Jennings explores French notions of a "white island" and of Dalat as a "model city" in "From Indochine to Indochic: The Lang Bian/Dalat Palace Hotel and French Colonial Leisure, Power and Culture," *Modern Asian Studies*

37, no. 1 (2003): 159–194, and Gwendolyn Wright, *The Politics of Design in French Colonial Urbanism* (Chicago: University of Chicago Press, 1991), 230.

4. For the address, 10 rue des Roses, and Diem's stay there, see CAOM, Haut Commissariat, carton 731, Ngo Dinh Diem.

5. Descriptions of the villa are from Madame Nhu's unpublished memoir, *Caillou Blanc,* and Hilaire du Berrier, *Background to Betrayal: The Tragedy of Vietnam* (Boston: Western Islands, 1965).

6. Gene Gregory, publisher of the *Times of Vietnam,* the pro-Diem newspaper in Saigon and the Nhus' mouthpiece, told this to Ed Miller in conversation; see Edward Miller, "Vision, Power, and Agency: The Ascent of Ngo Dinh Diem," *Journal of Southeast Asian Studies* 35, no. 3 (October 2004): 433–458.

7. A. J. Langguth, *Our Vietnam: The War, 1954–1975* (New York: Simon and Schuster, 2000).

8. Arnauld Le Brusq and Leonard de Selva, *Vietnam: A travers l'architecture coloniale* (Paris: Patrimoines et Medias/Éditions de l'Amateur, 1999).

9. Higgins, *Our Vietnam Nightmare,* 70.

10. Howard Sochurek, "Slow Train Through Viet Nam's War," *National Geographic* 126, no. 3 (1964): 443.

Chapter 8: The Miracle Man of Vietnam

1. Diem biographical overviews are drawn from Antoine Bouscaren, *The Last of the Mandarins: Diem of Vietnam* (Pittsburgh, PA: Duquesne University Press, 1965); Anne Miller, *And One for the People* (unpublished manuscript based on interviews with Diem and family, 1955), Douglas Pike Collection, Texas Tech University, Virtual Vietnam Archive, Box 5, Folder 2; Miller, "Vision, Power, and Agency"; Denis Warner, *The Last Confucian: Vietnam, Southeast Asia and the West* (Baltimore: Penguin Books, 1964).

2. For a description of the airport arrival, see Miller, *Misalliance,* 1–4.

3. For this book I have chosen to follow contemporary American convention in calling the country lying below the seventeenth parallel South Vietnam, despite the fact that the South Vietnamese government formally used the name Republic of Viet Nam (RVN) for the land it sought to control and administer.

4. Diem's political intrigue with the Viet Minh is from Miller, *Ascent,* 437–441. Diem's conversation with Ho Chi Minh is retold in Higgins, *Our Vietnam Nightmare,* 157–158, and in Bernard Fall, *The Two Vietnams: A Political and Military Analysis* (New York: Frederick A. Praeger, 1963), 240. The detail on walking out the open doors is from Madame Nhu, *Caillou Blanc,* 74.

5. Diem pronouncement of 1949 in Miller, *Ascent,* 441.

6. Du Berrier, *Background to Betrayal.*

7. Ellen J. Hammer, *A Death in November: America in Vietnam, 1963* (Oxford: Oxford University Press, 1988), 60–61.

8. Hammer, *A Death in November*, 23.

9. US Army Saigon to Department of Army, Washington, DC, October 23, 1954.

10. Diem's blind hatred of Bao Dai and the threat to the empoeror should he return are from Department of State secret file, July 4, 1954, from Saigon, document 44207.

11. On Virginia Spence and Harwood's friendship, see Thomas Ahern, *CIA and the House of Ngo: Covert Action in South Vietnam, 1953–63,* 2000, approved for release in 2009, http://www.scribd.com/doc/57818376/Vietnam-Declassified-Doc-1-CIA-and-the-House-of-NGO.

12. Madame Nhu told this to Charlie Mohr during eight hours of interviews for her profile, "Queen Bee," in *Time*, August, 9, 1963, 23.

13. For the limo speeding by Lansdale, see Robert Shaplen, *The Lost Revolution: The Story of Twenty Years of Neglected Opportunities in Vietnam and of America's Failure to Foster Democracy There* (New York: Harper and Row, 1965), 103; for the story in Lansdale's own words, see "Interview with Edward Geary Lansdale, 1979 [part 1 of 5]," January 31, 1979, WGBH Media Library & Archives.

14. Miller, *Misalliance*, 5.

15. Memo for the record, Gen. Joe Collins comments 4/22/55 DDE Library White House Office OSANSA NSC series, Briefing Notes Indochina 1954.

16. SHAT Archives 10H 4195, Bulletin de Renseignements No. 8312, September 21, 1954.

17. Madame Nhu, *Caillou Blanc;* "Queen Bee," *Time,* August 9, 1963; SHAT Archives Bulletin No. 8312.

18. SHAT Archives 10H 4198, Vincennes Bulletin de Renseignements, No. 96, May 10, 1955.

19. Ed Lansdale letter to James Nach, second secretary of the American embassy, Saigon, June 1972, Box 9, Edward Geary Lansdale Papers, Hoover Institution Archives, Stanford University.

20. John Osborne, "Diem, the Tough Miracle Man of Vietnam: America's Newly Arrived Visitor Has Roused His Country and Routed the Reds," *Life,* May 13, 1957, 156.

Chapter 9: A First Lady in Independence Palace

1. Frederick Nolting, *From Trust to Tragedy: The Political Memoirs of Frederick Nolting, Kennedy's Ambassador to Diem's Vietnam* (Westport, CT: Praeger Publishers, 1988). Net budget expenditures for foreign economic and technical development in fiscal year 1955 were estimated at $1.028 billion, of which $150 million was used to "support further the effort of our friends combating Communist aggression in Indochina." Dwight D. Eisenhower, "Annual

Budget Message to the Congress: Fiscal Year 1955," January 21, 1954, American Presidency Project, www.presidency.ucsb.edu/ws/index.php?pid=9919.

2. *Major Policy Speeches by Ngo Dinh Diem,* 3rd ed. (Saigon: Press Office, Presidency of the Republic of Viet Nam, 1957), 34.

3. For details on the 1955 elections, see Shaplen, *The Lost Revolution,* 201. Information on the National Assembly is in Robert Scigliano, *South Vietnam: Nation Under Stress* (Westport, CT: Greenwood Press, 1964), 28.

4. For more on proposal of Madame Nhu's name, see Robert Trumbull, "First Lady of Vietnam," *New York Times Magazine,* November 18, 1962, 33.

5. John Pham recalled Diem's menus in an interview with the author. His recollection conflicts with something that Diem's brother Ngo Dinh Thuc wrote in his autobiography: Diem had a severe allergy to fish as a boy and would vomit after eating it. Perhaps he outgrew the allergy. "Misericordias Domini in aeternum cantabo: The Autobiography of Mgr. Pierre Martin Ngô-dinh-Thuc, Archbishop of Hué," *Einsicht* 1 (March 2013): http://www.einsicht-aktuell.de/index.php?svar=2&ausgabe_id=180&artikel_id=1920.

6. For General Tran Van Don's details on Diem's relationship with Madame Nhu, see *Central Intelligence Agency Information Report: Major General Tran Van Don Details the Present Situation in South Vietnam; the Plan to Establish Martial Law; and, His Views on South Vietnam's Future—August 23, 1963,* Folder 11, Box 2, Douglas Pike Collection: Unit 1—Assessment and Strategy, Vietnam Center and Archive, Texas Tech University; on Diem's chastity, see "South Vietnam: The Beleaguered Man," *Time,* April 4, 1955.

7. Source is General Tran Van Don; see note 6.

8. Author's notes on national archive documents about Nhu's travel to Burma, December 20 to 23, 1957.

9. Ahern, *CIA and the House of Ngo,* 114, and DDE papers of Christian Herter, Box 1, Chron File, March 1957 (3).

10. Douglas Pike, *Viet Cong: The Organization and Techniques of the National Liberation Front and South Vietnam* (Cambridge: MIT Press, 1966), 174.

11. Scigliano, *South Vietnam,* 44–45.

12. The Nhus took out advertisements in several Saigon newspapers to explicitly deny charges on August 24, 1957, but their denials fed the rumors instead of silencing them; Fall, *Two Vietnams,* 252.

13. *FRUS*, Vol. 1, *Vietnam, 1958–1960*. For Chau's devalued position in the government, see "Second Conversation with Nguyen Huu Chau," December 31, 1958, FRUS, 1958–1960, 1:114–117

14. For Diem on Le Chi "acting like a prostitute," see "Ambassador Lodge's Telegram from Embassy in Saigon to Department of State," no. 805 (October 29, 1963), *FRUS,* 4:445. For Le Chi on suicide and saying that Madame regretted that she didn't succeed, see *Newsweek* 62, no. 2: 41; "Younger Sister Bitterly Criticizes Madame Nhu," *Arizona Republic,* October 27, 1963. For accounts of

the suicide attempt, see Nguyen Thai, *Is South Vietnam Viable?* (Manila: Carmelo & Bauermann, 1962); Etienne Oggeri, *Fields of Poppies: As Far As the Eye Can See* (Bloomington, IN: Trafford Publishing, 2007).

15. On Madame Nhu misunderstood, see "Interview with Edward Geary Lansdale, 1979 [part 1 of 5]," January 31, 1979, WGBH Media Library & Archives.

16. Nhu confided in Richardson; see John H. Richardson, *My Father the Spy: An Investigative Memoir* (New York: HarperCollins, 2005), 189.

17. For accounts of the coup, see Langguth, *Our Vietnam,* 108; Malcolm W. Browne, *The New Face of War* (Indianapolis: Bobbs-Merrill, 1968), 251. On Madame Nhu's power, see Richard Dudman, "Intrigue Tantrums," *St. Louis Post-Dispatch,* September 14, 1963.

18. As told to David Halberstam in David Halberstam, *The Making of a Quagmire,* edited with an introduction by Daniel J. Singal, rev. ed. (New York: Random House, 2008), 55.

Chapter 10: Tiger Skins

1. Martha T. Moore, "Interview with Jean Smith," *USA Today*, September 26, 2010.

2. LBJ quote in Richard Reeves, *President Kennedy: Profile of Power* (New York: Simon and Shuster, 1994), 118.

3. For the Johnsons' Saigon itinerary, see Howard Jones, *Death of a Generation: How the Assassinations of Diem and JFK Prolonged the Vietnam War* (Oxford: Oxford University Press, 2004), 61–65.

4. For Le Duan and the Viet Cong overthrow of Diem and colonial masters, see Langguth, *Our Vietnam,* 113–114.

5. Langguth, *Our Vietnam,* 389, 393, 399; "Telegram from the Department of State to the Embassy in Vietnam," *FRUS, 1961–1963,* 2:159–160.

6. For verbal orders and falsified body counts, see Neil Sheehan, *A Bright Shining Lie: John Paul Vann and America in Vietnam* (New York: Vintage, 1989), 123–125.

7. Info on Viet Cong terror tactics from United States Mission in Vietnam, "A Study: Viet Cong Use of Terror," May 1966, USAID, http://pdf.usaid.gov/pdf_docs/PNADX570.pdf.

8. Malcolm W. Browne, *The New Face of War* (Indianapolis: Bobbs-Merrill, 1968), 27–28.

9. Details of March 1961 bombing in *Times of Vietnam,* April 1, 1961.

10. LBJ Saigon itinerary details and Karnow quote in Jones, *Death of a Generation,* 61.

11. See memo of conversation between Elbridge Durbrow and Madame Nhu, Foreign Service Dispatch No. 28, July 8, 1960.

12. On skepticism, see Elbridge Durbrow, Foreign Service Dispatch, July 15, 1960. On the diplomat remarking that it doesn't make any difference if gossip is true, see Rene George Inagaki, W. Fishel Papers, Michigan State University, Archives and Historical Collections, Box 1223, Folder 40.

13. Halberstam, *Quagmire*, 101.

14. See Airgram A217 from Saigon, November 1, 1962, citing figures published in *Thoi Boi* Vietnamese news on October 24, 1962. Scigliano, *South Vietnam,* 173

15. Shaplen, *Lost Revolution,* 157.

16. Higgins, *Our Vietnam Nightmare*, 195.

17. For LBJ's "shit" comment, see Stanley Karnow, *Vietnam: A History* (New York: Penguin Books, 1997), 230. On Bigart's song, see William Prochnau, *Once upon a Distant War: Young War Correspondents in the Early Vietnam Battles* (New York: Random House, 1995), 48–49.

Chapter 11: Young Turks and Old Hacks

1. Clyde Haberman, "David Halberstam, 73, Reporter and Author, Dies" *New York Times*, April 24, 2007.

2. Halberstam, *Quagmire,* 27.

3. Lawrence Freedman, *Kennedy's Wars: Berlin, Cuba, Laos, and Vietnam* (New York: Oxford University Press, 2000), 388.

4. For a good summary of the tensions between the press and US intentions, see Jones, *Death of a Generation*, 208–210.

5. On the political agenda of the press in Saigon, see Prochnau, *Once upon a Distant War,* 354: "It could bring down Diem, and they would help it bring down Diem. They did not delude themselves about their goals."

6. Madame Nhu is quoted in Wilfred Burchett, *The Furtive War: The United States in Vietnam and Laos* (New York: International Publications Company, 1963), 17; the CIA carefully watched this book's publication because of Burchett's professed communism and support of the Viet Cong.

7. Halberstam, *Quagmire,* 28.

8. Halberstam, *Quagmire,* 27.

9. President Kennedy asked Henry Cabot Lodge to go to Saigon as the American ambassador in response to the Buddhist crisis. On Lodge's conception of his duty and his first instincts that the "Nhus had to go" because they were deliberately provoking the Kennedy administration, see Anne Blair, *Lodge in Vietnam: A Patriot Abroad* (New Haven, CT: Yale University Press, 1995), 22, 37, 40; and Jones, *Death of a Generation*, 280, 304.

10. Joyce Hoffman, *On Their Own: Women Journalists and the American Experience in Vietnam* (Cambridge, MA: Da Capo Press, 2008), 32.

11. "The Gregorys of Saigon," *Newsweek,* September 23, 1963, and "Mlle Readers in Saigon," *Mademoiselle*, March 1957.

12. Prochnau, *Once upon a Distant War,* 257.

13. Dorothy Fall, *Bernard Fall: Memories of a Soldier-Scholar* (Washington, DC: Potomac Books, 2006), 91–92, 117.

14. Carl Mydans, "Girl War Correspondent," *Life*, October 2, 1950, 51.

15. Higgins's luck finally ran out. On assignment in 1965, she contracted a fatal case of leishmaniasis, a tropical disease, and died at age forty-five. See also "1950: The Korean War," Columbia Journalism School, http://centennial.journalism.columbia.edu/1950-the-korean-war.

16. Higgins was quoted by Charlie Mohr, *Time* magazine correspondent in Saigon, in Prochnau, *Once upon a Distant War,* 350.

17. For the description of Madame Nhu down to her pink nails, see Higgins, *Our Vietnam Nightmare,* 62.

18. For the "Oriental Valkyrie" comment, see Higgins, *Our Vietnam Nightmare,* 63.

19. Correspondence with Madame Tran Van Chuong is from the Madame Ngo Dinh Nhu folders in Marguerite Higgins Papers, Box 10, Special Collections Research Center, Syracuse University Library.

20. Clare Booth Luce, "The Lady *Is* for Burning: The Seven Deadly Sins of Madame Nhu," *National Review,* November 5, 1963.

21. Box 223, Family and Personal Papers, Clare Booth Luce Papers, Manuscript Division, Library of Congress, Washington, DC.

22. On feminized descriptions of Asian leaders like Mao, Ho Chi Minh, and Diem, see Sheridan Prasso, *The Asian Mystique: Dragon Ladies, Geisha Girls and Our Fantasies of the Exotic Orient* (New York: PublicAffairs, 2006), 53, 56.

23. Michael Beschloss, ed., with a forward by Caroline Kennedy, *Jacqueline Kennedy: Historic Conversations on Life with John F. Kennedy, Interviews with Arthur Schlesinger, Jr., 1964* (New York: Hyperion, 2011).

Chapter 12: Burning Monks

1. On there being no mistaking the identity of Ngo Dinh Thuc, see Hammer, *A Death in November,* 103.

2. On Thuc getting concessions from the state, see "Secret Memorandum of a Conversation between Former Ambassador to Saigon Elbridge Durbrow and Vu Van Mau," Paris, POLTO 361, October 1, 1963, 3.

3. Hammer, *A Death in November,* 113–114.

4. Browne, *New Face,* 175–180.

5. On Diem and accommodating US demands, see "Edward Lansdale Secret Memorandum to Secretary of Defense Robert McNamara," January 19, 1961,

National Archives, General Lansdale, Bureau of Far Eastern Affairs; see also "Telegram Number g-383 from the Saigon Embassy to Department of State," March 18, 1961. For Diem's misconception of what the United States wanted from him, see "Memorandum from the Chief Adviser, Michigan State University Group in Vietnam (Fox), to James B. Hendry of Michigan State University," February 17, 1962, *FRUS, 1961–1963,* 2:152–155. For Diem's quote on the United States only wanting to send troops to Vietnam, see Hammer, *A Death in November,* 151.

6. Langguth, *Our Vietnam,* 493.

7. On policy being a disaster, see Halberstam, *Quagmire,* 127.

8. Halberstam, *Quagmire,* 130.

9. Madame Nhu, *Caillou Blanc,* 58.

10. For descriptions of the attack on Xa Loi pagoda, see Prochnau, *Once upon a Distant War,* 372–373; Halberstam, *Quagmire,* 146; and Denis Warner, "Agony in Saigon: The Lady and the Cadaver," *The Reporter,* October 10, 1963, 39.

11. Halberstam, *Quagmire,* 146.

12. "Secret Memorandum of a Conversation between Former Ambassador to Saigon Elbridge Durbrow and Vu Van Mau," Paris, POLTO 361, October 1, 1963.

13. On his meeting with Madame Chuong, see "Interview with Henry Cabot Lodge, 1979 [part 2 of 5]," 1979, WGBH Media Library & Archives.

14. For details on the Chuong resignations, see "Saddened Diplomat; Tran Van Chuong Wife Devout Buddhist Lived in Saigon," *New York Times,* August 22, 1963, 2; and Nan Robertson, "Ex-Saigon Envoy Starts Sad Exile: Mrs. Nhu's Parents Take a House in Washington; Daughter a Stranger," *New York Times,* September, 22, 1963, 3. On Diem recalling Ambassador Chuong before he quit, see "Secret Memorandum of a Conversation between Former Ambassador to Saigon Elbridge Durbrow and Vu Van Mau," Paris, POLTO 361, October 1, 1963, 3.

Chapter 13: Too Beautiful to Ignore

1. For Madame Nhu's quote that she was "caught by the skin of the neck," see "Interview with Madame Ngo Dinh Nhu, 1982," February 11, 1982, WGBH Media Library & Archives.

2. For the conversation between Vietnamese diplomat Buu Hoi and Harlan Cleveland about diplomatic efforts to quiet Madame Nhu, see Jones, *Death of a Generation*, 385.

3. For Madame Nhu's exchange of letters with Lyndon Johnson, dated September 7 to 30, along with accompanying memoranda documenting draft replies to Madame Nhu by the State Department and the White House

(including those extensively revised by the president and the president's request that Johnson sign the reply if it met with approval), see LBJ Library: LBJA: Famous Names, Box 7, Folder N. Kennedy's writing Madame Nhu a letter from the steam bath is recounted in Jones, *Death of a Generation,* 290.

4. See "Memorandum of Conversation," New York, October 2, 1963, Document 168, *FRUS, 1961–1963,* 4:347–349.

5. For Madame Nhu's belief that the Americans were well intentioned but arrogant, see "Interview with Madame Ngo Dinh Nhu, 1982," February 11, 1982, WGBH Media Library & Archives.

6. Ben Horman's interview with the young man outside of the Hotel Barclay on October 9, 1963, is CBS footage of Madame Nhu's visit. "Madame Nhu Picketed Outside of Her Hotel," October 9, 1963, WGBH Media Library & Archives.

7. See Central Intelligence Agency, "Vietnamese Summary Supplement, October 7–31, 1963," describing Madame Nhu's arrival in the United States, media appearances, and travels through the country.

8. For student comments, such as being sorry Madame Nhu wasn't feeling better, see "Madame Nhu at Fordham University: Bonze, Fordham/Student Comments Re: Madame Nhu [part 1 of 2]," October 11, 1963, WGBH Media Library & Archives.

9. "Visa to Mrs. Nhu Is Under Inquiry; Diplomatic Nature of Permit Questioned by Rep. Hays; Visa Issued Last Year; Mrs. Nhu Rests at Hotel Here; Telephones Kept Busy," *New York Times,* October 9, 1963, 10. The program director, Anita Berke Diamant, would go on to become a major literary agent, starting her own firm and representing best-selling author of gothic horror V. C. Andrews, whose plots were full of family secrets and incest.

10. On Oram Group, see "Oram Group, Inc. Records, 1938–1992," Ruth Lilly Special Collections & Archives, Indiana University–Purdue University Indianapolis, http://www.ulib.iupui.edu/special/collections/philanthropy/mss057.

11. Blair, *Lodge in Vietnam,* 64.

12. The NYC public events commissioner is quoted in "Vietnamese Summary Supplement, October 7–31, 1963," Central Intelligence Agency.

Chapter 14: Closed Doors

1. The details of Madame Chiang's visit to the United States in the spring of 1943 are described in Laura Tyson Li, *Madame Chiang Kai-shek: China's Eternal First Lady* (New York: Atlantic Monthly Press, 2006), 197–198.

2. On Tran Van Chuong choking up during his retirement speech, see "Saddened Diplomat," *New York Times*, August 23, 1963.

3. For the quote that Madame Nhu "has not the power she is supposed to have," see Henry Raymont, "Diem's US Envoy Quits in Protest," *New York Times*, August 23, 1963. For the quote about Nhu as the front man and Madame Nhu as his shadow, see Joseph Wershba, media review of Tran Van Chuong's appearance on CBS, *New York Post,* October 18, 1963.

4. The "I will have his head cut off" quote is from Nhu's interview with the Italian weekly *Espresso*; see "Telegram from the Embassy in Vietnam to the Department of State from Lodge Saigon, October 7, 1963, 7 p.m.," Document 186, *FRUS, 1961–1963*, 4:385–386.

5. For the description of the Chuongs' house and furnishings, see Nan Robertson, "Ex-Saigon Envoy," *New York Times*, September 22, 1963.

6. For the Kennedy aide's conversation with Madame Chuong about running Madame Nhu over with a car, see "Memorandum of Conversation Between the Director of the Vietnam Working Group and Madame Tran Van Chuong," September 16, 1963, *FRUS, 1961–1963,* 4:237–238.

Chapter 15: Coup d'État

1. For Madame Nhu in Dallas on US Day, see Peter Dale Scott, *Deep Politics and the Death of JFK* (Berkeley: University of California Press, 1996), 214. For Madame Nhu figuring in conspiracy theories, see Bradley S. O'Leary and L. E. Seymour, *Triangle of Death: The Shocking Truth about the Role of South Vietnam and the French Mafia in the Assassination of JFK* (Washington, DC: WND Books, 2003), and radio show host Michael Cohen on Madame Nhu's instigating the assassination of JFK in his "JFK Assassination Special X," Coast to Coast AM with George Noory, November 21, 2012, http://www.coasttocoastam.com/show/2012/11/21.

2. For skeet shooting on the Dougherty ranch and details on Bruce Baxter as Le Thuy's boyfriend, see *Life,* November 8, 1963, and the *Victoria Advocate* (Beeville, Texas), October 28, 1963. For the quote from California governor Pat Brown, see *Time,* November 1, 1963.

3. The momentous decision to get rid of Diem and Nhu, with all the implications this would have for the war, was reached in the space of a few hours on a Saturday afternoon. The president received a draft of a cable implying US support for a coup while he was with his wife and two children in Hyannis Port, still mourning the death of their infant son Patrick only two weeks before. Assistant Secretary of State for Far Eastern Affairs Roger A. Hilsman and Deputy Secretary of State W. Averell Harriman wrote the cable. Secretary of State Robert McNamara was unreachable, and President Kennedy asked, "Can't we wait until Monday, when everyone is back?" But when told that his aides really wanted to get the cable out of the way, JFK finished by telling them, "Go see

what you can do to get it cleared." Secretary of State Dean Rusk, Undersecretary of State George Ball (who was on the golf course at the time), and Special Assistant for Counter Insurgency Activities on the Joint Chiefs of Staff Victor "Brute" Krulak, all gave their okay once they heard the president was on board, as did Deputy Secretary of Defense Roswell Gilpatric, who summed up the inertia that led him to sign by saying, "I felt I should not hold it up, so I went along with it just like you countersign a voucher" (Jones, *Death of a Generation,* 315–316). See John F. Kennedy Library, Kennedy Papers, National Security File: Meetings and Memoranda Series, Box 316, Folder "Meetings on Vietnam 8/24/63–8/31/63."

4. For Nhu eavesdropping in the American embassy in Saigon, see Karnow, *Vietnam,* 311–312.

5. Lodge's imperious manner is detailed in Seth Jacobs, *Cold War Mandarin: Ngo Dinh Diem and the Origins of America's War in Vietnam, 1950–1963* (Lanham, MD: Rowman & Littlefield, 2006), 158.

6. For details about the end of John Richardson's CIA career in Vietnam, see his *New York Times* obituary, June 14, 1998; Blair, *Lodge in Vietnam*; and Richardson, *My Father,* 193.

7. Harold P. Ford, "CIA and the Vietnam Policymakers, Episode 2, 1963–1965," Center for the Study of Intelligence, CIA Books and Monographs, 2007.

8. Ford, "CIA and the Vietnam Policymakers."

9. For details on Nhu's talks with the north, see the memo of the conversation between Eisenhower and John McCone, dated September 19, 1963, Dwight D. Eisenhower Library, Special Name Series, Box 12. Also see Margaret K. Gnoinska, "Poland and Vietnam, 1963: New Evidence on the Secret Communist Diplomacy and the Maneli Affair" (Working Paper 45, Cold War International History Project, Woodrow Wilson Center for International Scholars, Washington, DC, 2005).

10. For details on the meeting with Lodge and Felt, see Joseph Buttinger, *A Dragon Embattled* (Westport, CT: Praeger Publishing, 1967), 2:1005; and "Revolution in the Afternoon," *Time,* November 8, 1963.

11. For Nhu's "It's alright" quote, see Karnow, *Vietnam,* 44.

12. For the false coup plans, see Neil Sheehan, *A Bright and Shining Lie: John Paul Vann and America in Vietnam* (New York: Vintage Books, 1989), 367–369; and Karnow, *Vietnam,* 316–320.

13. For a description of Dinh's betrayal, see Buttinger, *A Dragon Embattled,* 2:1003–1004.

14. For Diem and Nhu last being seen by Ma Tuyen, see Fox Butterfield, "Man Who Sheltered Diem Recounts '63 Episode," *New York Times,* November 4, 1971, 5.

15. Higgins, *Our Vietnam Nightmare,* 225.

16. "The Overthrow of Ngo Dinh Diem, May–November, 1963," in *The Pentagon Papers: The Defense Department History of United States Decision Making on Vietnam,* ed. Mike Gravel (Boston: Beacon Press, 1971), 2:201–276.

17. Khanh played a role in the military intrigue that led to the 1963 coup, but he was not selected to be on the twelve-man Military Revolutionary Council headed by Big Minh. In January 1964, Khanh led the overthrow of Big Minh "without a shot being fired" and became the next leader of South Vietnam—but his rule lasted only one year. In February 1965, he was overthrown by four junior officers.

18. Fred Flott, *The Foreign Affairs Oral History Collection of the Association for Diplomatic Studies and Training* (Washington, DC: Library of Congress, Manuscript Division, July 22, 1984).

19. On Colby's assessment of Diem's coup being the "worst mistake" America made, see "Transcript, William E. Colby Oral History Interview II, 3/1/82," by Ted Gittinger, Internet Copy, LBJ Presidential Library, 32–33.

20. On Kennedy's reaction to the deaths of Diem and Nhu, see Jones, *Death of a Generation,* 425–436.

21. Kennedy's "That goddamn bitch" reaction is paraphrased by his personal friend Red Fay; see John F. Kennedy Library, Paul B. Fay Jr., Oral History Interview—JFK #3, November 11, 1970.

22. John F. Kennedy, Telephone Recordings: Dictation Belt 52.1. Dictated Memoir Entry, November 4, 1963, Papers of John F. Kennedy, Presidential Papers, President's Office Files, John F. Kennedy Library.

Chapter 16: In Exile

1. "Letter from Professor Wesley R. Fishel of MSU to the President of the Rep. of Vietnam (Diem)," *FRUS, 1958–1960,* 1:426–433. See also Chuong's character in Hammer, *A Death in November,* 303.

2. "Interview with Everett Bumgardener [2], 1982," August 24, 1982, WGBH Media Library & Archives.

3. Buttinger, *A Dragon Embattled,* 2:956–957.

Index

JESSICA TAMPAS PHOTOGRAPHY

Monique Brinson Demery took her first trip to Vietnam in 1997 as part of a study-abroad program with Hobart and William Smith Colleges. She received a United States Department of Education grant to attend the Vietnamese Advanced Summer Institute in Hanoi, and in 2003, she received a master's degree in East Asia regional studies from Harvard University. Demery's initial interviews with Madame Nhu in 2005 were the first the former South Vietnamese First Lady had given to any Westerner in nearly twenty years. Demery lives in Chicago.

PublicAffairs is a publishing house founded in 1997. It is a tribute to the standards, values, and flair of three persons who have served as mentors to countless reporters, writers, editors, and book people of all kinds, including me.

I. F. Stone, proprietor of *I. F. Stone's Weekly*, combined a commitment to the First Amendment with entrepreneurial zeal and reporting skill and became one of the great independent journalists in American history. At the age of eighty, Izzy published *The Trial of Socrates*, which was a national bestseller. He wrote the book after he taught himself ancient Greek.

Benjamin C. Bradlee was for nearly thirty years the charismatic editorial leader of *The Washington Post*. It was Ben who gave the *Post* the range and courage to pursue such historic issues as Watergate. He supported his reporters with a tenacity that made them fearless and it is no accident that so many became authors of influential, best-selling books.

Robert L. Bernstein, the chief executive of Random House for more than a quarter century, guided one of the nation's premier publishing houses. Bob was personally responsible for many books of political dissent and argument that challenged tyranny around the globe. He is also the founder and longtime chair of Human Rights Watch, one of the most respected human rights organizations in the world.

• • •

For fifty years, the banner of Public Affairs Press was carried by its owner Morris B. Schnapper, who published Gandhi, Nasser, Toynbee, Truman, and about 1,500 other authors. In 1983, Schnapper was described by *The Washington Post* as "a redoubtable gadfly." His legacy will endure in the books to come.

Peter Osnos, *Founder and Editor-at-Large*